全国商务英语实训规划教材

商务英语实训教程

A Practical Course for Business English

主　编　牛洁珍　张翠波
副主编　计　晗　崔肖菡　贾增艳
编　委　牛洁珍　张翠波　计　晗
　　　　崔肖菡　贾增艳

本书获北京联合大学"十三五"规划教材建设项目资助。

苏州大学出版社

图书在版编目(CIP)数据

商务英语实训教程 = A Practical Course for Business English / 牛洁珍,张翠波主编. —苏州:苏州大学出版社,2019.7(2021.1重印)
全国商务英语实训规划教材
ISBN 978-7-5672-2763-7

Ⅰ.①商… Ⅱ.①牛…②张… Ⅲ.①商务-英语-教材 Ⅳ.①F7

中国版本图书馆 CIP 数据核字(2019)第 142992 号

| 书　　名:商务英语实训教程 |
| A Practical Course for Business English |

| 主　　编:牛洁珍　张翠波 |
| 责任编辑:汤定军 |
| 策划编辑:汤定军 |
| 封面设计:刘　俊 |

| 出版发行:苏州大学出版社(Soochow University Press) |
| 社　　址:苏州市十梓街1号　邮编:215006 |
| 印　　装:镇江文苑制版印刷有限责任公司 |
| 网　　址:www.sudapress.com |
| E - mail:tangdingjun@ suda.edu.cn |
| 邮购热线:0512-67480030 |
| 销售热线:0512-67481020 |

| 开　本:787mm×1092mm　1/16　印张:16　字数:354 千 |
| 版　次:2019 年 7 月第 1 版 |
| 印　次:2021 年 1 月第 2 次印刷 |
| 书　号:ISBN 978-7-5672-2763-7 |
| 定　价:49.00 元 |

凡购本社图书发现印装错误,请与本社联系调换。服务热线:0512-67481020

前言

本书是北京联合大学"十三五"规划教材。编写本书,旨在通过一系列商务英语情景模拟实训,培养和提高学生在商务环境下运用英语从事各类商务活动的基本技能和素养,以期能够把英语语言知识技能和商务专业知识有机融合并运用到未来的实际工作当中,从而满足社会对应用型商务英语人才的需求。

本书力求吸收二语习得的最新研究成果,通过章节结构的设计和内容的编排,努力达到科学高效地引导学生"课下输入为主,课上输出为主",把所学的语言点和技能自然转化,由被动接受变为主动参与,让学生把错误犯在课堂上,从而进行有针对性的查漏补缺,提高学习效率和效果。同时,本书还结合应用型本科学生的认知规律,在具体学习内容和课内练习编排时,尽力关照到语言技巧与商务知识的传授比例、商务英语核心词汇的涵盖程度、词汇的重复率等方方面面,做到课前任务、课中任务和课后任务兼顾,以期达到理想的学习效果。此外,本书通过对国际商务活动一般规则和惯例的简要介绍,还能够达到强化学生跨文化商务交际的意识和能力的培养之目的。

全书设计了五个实训模块,共15个单元,涵盖了常见的商务活动各类主题。每个单元以商务情景展现进行编写,分别设有单元实训目标、话题讨论、阅读训练、听力训练、会话样本、常见句式表达、书面训练、拓展阅读和BEC真题练习。各部分之间环环相扣,紧密相连,着力突出了"语言知识""交际策略""商务实践"的有机融合。

本书由具有丰富教学和实践经验的教师编写。牛洁珍、张翠波负责全书的组织、策划和统稿工作。具体编写分工为:牛洁珍编写Module 5(Unit 13,Unit 14,Unit 15)以及附录和后两个模块的BEC真题部分;张翠波编写Module 3(Unit 7,Unit 8,Unit 9)以及前三个模块的BEC真题部分;计晗编写Module 1(Unit 1,Unit 2,Unit 3);崔肖菡编写Module 2(Unit 4,Unit 5,Unit 6);贾增艳编写Module 4(Unit10,Unit 11,Unit 12)。在编写过程中,编者参考了国内外近年来出版的相关教材和网站,吸取了国内外众多学者和专家研究的最新成果。同时,本书的出版得到了北京联合大学经费支持。在此一并致谢。

由于时间仓促,编者的水平和经验有限,书中的缺点错漏和不足之处在所难免,恳请广大读者批评指正。

编者
2019年4月1日

Contents

Module 1 **Business Reception** / 1
- Unit 1　Welcome and Farewell　/ 2
- Unit 2　Company Tour　/ 20
- Unit 3　Entertainment　/ 38

Module 2 **Business Travel** / 56
- Unit 4　Making Reservations　/ 57
- Unit 5　On the Journey　/ 72
- Unit 6　Hotel Accommodation　/ 88

Module 3 **Business Communication** / 103
- Unit 7　Job Interview　/ 105
- Unit 8　Job Description　/ 127
- Unit 9　Business Calls　/ 140

Module 4 **Business Planning** / 155
- Unit 10　Activity Planning　/ 157
- Unit 11　Advertising Planning　/ 171
- Unit 12　Marketing Planning　/ 184

Module 5 **Business Meetings** / 197
- Unit 13　Staging a Meeting　/ 198
- Unit 14　Chairing a Meeting　/ 209
- Unit 15　Attending a Meeting　/ 222

Glossary　/ 237

References　/ 250

Module 1 Business Reception

Reception—the business card of your company

 Into the Module

Business reception represents the corporate identity of a company. Welcoming your clients in an appropriate way sets a mark and shapes the first impression. During a company or factory tour, the operation, products and culture of your company can be well presented and your professionalism well demonstrated. Entertaining your clients to dinner or sightseeing can soften up your business negotiation and improve the chances of cooperation.

 Training Objectives

By the end of this module, you are expected to:
- learn useful expressions for greeting and saying farewell in business reception;
- learn how to accompany clients in a company or factory tour;
- learn useful expressions for entertaining clients to dinner or sightseeing;
- know the etiquette in business reception.

What I've realized is that the joy of meeting and greeting people from all over the world is universal.

—Joe Gebbia (American designer, Co-funder of Airbnb)

Unit 1 Welcome and Farewell

Make a great first impression

 **Training Objectives**

> By the end of this unit, you are expected to:
> - know how to meet or see off clients at the airport;
> - know how to start conversations with clients;
> - know the etiquette of welcoming and seeing off clients.

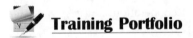 **Training Portfolio**

Part I Starting up

Section 1 To discuss

Discuss with your partner and collect your thoughts on the following questions.

(1) What preparations do you think should be made before meeting your client?

(2) What preparations do you think should be made before your client's departure?

(3) What kind of gifts could be sent to your client?

Section 2 To read

Read the tips for welcoming and seeing off clients in business reception, and then discuss what impresses you most.

Tips for welcoming clients

- On formal occasions, you should address someone as "Mr." (for man) or "Ms" (for woman) with the person's last name or surname unless the person asks you to call him/her by his/her first name.
- Professional dressing is appropriate in the Western business culture. Many companies require that their employees dress in a professional manner.
- In the Western culture, people are used to maintaining a relatively large physical distance between each other during conversations or social meetings.
- Men always shake hands firmly when meeting each other for the first time, while some women prefer verbal greeting only.
- English speakers often ask "How are you?" or "How are you doing?" when you meet them. These are usually more greetings than real questions, and they do not always expect an honest answer. If you are well acquainted with this person, you might say how you are truly feeling. If not, the accepted response is usually "Fine, thank you. How are you?" even if you are not feeling very well.

Tips for seeing off clients

- If your client wants to leave during the farewell dinner, never be the first one to rise and say goodbye to him/her, or you will be considered impatient and insincere.
- A gift is used as the lubricant to make communication easier and also helpful to conclude business with your client.
- You'd better present a gift to your client's taste. The gift whose package is attractive and exquisite should be neither too expensive nor too cheap.
- Help your client make flight reservations and book an air ticket if it is necessary.
- Consequently sending regards or email to him/her can be helpful to strengthen the friendship between you and your client.

Part II Listening in

Task 1 Listen to the conversation and try to fill in the blanks.

At the airport, Mr. Brown sees a board with his name on it held by a young woman, so he walks towards her.

Wang Jia: Hello! Are you Mr. Brown?

Mr. Brown: Yes. And you are?

Wang: How do you do, Mr. Brown? I'm Wang Jia, (1)_____ of Shanghai Sunrise Trading Corporation. Nice to meet you.

Brown: How do you do, Wang Jia? Nice to meet you, too.

Wang: Let me help you with the (2)_____.

Brown: Thanks a lot.

Wang: My pleasure. (3)_____?

Brown: A pleasant one. Good food and good service. But I'm catching a little jet lag.

Wang: Oh, you need a good rest to (4)_____. We've booked a room at the Shangri-La. Shall we go?

Brown: Great. You are so nice.

Wang: This way, please. Our car is outside.

Brown: Thanks.

Mr. Brown and Wang Jia are on the way to the hotel. They are talking in a friendly way.

Wang: So it's the first time for you to visit Shanghai, isn't it?

Brown: Yes. I felt quite excited when I had a splendid bird's-eye view of Shanghai on the plane. It has a clear skyline dominated by (5)_____.

Wang: Yes, it is. Shanghai is a very beautiful modern city. I can assure you that you would enjoy staying here.

Brown: Oh, I bet I will. Could you make some (6)_____ for me?

Wang: No problem, I'll do it. By the way, you'll be staying at Shangri-La, one of the best hotels in our city. The hotel has nice restaurants, bars, a boutique, 24-hour room service, laundry service, and facilities such as fax, copying and typing, etc. We've booked a room with a

Module 1 Business Reception

(7)_____ of the Bund and Huangpu River.
Brown: Sounds great. But is it conveniently located?
Wang: Sure. Oh, here we are.
Brown: Wow! It looks very grand. That's very kind of you.
Wang: You're welcome.

They arrive at the Shangri-La Hotel. At the front desk Wang Jia helps Mr. Brown to check in.

Wang: This way, please. Let's go to the front desk for check-in.
Receptionist: Good morning. Welcome to Shangri-La. Can I help you?
Wang: Good morning. This is Mr. Brown from the United States. We've booked one room for him.
Receptionist: Let me see ... Oh, a reservation of a single room for 3 days in the name of Mike Brown, right? (8)_____?
Brown: Certainly. Here you are.
Receptionist: Thank you for showing your passport. And how would you like to pay?
Brown: Is Visa Card OK here?
Receptionist: Certainly.
Brown: Oh, could you tell me where I can find a supermarket?
Receptionist: Well, it is on the second floor. The Health Club and the bar are on the third floor.
Brown: I see.
Receptionist: If there's anything we can do for you, please let us know. The extension for the front desk is "6". And breakfast starts from 6:30 until 10:00.
Brown: OK. Thank you.
Receptionist: Please sign your name here, Mr. Brown. It's your keycard, and your room number is 1802. I'll get a bellboy to take you to your room. Hope you enjoy your stay here.
Brown: Thank you for your help.
Receptionist: You're welcome.

After Mr. Brown settles down, they begin to talk about the arrangement of his visit.

Wang: Here we are.
Brown: I like it. Thank you.
Wang: By the way, you probably know you can't drink the (9)_____,

Brown: right? You may drink boiled water, or you can drink bottled water.
Brown: Oh, thanks for telling me.
Wang: Mr. Brown, may I discuss with you about the two-day visit here now? We plan to spend one day (10)_____ our factory and the other day sightseeing. Which do you prefer to do tomorrow, going around the factory or the city? Or you just want to have a day of good rest?
Brown: It's really kind of you, but I'm eager to have a look at your factory and the products we've mentioned before.
Wang: I see. How about picking you up at 9:00 tomorrow? Is it OK?
Brown: Fine. Thank you for everything you've done for me.
Wang: It's my pleasure.

Task 2 Listen to the conversation and try to fill in the blanks.

About one week ahead, Monica Huang notifies the restaurant of a farewell dinner and discusses with the chef about the menu. Now the farewell dinner is coming.

Huang: Good evening, Mr. Wilson. I'm glad you've come.
Wilson: Good evening, Ms. Huang. It's very kind of you to invite me to dinner tonight.
Huang: Take a seat, please. The dinner will be ready in a few minutes.
Wilson: Thanks.
Huang: It's a pity that you're leaving tomorrow. Hope you'll visit our company again.
Wilson: I am sure I will. Ms. Huang, I truly (1)_____ everything you've done for me. It has been a very pleasant and productive trip for me. Your company has left me a very good impression, and I am deeply moved by your hospitality.
Huang: Thank you very much. I hope you have enjoyed your trip in China.
Wilson: Oh, yes. This trip is excellent. Besides our business, I visited different places, which has helped me a lot to know more about China.
Huang: Mr. Wilson, here is something I'd like you to give to your wife.
Wilson: Thank you. I'll open it ... Oh, it is an embroidered picture. It's really (2)_____.
Huang: I'm glad you like it.
Wilson: I believe my wife will like it too. I don't know how to thank you for your kindness.

Module 1　Business Reception

Huang: It's very kind of you to say so. Well, Mr. Wilson, this is the air ticket we booked for you. The flight number is CA985, and the plane will take off at 10:55 tomorrow morning. I will arrange a car to pick you up at 8:30. Please get everything ready before that.

Wilson: You are so (3)_____. I've given you too much trouble.

Huang: No trouble at all. And I should say thank you for placing an order with us. You won't be disappointed. En ... Now the dinner is ready. Please come to the table. Take this seat here, please.

...

Wilson: Thanks. How delicious the food is!

Huang: Mr. Wilson, here's to our friendly cooperation.

Wilson: To your health and our everlasting friendship.

Huang: (4)_____ to whatever you like.

In the morning, Monica Huang comes to the hotel and waits for Mr. Wilson at the lobby.

Wilson: Good morning, Ms. Huang.

Huang: Good morning, Mr. Wilson. Have you checked out?

Wilson: Yes.

Huang: OK. We should be at the airport two and a half hours earlier as you need time for customs formalities and (5)_____.

Wilson: Sure.

Huang: I've arranged a car to the airport. I'll call the porter to take your suitcase to our car.

Wilson: Thank you.

Mr. Wilson and Monica Huang get into the car and head for the airport. 30 minutes later, they get to the airport.

Huang: My driver will help you unload the luggage. This way, please.

Wilson: Thank you.

Wilson is at the check-in desk now.

Clerk: May I have your passport, please?

Wilson: Here you are.

Clerk: Thank you, Sir. The flight number is CA985 to San Francisco. How many

(6)_____ do you wish to check?

Wilson: Two.

Clerk: Put your baggage on the conveyor, please.

Wilson: By the way, can I have an (7)_____?

Clerk: Let me see. Yes, you may take one. All settled down. Here are your passport, boarding pass and the receipt to (8)_____. You may proceed to Boarding Gate Number 12.

Wilson: Thank you.

Mr. Wilson finishes check-in, and the departure time is coming.

Huang: I've checked the departure time. We still have 40 minutes. Let's wait at the departure lounge.

Wilson: Thank you so much, Ms. Huang. I'm so grateful to you.

Huang: It's my pleasure. I hope we can keep in touch.

Wilson: I hope so, and I believe we will.

The airport broadcast announces the boarding for the flight CA985 to San Francisco.

Wilson: Now, time for boarding. I'm afraid I have to say good-bye now. Ms. Huang, my dear friend. Thank you for all your help. I believe Mr. Jin is very lucky to (9)_____.

Huang: Thank you. It's very kind of you to say so. I wish you a very pleasant journey.

Wilson: Please (10)_____ your boss and other colleagues.

Huang: Sure. Keep in touch!

Wilson: See you!

Huang: Take care, and have a nice flight.

Part Ⅲ Language focus

■ **Meeting at the airport**

1. Excuse me, but are you ... from ...?

2. Did you have a good trip? / How was your flight? / Was it comfortable?

3. The journey was pleasant and the service on board was excellent.

4. I'm catching/feeling a little jet lag.

5. How many pieces of luggage do you have?

6. Let me help you with your luggage.

7. It's very nice of you to come and meet me.

8. We have already reserved you a standard/single room/suite at … Hotel.

9. Anyhow, it's a long way to China, isn't it?

10. If all is ready, we'd better start for the hotel.

11. Our car is in Parking Lot 3.

■ **Breaking the ice**

1. I didn't expect the airport to be so efficient.

2. Well, I'm so glad to be able to come to …

3. We're glad to have you here …

4. We have a shuttle bus for … visitors over there.

5. It's also very convenient to travel from the airport to the downtown area.

6. Have you ever been to …?

7. I hope you could tell me the most convenient way to …

8. You can take a shuttle bus as well as the subway.

9. It is a 10-minute drive to get there.

10. I certainly will take this opportunity to visit the city this time.

11. The hotel is conveniently located.

12. It is a bright and clean room facing the garden on the sunny side.

■ **At the farewell dinner**

1. Good evening … It's very kind of you to invite me to dinner tonight.

2. I'm glad you have enjoyed your stay here.

3. I really appreciate all of your help/hospitality.

4. Here is something for you and your … I hope you will like it.

5. I'd like to give you something (to take home).

6. Please accept this gift. It's a token of our friendship.

7. How nice of you! I'll open/unroll it right now … Oh, it's lovely!

8. How skillfully it's done. It's hand-made, isn't it?

9. To your health and our friendship / friendly cooperation / brilliant future.

■ **Farewell at the airport**

1. It's very kind of you to come all the way to see me off.

2. Please send your family my best regards.

3. I wish you a very pleasant journey.

4. Take care. And don't forget to keep in touch.

5. Farewell and all the best.

Part Ⅳ   Speaking out

Section 1   Sample dialogues

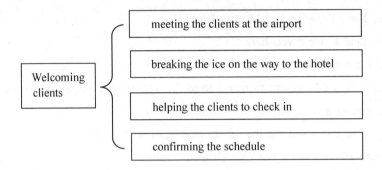

Dialogue 1

Howard Yang is the director of Purchasing Department (PD) of Active Sports, Beijing, and Tom Chambers from the U. S. has been the largest client for Active Sports in the past few years. Today Howard picks up Tom in person at the airport, and they will discuss the likely further cooperation.

Tom: Howard! Great to see you again!

Howard: Good to see you too, Tom. How was your flight?

Tom: Good. No holdups at the airport, and the flight was comfortable. I was able to take a nap on the way over.

Howard: Good. Do you have any jet lag?

Tom: No, not now. I adjusted to the time difference while I was in Korea, so I'll be all right.

Howard: That's good. I always get bad jet lag when I travel.

Tom: So, how is your wife doing, Howard?

Howard: She's doing fine, thank you. How is your family?

Tom: Fine, thanks. My wife wanted me to say thank you for your gift last time. She liked the jewelry box very much.

Howard: Oh, it was nothing. I'm glad she liked it.

Module 1 Business Reception

Tom: I heard you had a haze recently.

Howard: Yes, but it wasn't too serious. The weather forecast for the next few days looks very good, so we don't need to worry about it.

Tom: Wonderful. I was hoping to get some exercise and go sightseeing. Will we have enough time?

Howard: Sure. Your schedule is very flexible. The only firm appointments are to spend a day at the factory tomorrow, and a half day at the office on Wednesday.

Tom: There must be a lot of places of interest in Beijing. Last time I only visited the Forbidden City, but it was really unforgettable.

Howard: This time we can go to the Summer Palace, and the Temple of Heaven.

Tom: Sounds very exciting.

Howard: And we can take you shopping before you leave.

Tom: Great. It's good to be here, Howard. And it's really good to see you again.

Howard: It's good to have you, Tom.

Dialogue 2

Tom: All my bags are checked in. I guess I'm all set to go.

Howard: I know you must be excited to go home after such a long business trip.

Tom: I'm sure. So we'll be expecting the first shipment in less than a month?

Howard: Yes, that's right. They'll be there in no time.

Tom: Good. Tell Mr. Cao at the factory to keep up the good work. I think all the products are going to sell very well.

Howard: We hope so! It's always good to work with you, Tom. I want to thank you for placing such a big order with us. You won't be disappointed.

Tom: I'm sure I won't. I really appreciate all of your hospitality.

Howard: It was my pleasure. And I'd like to give you something to take home. Let me unroll it.

Tom: This is beautiful! Chinese calligraphy. What do these characters mean?

Howard: They mean longevity. I remembered you like the calligraphy at the Palace Museum, so I thought you might like it.

Tom: That's very nice of you. Where did you get it? It's not a print.

Howard: No, it's an original. My father's friend is a calligrapher, and I had him make it for you. His name and the date are at the bottom.

Tom: I'll hang it in my office. But I feel bad, and I didn't get you anything.

Howard: Don't worry about it. It's a token of my appreciation for your business and friendship.

Tom: If you have time around Christmas, please come to visit my family. I'll show you around our city.

Howard: Thanks for your invitation. And please give my regards to your wife.

Tom: You do the same. Well, I'd better go. Thanks again for everything.

Howard: Take care, and have a nice flight.

Section 2 Creating your own

Task 1 Pair work: Make a conversation according to the given information.

Tips for you (A)

You are waiting at the airport for a new client who is going to visit your company. The tips are for you to prepare a conversation.

- You are

    from China

    the sales representative of a food company in Hangzhou, China

- You

    meet your client at the airport

    talk about his/her journey

    want to help him/her with his/her luggage

Tips for you (B)

The supplier is waiting for you at the airport. The tips are for you to prepare a conversation.

- You are

    from Mexico

    the head of a food corporation in Mexico

- You

    express your thanks to him/her

    express your feeling about your journey

    refuse his/her help and carry the luggage yourself

Module 1 Business Reception

Task 2 Pair work: Make a conversation according to the given information.

Tips for you（A）

You are ready to say farewell to a client who has just visited your company. The tips are for you to prepare a conversation.

- You are

    from China

    the sales representative of Glamour Trading Co., Ltd., Ningbo, China

- You

    see him/her off at the airport

    present a small gift to him/her

    express your thanks for his/her order

    send your wishes

Tips for you（B）

You are going to leave for your country. The host is saying farewell to you. The tips are for you to prepare a conversation.

- You are

    from Singapore

    the market manager of MAP Corporation, Singapore

- You

    express your thanks for her/his hospitality

    accept the gift and express your appreciation

    hope they will execute your order on time

    say goodbye

Part V Writing

Name card

A name card, more often called a business card or visiting card, usually bears such personal information as one's work unit, professional title, e-mail address, zip code, telephone numbers and so on. Today, it has often become a must for people to exchange name cards in social activities.

Design a business card for Mr. Liu, the Personnel Manager, according to the following ad.

> Grace China Ltd. Hangzhou is seeking for an OFFICE ADMINISTRATOR to assist with the office administration duties. Interested candidates please send your detailed resume in both English and Chinese to Mr. Liu Hai, Personnel Manager, Personnel Department, 24th floor, Zhongguancun, Haidian South Road.
> E-mail: hailiu@gmail.com
> Tel: 86 + 10 + 65920352
> Fax: 86 + 10 + 65920352

Part VI Follow-up reading

Passage 1

Read the following passage and decide whether each of the following statements is true (T) or false (F).

If foreign clients pay a visit to your place, it indicates that a business trade will be probably concluded. Welcoming your clients in an appropriate way can leave a good impression and lay a positive foundation for your business.

Before the foreign clients start their activities in your place, you need to prepare a schedule concerning activities and arrangements in order of time. You also need to learn how to address your clients acceptably on a formal occasion and how to dress properly for the first meeting. It is of great importance to confirm the time of their arrival and the flight number.

It is also necessary to reconfirm whether the airplane is due to arrive on time. You are supposed to reach the airport in advance. You'd better take the clients' photos along with you or prepare a piece of poster with their names on it which can be easily recognized. When meeting the clients, you need to shake hands with them to convey your friendliness in China. Japanese always give their clients gifts after bowing. In some Western countries people are likely to hug or kiss as a gesture of goodwill. Therefore, when a Westerner expresses his/her friendliness this way, you'd better follow suit lest your client feel embarrassed.

Be helpful to your clients with their baggage. They will think you are nice to offer them a hand for the baggage and arrange the transportation and accommodation for them. Talking about weather, trip and hobbies is a good way to break the ice on the way to the hotel and get closer in relationship. Avoid comments that could be taken as boastful on religion, politics, or private topics, such as salary, marriage, clothes price and so on. Conversations can be ignored if your clients seem tired or take little interest in them.

As for the arrangement of accommodation, you need to consider its location, cost, service, convenience, etc. Help your clients check in when you arrive at the hotel. Show the clients to the rooms and tell them where the dining room is. Before saying goodbye to the clients, you should know when to ring them up and discuss with them about the schedule in case there might be some changes. Do not spend too much time on this in that the clients need a rest after a long trip. The schedule should be updated immediately if any change occurs. Moreover, you also need to inform those people who will meet the clients of their activities or appointments by telephoning or sending e-mails respectively. The secretary must inform all parties involved of any change immediately.

(From: JI Shujun, 2010: 23)

(　) (1) It is highly recommended to arrange activities in order of time.
(　) (2) It's no use checking the arrival time of your clients' plane.
(　) (3) Giving clients gifts at the first meeting is acceptable in Japanese culture.
(　) (4) It's appropriate to talk about the religion with your clients on the way to the hotel.
(　) (5) You should update any change of schedule to all people involved.

■ Passage 2

Read the following passage and fill in the blanks.

Farewell is the last, but not the least work of reception. You should get farewell well arranged to make the foreign client feel at home and want to come back again.

To follow a prescribed order in farewell arrangement is essential to you. Farewell arrangements begin with arranging the farewell dinner if there is one. Usually, before dinner, you notify the staff canteen (or some preferable restaurants) of the farewell dinner and discuss with the chef about the menu. If a farewell speech is needed, telephone or send emails to the person who is going to deliver the speech and remind him/her of the speech, the time and place of the dinner.

A farewell speech is delivered to a person who is leaving, usually by the boss or manager. In the speech, the speaker refers to the positive memories of the person who is leaving and expresses his appreciation for having cooperated with the person. The speaker also extends the best wishes to the person. After dinner, accompany your client to the hotel and ask for comments and proposals for this business travel. Inquire about the check-out time and present a gift before you leave.

Next, a car or a coach should be arranged to pick up the client from the hotel to the airport on the departure day. You should call the administration office two or three days in advance, and confirm the car arrangement one day before departure. Some people may wish to see off the client personally. In such a case, you should notify these people of the client's departure time from the hotel or the departure time of the plane if they like to go to the airport directly.

Checking ETD (Estimate Time of Departure) is a must. You can telephone the airport several hours ahead to confirm the flight and see if there is any change.

The airport sets the time for check-in and boarding. It is set as follows:

	Domestic Flights		International Flights	
Check-in	Start 1.5 hours before take-off	Close 0.5 hour before take-off	Start 2 hours before take-off	Close 45 minutes before take-off
Boarding	Start boarding about 0.5 hour before take-off			
	Close the boarding gate about 10-15 minutes before take-off			

Therefore, before heading for the airport, you should go to the hotel several hours before the plane takes off and help the client to check out. You should make sure the client has collected all his/her belongings, documents (especially passport), and has taken all the luggage.

After you arrive at the airport, it is your job to help the client with the customs formalities and check-in. It is essential for you to wait in the departure lounge with the client till the time for boarding. When the client starts boarding, you should wave goodbye to him/her.

Module 1 Business Reception

Make a report to your chief after you accomplish the task. In the meantime, keep in touch with your client by telephone or email even after he/she goes back to his/her place.

(From: JI Shujun, 2010: 118)

(1) Farewell arrangements begin with arranging the farewell _____.
(2) In a farewell speech, the speaker could mention positive _____ of the person who is leaving.
(3) It is advisable to confirm car arrangements one day before _____.
(4) The client can check in 2 hours before _____ for an international flight.
(5) You are supposed to wait in the departure lounge with the client until the time for _____.

Training Assessment

Part I Self-study

Some greetings behavior are listed below which, in some cultures, may be seen as appropriate but in others would be inappropriate or even shocking. Select adjectives from the box which suggest appropriate and inappropriate behavior and fill in the list below.

threatening	respectful	insulting	reassuring
overhearing	warm	welcoming	easy-going
rude	impolite	cold	polite
hostile	supportive	offensive	professional

"appropriate" behavior   "inappropriate" behavior

_____   _____
_____   _____
_____   _____
_____   _____
_____   _____
_____   _____
_____   _____
_____   _____

Part II BEC exam focus

Reading Test

- Read the article below about the changing role of human resources departments.
- Choose the best sentence from A – G to fill each of the gaps (1 – 5).
- Do not use any letter more than once.
- There is an example at the beginning (0).

The best person for the job

Employees can make a business succeed or fail, so the people who choose them have a vital role to play.

Employees are a company's new ideas, its public face and its main asset. Hiring the right people is therefore a significant factor in a company's success. (0) __G__ If the human resources department makes mistakes with hiring, keeping and dismissing staff, a business can disappear overnight. Many companies now realize that recruiting the best recruiters is the key to success.

Sarah Choi, Head of HR at Encoplc, believes that thinking commercially is a key quality in HR. Every decision an HR manager makes needs to be relevant to advancing the business. (1)_____ That's no longer the case. HR managers have to think more strategically these days. They continually need to think about the impact of their decisions on the bottom line. (2)_____ For example, a chief executive will expect the HR department to advise on everything from the headcount to whether to proceed with an acquisition.

Why do people go into HR in the first place? Choi has a ready answer. I think most people in the profession are attracted by a long-term goal. (3)_____ Nothing happens in the company which isn't affected by or doesn't impact on its employees, so the HR department is a crucial part of any business.

Not all operational managers agree. An informal survey of attitudes to HR departments that was carried out last year by a leading business journal received comments such as "What do they actually contribute?" (4)_____

As Choi points out, salaries have never been higher and, in addition, HR managers often receive substantial annual bonuses.

Despite the financial rewards, HR managers often feel undervalued, and this is a major reason for many leaving their jobs. (5)_____ However, a lack of training and development is a more significant factor. These days, good professional development opportunities are considered an essential part of an attractive package, Choi explains.

A. But rising levels of remuneration demonstrate that the profession's growing importance is widely recognized.
B. At one time, a professional qualification was required in order to progress to the top of HR.
C. Other departments and senior executives used to see HR managers as having a purely administrative role.
D. Since it's one of the few areas where you can see the whole operation, it can lead to an influential role on the board.
E. Being seen as someone who just ticks off other people's leave and sick days does not help build a sense of loyalty.
F. They therefore need to be competent in many aspects of a company's operations.
G. On the other hand, recruiting the wrong staff can lead to disaster.

Unit 2 Company Tour

Solidify professional reputation of your company

 **Training Objectives**

> By the end of this unit, you are expected to:
> - know the common expressions of company profile;
> - know how to talk about company operation and performance;
> - master the basic expressions of showing clients around a factory;
> - know how to describe the quality and performance of a new product.

 **Training Portfolio**

Part I   Starting up

Section 1   To discuss

(1) Can you name the main departments of a company or a factory?

(2) Can you translate the following common expressions of company management into Chinese?

corporate strategy	assume the sole responsibility for one's own profits or losses
development plan	logo
corporate identity	be bold in the reform
poor management	bankrupt
assembly line	equipment upgrading
batch production	mass production
in the red	production line
pioneering spirit	technical innovations
talents	catalogue
a bright prospect	environmentally-friendly packaging
gross profit	crease-resistant
foldable	patented
superior quality	complete in specification
wide varieties	quality and quantity assured
durable in use	well-known for its fine quality
reliable reputation	sophisticated technology

Section 2 To read

Discuss the following questions with your partner after reading the passage.

(1) What is the main purpose for foreign clients to visit a factory?

(2) What are you supposed to introduce during the visit?

Showing clients around a factory

For those who intend to purchase in large quantity, they would be rather careful, and may hold the attitude of "seeing is believing". Therefore, it is commonly seen that the clients demand a visit to exporting enterprises. The main purpose for foreign clients to visit the factory is to know the manufacturing procedure, quality and types of the products, etc.

When the clients arrive at your factory, you could first introduce the factory manager and leaders to the clients. Then you could introduce the factory and its main products through PPT or photos to give the clients a general impression before they visit the factory. The visit could start from the most well-known department. The items that the clients are most interested in should also be in priority. Consequently, the clients will not regret for this visit.

Quality is the most concerned element for the clients. Superior equipment makes for superior products. Therefore, quality manufacturing equipment and quality control system should be listed in the visiting schedule if there are. The number of employees, annual output, sales and distribution channel and market shares are also important factors during introduction. Furthermore, the staff dormitory, recreation facilities and staff restaurant could better indicate the excellent capacity and system of the company. The receptionist may come across some technical terms during the translation, and some technical questions may be raised by the clients during the visit. So as a receptionist, you should make full preparation beforehand, and you can also give explanations with the help of diagrams and statistics as well as consultation from technicians in place.

The visit of exhibition room or showroom is beneficial in that the clients will be more confident in the products of the company. It is a golden chance for you to promote your new products once the clients step into the exhibition room. "Please take a look at this. It's an innovative product just developed." Then you can introduce the advantages of the new products to arouse their desire to place an order. You can also highly recommend the products which are still in the experimental stage, because new products are always more attractive for most people. But don't forget to add this sentence: "It's still in the experimental stage."

At the end of the visit, it is important to ask the clients about the impression on the factory. It is a good chance to review what the clients see and hear during the whole day. The important and interesting moment during the visit can be mentioned again to deepen the impression of the clients on the factory. This will create a harmonious atmosphere while strengthening the purpose of this visit. For example, you can say, "I certainly hope you found the trip as interesting as I did." or "I am surprised you knew so much about …", etc. In the end, the photos taken during the visit or an exquisite product of the company could be made as presents for the clients to enhance the understanding between each other.

(From: JI Shujun, 2010: 37)

Part II Listening in

Task 1 Listen to the conversation and try to fill in the blanks.

A: May I take a look around your company?

B: Yes, of course. (1)_____. I hope you can get a picture of what our business is from my introduction. Let's get outside.

A: Your buildings are very large.

B: Yes, we are still (2)_____.

A: What's that red building?

Module 1 Business Reception

B: That's our research and development center.
A: Would you mind showing me your showroom?
B: Of course. It's on the fourth floor.
A: What do you specialize in?
B: We specialize in manufacturing electronics.
A: Does most of your business deal in exports?
B: Yes, most of our business is (3)_____ America.
A: How about Europe?
B: Well, at the moment, not much. But with a view to future trade, we have (4)_____ in New York and Chicago. We are planning to open a new office in Paris, too.
A: That's impressive, indeed. What about your annual turnover?
B: We grossed about US $10 million last year, and our business is (5)_____.
...
A: May I take a look at the Purchasing Department?
B: Sure, please. It could also be called the Stock Control Department.
A: (6)_____?
B: We have several functions to carry out: buying, stock control, and goods inwards. Usually, these functions are (7)_____ in larger firms.
A: Aren't you very busy?
B: Yes. Each of the responsibilities is complex, so the Purchasing Department is a busy one. We have to deal with around 1,000 different (8)_____. Many purchasing departments would have nightmares over these sorts of figures.
A: So that means you have to plan well ahead and (9)_____ stock levels very carefully. Right?
B: Exactly. We invented a computer system to deal with the stock control.
A: That's quite efficient.
B: Yes, it's worth putting a lot of (10)_____ and energy into devising the system.
A: Thank you so much for giving me a tour of the company. I wonder if I could take a look at your factory.
B: Sure, this way, please.

Task 2 Listen to the conversation and try to fill in the blanks.

In the morning, Gloria Cai is sent to pick Mr. Black up to the factory. Gloria Cai briefly introduces the visiting arrangement before they start off.

(at the hotel lobby)

Gloria Cai: Good morning, Mr. Black. Did you sleep well last night?

Mr. Black: I slept like a log. And you?

Gloria Cai: Just fine. I think we should discuss today's visiting arrangement.

Mr. Black: OK.

Gloria Cai: We'll drive to my corporation's factory, which is about 45 minutes from here. We're (1)_____ here by 4:00 this afternoon. When we arrive at the factory, we will look around the factory and visit the workshop. After that we'll go to the showroom. Is that OK?

Mr. Black: That would be (2)_____.

(at the factory)

Gloria Cai: Here we are.

Mr. Black: Oh, I expect it would take a longer time.

Gloria Cai: I'll show you around and explain the (3)_____ as we go along. So you can get a good idea of how things work.

Mr. Black: That will be perfect.

Gloria Cai: And I shall be very glad to answer any of your questions.

Mr. Black: Thanks a lot.

Gloria Cai: It's my pleasure. This way, please.

Mr. Black: How large is the factory?

Gloria Cai: It covers 30,000 square meters.

Mr. Black: That is much larger than I expected. When was the factory (4)_____?

Gloria Cai: It was built 10 years ago. At present, there are 900 people at the factory. We've spent a great deal of money on the manufacturing equipment.

Mr. Black: Your buildings are very large, aren't they?

Gloria Cai: Yes. Look! This is our administration building. We have all the administration departments here.

Mr. Black: What's that long building?

Gloria Cai: That's the recreation center and restaurant.

Mr. Black: What's that building opposite us?

Gloria Cai: That's the warehouse.

Mr. Black and Gloria Cai are walking around the factory and come in front of the production block.

Mr. Black: Miss Cai, can you show me around your workshops?

Gloria Cai: Sure. We have in all seven workshops. Mr. Black, this way, please.

(*at the workshop*)

Gloria Cai: This is one of our workshops. We produce various garments of cotton, silk, wool and embroidery.

Mr. Black: What a large workshop! How much do you spend on design development every year?

Gloria Cai: About 4% of the gross sales.

Mr. Black: Good! That's what we need. Do you have an R&D department?

Gloria Cai: Yes. We have an R&D department, a sales department, an accounting department and a (5)_____ department.

Mr. Black: Do you have a design development department?

Gloria Cai: Of course. The staff of designers is big enough to work out the new technology and design new products.

Mr. Black: If I (6)_____ now, how long would it be before I got delivery?

Gloria Cai: It would largely depend on the size of the order and the items you want.

Mr. Black: I see. What's (7)_____ per month?

Gloria Cai: About 8,000 items per month now. But we'll be making 9,000 items next year. Mr. Black, may I introduce you to Mr. Liu Hu, director of our factory?

The showroom has a large collection of their products. It's a good chance for Gloria Cai to promote their products.

Gloria Cai: Mr. Black, shall we go and see the products in the showroom?

Mr. Black: After you.

(*in the showroom*)

Gloria Cai: Here we are. This is our showroom. Almost all of our company's products can be found in this showroom.

Mr. Black: Do you sell your products abroad?

Gloria Cai: Yeah, we are exporting a great variety to the world market.

Mr. Black: These samples are lovely.

Gloria Cai: (8)_____. This gown is very colorful and feels nice. It's pure silk. Our clothes are all of high quality.

Mr. Black: How do you ensure the quality control?

Gloria Cai: Well, it's done by our strong quality control department. Before delivery, all the goods will be inspected carefully.

Mr. Black: (9)_____ in these items.

Gloria Cai: Why don't you order some samples before you decide?

Mr. Black: Can I do this?

Gloria Cai: That's all right with us.

Mr. Black finishes his visit with Gloria Cai, and Gloria Cai is asking for the feedback from Mr. Black.

Gloria Cai: It's a great pleasure to have you visit us today.

Mr. Black: It's also my pleasure.

Gloria Cai: Thank you for your interest in our corporation. Mr. Black, what do you think of the factory?

Mr. Black: I have been very impressed by what I have seen today. The equipment is quite modern while the workers are so diligent.

Gloria Cai: Thank you for saying that.

Mr. Black: After visiting your factory, I believe (10)_____ for us to work together.

Gloria Cai: I am very glad to hear that. Mr. Black, this is our latest catalogue. If you are interested in any of the items, please do not hesitate to contact us.

Mr. Black: Thank you.

Gloria Cai: Then I hope you will come here again.

Mr. Black: I hope so.

Part III Language focus

■ **Clients may say**

1. We look forward to our tour of your plant.

2. Can you show me around …?

3. If it is not too much trouble, we would like to talk to some of the technicians.

4. Can you brief me about the company/factory system organization?

5. It was very kind of you to give me a tour of the company/factory.

6. Can you give me some details about this?

7. What is the total annual output of the factory?

8. Do you spend a lot on research and development?

9. How do you ensure the quality control …?

10. I think we may be able to work together in the future.

■ **Receptionist in an office or a factory may say**

1. I'll show you around.

2. I'll arrange this for you.

3. The company is an export-oriented company with a history of twenty years.

4. Our company started out as a small family company.

5. This company started as a subsidiary of … Company.

6. We mainly engage/specialize in the manufacture/production and sale of …

7. We deal exclusively in …

8. Our company covers/occupies/has an area of … square meters.

9. It has a staff of around … / The total number of employees is over …

10. We've been working to improve …

11. Our market share in … has increased by …%/making up/accounting for …% of total sales.

12. Our company has an annual turnover of …

13. Let me introduce to you some of the staff members of our factory, here's Mr. …, the director of …

14. Please go this way. I'd like to show you our showroom/warehouse …

15. We can offer a superior product at the same price as our competitors'.

16. Thank you for sparing time to visit us. What do you think of …?

Part Ⅳ　Speaking out

Section 1　Sample dialogues

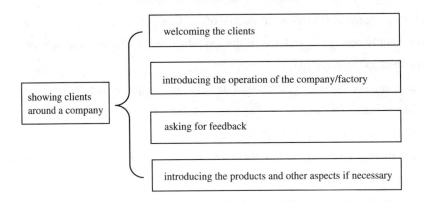

📘 Dialogue 1

Alice Wong welcomes Mr. Taylor at the company's reception office.

Alice： Welcome to our company. Please be seated. What would you like to have?

Mr. Taylor： Tea, please.

Alice： (*to her personal assistant*) I'd like to have some coffee. Thank you.

Mr. Taylor： We have heard much about your company. When did it come into being?

Alice： Actually, it started as a subsidiary of Sunrise Corporation in 2000. In total, it's over 18 years.

Mr. Taylor： Oh, it is still a young company, but your development of electric appliances has been remarkable.

Alice： You said it, and our research has told us our products enjoy a relatively large market share both at home and abroad.

Mr. Taylor： We are quite interested in your products. Could we have detailed information about your products?

Alice： Sure, please have a look at our samples. There are the latest models.

Mr. Taylor： Very impressive. I think we have already seen some items we might like to order, although we would still like to study them a bit more.

Alice： Good, we are willing to be at your service as always.

Dialogue 2

Mr. Parker (P) was invited to a dinner held in his honor. The next morning, he paid a visit to GFTD and, together with Ms. Liu (L), drew up an agenda for the following days. After visiting the corporation, he was invited to visit one of the factories of GFTD. Mr. Zeng (Z), the factory manager, will show him around.

L: Mr. Parker, would you like to go through to tour our factory? You will understand our product better if you visit the plant.

P: That is a good idea. If it will not take too long to arrange.

L: No, it won't. I will arrange this for you. We can make it tomorrow. What do you think about it?

P: That is great! I am already looking forward to this.

L: The tour will last about three hours altogether. I will accompany you on your tour.

P: It is very kind of you to do that. Will you show me around the factory?

L: No problem. Mr. Zeng, the manager of the factory, will show you around and answer any question you will pose.

P: Thank you for your consideration.

...

L: Mr. Zeng, may I introduce to you Mr. Parker, the manager of the Import Department of Pacific Industries Co., Ltd., Canada? And Mr. Parker, this is Mr. Zeng, the manager of this factory.

P: It is a pleasure to meet you.

Z: Welcome to our factory. We have been expecting you. Knowing you will come, we are all set for you in advance.

L: Is everything ready?

Z: Yes. We can start any time.

P: I have wanted to see your factory for a long time. Shall we get started on our tour?

Z: Of course. I suggest we start at the beginning of our production line.

P: I will just follow you.

Z: You will have to wear this helmet during the tour.

P. This one seems a little small for me.

L: Here, try this one.

P: That is better. Mr. Zeng, your factory is much smaller than I expected.

Z: Our small size makes us very flexible. Because we are small, we can respond quickly to changes in market.

P: The factory looks very busy.

Z: Yes, it is peak season. We are always flooded with orders during this season each year.

...

Z: Thanks for coming today, Mr. Parker. We'd like to give a complete picture of our operation.

P: Thank you. That is why I am here. I know the factory is operating at full capacity.

Z: Since it is peak season now, our factory is working at full capacity.

P: How long does this peak season usually last?

Z: Our factory's peak manufacturing period is from August to February.

P: How many employees do you have in this plant? Are you in three shifts? Is the production line fully automated?

Z: We have 300 employees. Yes, we are running in three shifts. But the production line is not fully automated.

P: I see. Then what is your monthly output?

Z: 1,000 units per month now, but we will make 1,200 units in October.

P: What about your control of quality?

Z: It is extremely tight. Quality is one of our primary considerations.

P: Good! What is your usual percentage of rejects?

Z: Around 4% in normal operations.

P: That's wonderful. Do you fulfill the entire manufacturing process in your factory?

Z: Almost. Only a few necessary items are made elsewhere.

P: How much do you invest in developing new products each year?

Z: About 3%~4% of the gross sales. We believe technical development is the key to the future.

P: Very good. One more question: How long have you been in this line?

Z: Almost 20 years. So our factory was set up in 1999.

P. Well, that is quite a long history.

Z: You have asked me so many questions, Mr. Parker. And I have one question, too. What do you think of our factory?

P: Very impressive. I believe we may be able to work together in the future.

Module 1 Business Reception

Section 2 Creating your own

Task 1 Pair work: Make a conversation with your partner according to the given information.

Tips for you (A)

You are introducing your factory to a new client who is visiting your factory. The tips are for you to prepare a conversation.

- You are

    from China

    the sales representative of Century Sportswear Co., Ltd, Shanghai, China

- You

    describe your factory operation

    talk about your major business line

    talk about the advantages of your products

Tips for you (B)

The supplier is introducing their factory to you. The tips are for you to prepare a conversation.

- You are

    from Australia

    the head of the Import Dept. of the Island Sportswear Imp./Exp. Corp., Sydney, Australia

- You

    ask questions about their factory operation

    inquire about their major business line

    ask about the advantages of their products

Task 2 Role-play

You are a salesman of a local foreign trade company. One of your clients from France is interested in your products, and he asks to come to your place and visit the factory. Please act out how you show your client around the factory. The following items should be included:

- inform the arrangement of the visit;
- introduce staff members;

- describe your factory operation;
- recommend newly developed products in your showroom;
- answer technical questions;
- inquire feedback from your client.

Part V Writing

A memo (memorandum) is a type of document used for internal communication between company employees. Memos are a time-tested aspect of the business world and, when written properly, help keep everything running smoothly.

Super J IT. Enterprise
MEMO

To: Office Manager
From: Tan Jin Nee, Manager
Date: 15 June 2012
Subject: Sales exhibition—UUM

For your information, we accepted an invitation from UUM to set up a stall on the campus for three days from 18 to 20 June 2012 as part of a sales exhibition. The details are as below:

1) Six sales personnel and two company cashiers.
2) Two shifts, the first 9.00 a.m. to 1.00 p.m. and the next from 1.00 p.m. to 5.00 p.m.

I would like to call for volunteers from your sales personnel to manage the stall on the three days concerned. Please arrange the transportation to take the computers and other equipment to UUM and back.

Please contact me if you have any problems.

Read the information below and then write a memo to all the staff in your company.

You are a PR manager for a large manufacturing firm. Tom Parker, a representative from an American company is visiting your company as well as the factory. In your memo you should:

- announce the representative's visit;
- say when and where he will tour;
- ask the related departments to be well prepared for his visit.

Write 30~40 words only. Remember to include a *To*, *From*, *Date* and *Subject* line.

Part VI Follow-up reading

Passage 1

Read the following passage and choose the best answer to each of the following questions.

The main purpose for making a good "Company Profile" is to approach your potential customer with your company's strengths in terms of capacity, quality, financial leverage and experience, and to show your ability to start the business and to develop it in a trustworthy way. The idea behind it is to convince your potential customer to rely on you by giving him relevant information in a stage where he has to evaluate your offer. He is now looking at your quotation or offers and there may still be doubts in his mind. The "Company Profile" increases your value compared with your competitors by influencing positively the decision of your potential customer to start business with you. The impression a potential customer has about your organization is strongly influenced by the way you have fulfilled his expectations. Not fulfilling the expectations causes disappointment. Fulfilling the expectations, however, is not enough. You will only score when you exceed them.

The content of your "Company Profile" should include or contain introduction, company data, structure and infrastructure. Most importantly you need to clearly and professionally present your products, capacity, equipment, quality policy, experience, financial statements, short and long-term plans and good references. It is also professional to present your company using a mission statement.

As your "Company Profile" represents your company, it is absolutely essential to prepare it professionally. This includes a good layout, no typing errors, laser printing on quality paper and proper coloring and structuring. Of course it is entirely up to your imagination and creativity to add or delete chapters or subjects and give it its final form and outlook. However, including the contents we mentioned above is crucial.

The size of your "Company Profile" should be 12 to a maximum of 15 pages, thinking about the time that your potential customer is willing to give to read your profile. Put yourself in the position of your potential customer and only include information that you think he would like to know to enable him to do the business with you. Follow the AIDA structure step by step. First catch the **Attention**, and then generate **Interest** and create **Desire** to get him into **Action**. Be informative and businesslike.

Timing is very important. Do not send the profile together with your brochure in the first glance. Wait by making a final version until you have met with some customers and know their preferences.

Make sure that sending this "Company Profile" is an integral part of your approach strategy and test its effectiveness. Do not forget that there is a wide gap to bridge before creating the first realistic chance to book an order. With this "Company Profile" you have a tool to approach him once more but in a positive contributing manner.

(From: Yao Jianhua, 2014: 54)

( ) 1. The main purpose for making a company profile is to _____.

  A. make your potential customer evaluate your product

  B. show your potential customer your ability to start the business

  C. fulfill the expectations of your potential customer

  D. make your company known

( ) 2. The impression a potential customer has about your company is based on _____.

  A. your brochure   B. your quotation

  C. your company profile   D. your expectations

( ) 3. The content of your company profile should include _____.

  A. introduction about your company

  B. introduction about your products

  C. introduction about your future plans

  D. All of the above

( ) 4. _____ is very important in the presentation of a company profile.

  A. A good layout   B. Good printing

  C. An appropriate coloring   D. All of the above

( ) 5. You should send the company profile _____.

  A. together with your brochure

  B. after sending your brochure

  C. before sending your brochure

  D. anytime

Passage 2

Read the passage and decide whether each of the following statements is true (T) or false (F).

An office reception area is an important part of a business. Before someone even gets to the receptionist, he or she will walk through the office reception area first. If you are in charge of decorating that area, it is important to do so in a way that appeals to the majority of the people that will walk through the front door. A few simple changes can help you turn the area from uninviting to appealing.

Adding greenery is a good way to brighten up any room.

Put out some plants. Greenery is a simple and inexpensive way to brighten up any room. The best place to keep small plants is on a side table where they can be out of the way and will not get knocked over. If you have a large floor plant, you can tuck it in the corner, out of the way.

A modern mural on the wall will give your business a sophisticated feel.

Hang a painting or photograph on the wall. It does not matter what type of business you have, you can always find a painting or photograph that matches it and reflects your style. It should be something that is eye-catching and has a sophisticated feel to it. For example, if you have a motorcycle shop, hang a large close-up photo of a beautiful motorcycle. Even if you cannot afford to spend a lot of money, you can check online auction sites or commission a local painter to paint it for you.

Coffee-table books can be used as decor.

Use books as decor. Almost every office reception area has magazines, but you may also want to incorporate some interesting coffee-table books. Consider travel books of favorite places you have been or would like to go to some day. It can give your clients something interesting to browse through while they are waiting.

Consider hanging a TV on the wall.

Hang a TV on the wall. While some businesses choose to put a TV on a stand, it leaves open the opportunity for it to get dirty or damaged. It can also take up quite a bit of space. Opt for hanging a flat-screen TV on a wall across from where the clients will sit.

Select an appropriate number of chairs.

Select chairs for the office reception area that are easily washable. If someone makes a mess, it is much easier to wash it off than to have to throw out the entire chair. There should be enough chairs to accommodate your clients at any given time, but not so many that there is an excess. For example, if you see three clients in an hour, have only five chairs in the room.

Do not overwhelm the office with large pieces of furniture. It can look cluttered and can make the area appear uninviting.

(From: https://bizfluent.com/13642641/how-to-decorate-an-office-reception-area)

(　　)(1) It is appropriate to put a large floor plant just in the middle of the office.
(　　)(2) If you are short of money, you can check online auction sites for some paintings to decorate your office.
(　　)(3) Offering some coffee-table books while your clients are waiting is a good idea.
(　　)(4) It's recommendable to put a TV on a stand in a reception office.
(　　)(5) Chairs should be placed in a reception area as many as possible.

Training Assessment

Part I Self-study

Choose the correct phrase to complete each sentence, and change the forms when necessary.

| shoot up | start rolling on | get a good idea of |
| sell like hotcakes | show one around | |

(1) Let me _____ the factory so you can see how these machines work.
(2) Because of the humorous dialogue and the funny characters, "Garfield Comic" _____.
(3) In order to keep up with market trends, we _____ some changes for our old products.
(4) In order to _____ the operation system, we attend a one-day workshop for all new employees.
(5) Housing prices in Hong Kong have been _____ recently.

| keep an eye on | solid reputation | branch out |
| get in touch with | I appreciate your time | |

(6) They have _____ into higher quality products over the past years.
(7) Don't fool around at your work again. Our manager has been _____ you.

(8) Switzerland has a _____ for making first-class watches.

(9) Through a number of e-mails and phone calls, we _____ overseas buyers.

(10) Thanks for helping me with this project. _____.

Part II BEC exam focus

Reading Test

- Read the article below about a manufacturing company called Lebrun.
- In most of the lines (1 – 12), there is one extra word. It either is grammatically incorrect or does not fit in with the meaning of the text. Some lines, however, are correct.
- If a line is correct, write **CORRECT** on your Answer Sheet.
- If there is an extra word in the line, write **the extra word** in CAPITAL LETTERS on your Answer Sheet.
- The exercise begins with two examples (0 and 00).

Examples:

0   AS

00   CORRECT

0 After 98 years of trading, the steel manufacturer Lebrun knows from experience as show

00 difficult fluctuations in the economic cycle can be for suppliers such as themselves.

(1) Since many of the nation's largest production companies which are its customers,

(2) Lebrun is adversely affected by any change for the worse in the economy. Yet Lebrun

(3) has managed to keep on sales steady (in the region of approximately $2.5 billion)

(4) and has recorded only one annual loss during the difficulties of the past five

(5) years, but despite the effects of the ongoing industrial slowdown. James Griffith,

(6) president of Lebrun, now has the task of turning up survival into growth, and

(7) his strategy is already becoming clear to those industry observers. In February of

(8) this year, the company acquired Bronson plc, additionally a one-time competitor.

(9) This merger will greatly expand the size of both Lebrun's labor force, and

(10) Griffith estimates it will boost its revenue by nearly 50%, while too increasing

(11) the number of plants and R&D centers in much a similar way. Griffith is

(12) optimistic that while the steel industry is about to pull out of recession, and he wants Lebrun to be ready for this.

Unit 3 Entertainment

Soften up your clients

 **Training Objectives**

> By the end of this unit, you are expected to:
> - know how to entertain foreign business clients;
> - know how to entertain clients to dinner;
> - know how to accompany clients for sightseeing.

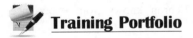 **Training Portfolio**

Part I Starting up

Section 1 To discuss

Discuss with your partner and collect your thoughts on the following questions.

(1) Which cuisine does your local food belong to? Can you describe its features?

(2) Where would you like to guide your foreign clients to go sightseeing?

Section 2 To read

Read the following passage and discuss with your partners the following questions.

(1) What are the most popular forms of entertaining?

(2) What are you supposed to prepare before arranging corporation entertaining?

The ability to entertain clients is one of the best skills to have in any corporate setting. If you impress your clients, it means to repeat business and other perks down the road. To care for your clients, you must learn what services and perks your clients expect. A determination to serve your clients, even if you don't see immediate results, will pay off in better relationships over time. Genuine concern, good communication and efficient business practices combine to raise the level of trust people have for you. Trust is the currency of good client relations.

Smile and make eye contact when meeting clients. Repeat the client's name when you meet her and when you leave her. Dale Carnegie, who wrote *How to Win Friends and Influence People* said, "Remember that a person's name is to that person the sweetest and the most important sound in any other language."

Ask questions and listen attentively. Begin questions with "Tell me about …" or "What do you think about …?" These questions encourage thoughtful answers and give more opportunity for the client to tell you more about himself. People give out copious amounts of information if you just pay attention.

Keep a file on your clients. Note the information you have gained through casual conversation, including: spouse names, where your clients are originally from, how many children they have and any important events they have mentioned to you. Whatever is important to your clients should be important to you. Note all business information as well.

Communicate regularly with your clients. Send an e-mail, a text or phone. Keep the tone casual and friendly. Work from polite personal interest topics to business. Keep clients apprised of any sales, special services offered or promotions.

Respond to clients' inquiries during the same business day, when possible. Think about how you would want to be treated if you were the client, and how quickly you would want a response to your questions or concerns. With some preparation, you can have a lot of fun entertaining clients.

* **Feed them.** Taking clients out to a nice dinner is a basic and expected part of entertaining. A nice meal sets the stage for great conversations and potential business deals. Find out if they have any dietary restrictions before making reservations to ensure that they will have a good time.

* **Take them to a sporting event.** Depending on where you live, you could entertain your clients with a round or two of golf, or by getting them courtside seats at a basketball game.

* **Show them around your city.** It's disappointing when you take a business trip to another city and don't have a chance to take in some of the local flavor. So entertain your clients by taking them to the best local restaurant or even to the lake for a casual dinner under the stars.

* **Think outside the box.** If you take the time to get to know your clients, you may be able to come up with some creative ways to entertain them. They may love to go skydiving, go snorkeling or attend a rock concert if they're the adventurous types.

(From: http://www.ehow.com)

Part II Listening in

Task 1 Listen to the passage and try to fill in the blanks.

How to entertain business clients

To entertain clients successfully will require (1) _____ and extra effort on your part. What does your clients like to do? Do they enjoy playing golf? Golf is always a popular choice. It offers an opportunity to spend an extended amount of time in a (2) _____ setting relatively free from distraction. This allows plenty of time for you and your clients to get to know each other and chat about business (3) _____.

Everyone enjoys eating out at fine restaurants. There are something about good food and a glass of wine that reduces (4) _____ and makes people feel at ease. Eating out can be rather a routine, so find an exclusive restaurant with a fine chef and entertainment. Make it a (5) _____ experience for your clients.

Cultural events such as plays, concerts and sports events are a nice touch as well. However, there is little opportunity to talk business during these types of (6) _____, so consider events such as these as simply an opportunity for you and your clients to get to know each better.

Task 2 Listen to the passage and decide whether the following statements are true (T) or false (F).

(   ) (1) You should complain if your meeting seems to be hindered by bad restaurant service.

(   ) (2) It is okay to ask for a discount on bad service when you are with a business associate.

(   )(3) If you are meeting someone at a restaurant, you should arrive at least five minutes earlier.

(   )(4) You can recommend and order for your business associate.

(   )(5) When the waiter arrives at the table and let your associate order first.

■ **Task 3   Listen to the passage and answer the following questions.**

(1) What are the problems caused by cultural differences in business entertaining?

(2) Why can't we invite people of different statuses to the same dinner party?

(3) Is home a proper place for business entertaining in some societies except in America? Why or why not?

(4) Which method of entertaining is popular in the Americans' home?

Part III   Language focus

■ **Inviting clients**

1. We are planning to have a casual get-together, and I wonder if you can join us.
2. We want to hold a party for you. We hope you'll be able to attend.
3. Our president wants to have dinner with you while you're here. When would be convenient for you?
4. I'd like to take you out to dinner this evening.
5. May I invite you to dinner at a Chinese restaurant?
6. I will certainly come if I have time.
7. I'm sorry I can't come. I have already accepted another invitation. Thanks all the same.

■ **Inquiring about the flavor of clients**

1. What would you like to have for lunch?
2. Would you prefer Japanese food, Chinese food, or some other kind of food?
3. Are you in the mood for Japanese cuisine, Chinese cuisine, or some other cuisine?
4. Is there anything you don't eat?
5. Have you ever had … before?

■ **Talks before dinner**

1. Thank you for your invitation to dinner. It is very kind of you.
2. I'm glad you are able to come. I know how busy you are.
3. This is a nice-looking place, nice atmosphere, pleasant decor, and polite service.

4. Let's sit here by the window, shall we?

5. I hope you like French cuisine, Mr. …, because that's what this restaurant specializes in.

6. This is a restaurant with a cheerful atmosphere.

■ **Talks in dinner**

1. Do you have vegetarian dishes?

2. What is the specialty of the restaurant?

3. What kind of drinks do you have for an aperitif?

4. I'll try … first. How about you, Mr. …?

5. Next, I think I'll have the flatfish. What kind of fish would you like?

6. How about another glass of wine?

7. Please help yourselves to whatever you want. But you'd better have a taste of each dish because each has different flavor.

8. Make yourself at home and eat it while it is hot.

9. Let's all drink a toast for the success of our future cooperation.

■ **Talks after dinner**

1. Thank you for your hospitality and your dinner.

2. Thank you for preparing such a wonderful dinner especially for us.

3. I must thank you again for the very enjoyable dinner.

4. I've had a wonderful evening. Not only did you make me a good business offer, but you treated me to a great dinner.

5. This is not just an evening of business. It's also for the cultivation of friendship.

■ **About traveling itinerary**

1. I'll take you to … in the morning, and then we'll go to …

2. In the evening we'll go to … I think we'll be able to get you back to your hotel by nine or so.

3. We will take the 10 o'clock train to Tianjin, where we'll see … We'll stay at a Chinese inn there and then go to Beijing the next day.

4. How long does it take to go to the destination?

5. We'll be leaving here by car now and should reach … by 10:30.

6. We'll drive to the mountain villa, which is about 40 minutes from here.

■ **About the sights**

1. Could you give me a general idea of the layout?

2. It shows the wisdom and talent of the Chinese working people in ancient times.

3. It occupies an area of 200 square kilometers.

4. It has a history of 1,500 years.

5. It has been put down on the list of the important historical sites to be given special protection.
6. It was renovated in 1980.
7. In heaven there is the paradise, and on earth there are Suzhou and Hangzhou.
8. Guilin scenery tops those elsewhere. / Guilin scenery stands out as the world's best.

■ **During the sightseeing**

1. Shall we take a rest for a while now? You must be tired after seeing …
2. You might be tired after walking all morning. Shall we have a cup of coffee at that coffee shop?
3. Please excuse me, I have to use the men's room.
4. Are you all right? Let's sit down on that bench for a while.
5. Will you pose with me for a picture?
6. Shall I take a picture of you in this scenic spot?
7. Let's find someone to take our picture together in front of that building.

■ **After the sightseeing**

1. I hope you enjoyed the day.
2. I hope you had a wonderful time today.
3. I've enjoyed your company.
4. How did you like …?
5. Thank you so much for coming with me and telling me so much about …

Part Ⅳ Speaking out

Section 1 Sample dialogues

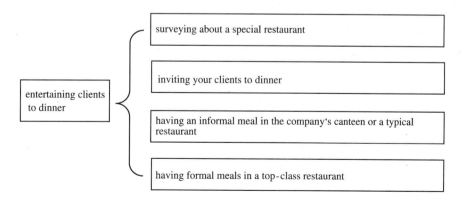

Dialogue 1

As the lunchtime is very short and they still have to do investigation in the afternoon, Sally Liu invites Mr. Williams to have business lunch in the canteen of the company.

Ms. Liu: Mr. Williams, you must be very hungry.
Mr. Williams: Not really. I've had quite a lot at breakfast. How about you?
Ms. Liu: A little. Mr. Williams, what would you like to eat? Rice or noodles?
Mr. Williams: A set meal, please.
Ms Liu: OK. What would you like to drink?
Mr. Williams: A bottle of Fanta, please.
Ms. Liu: OK. Would you like anything else, Mr. Williams?
Mr. Williams: No, thank you. We usually take lunchtime as part of working hours.
Ms. Liu: Yes. We only have one-hour lunchtime. It is so short.
Mr. Williams: We take efficiency as the top.

Sally Liu invites Mr. Williams to have dinner in the evening.

Ms. Liu: Hello, Mr. Williams. How do you find the room service and food here?
Mr. Williams: The room service is quite satisfactory and the food very delicious. This is a very good hotel.
Ms. Liu: I'm glad you find the hotel service satisfactory. Mr. Williams, I wonder if you've made any plan for tonight.
Mr. Williams: I'm not sure, but let me check my memo. Ah, no, I'm at your disposal.
Ms. Liu: Great! We'd like to hold a dinner in your honor.
Mr. Williams: Well, that's very kind of you. I'd be delighted to go.
Ms. Liu: You'll meet Mr. Pan, the GM of our company.
Mr. Williams: Good! I'm sure he's the very person I would like to meet. Thank you!
Ms. Liu: So I'll be at the hotel to pick you up. Is that OK with you?
Mr. Williams: That's good. It's awfully thoughtful of you to do this, Ms. Liu.
Ms. Liu: That's all right. Well, then, I'll say good-bye.
Mr. Williams: Good-bye and see you tonight.

During the dinner, Mr. Williams will be introduced to Mr. Pan, the general manager of SIM.

Ms. Liu: Good evening, Mr. Williams. How nice to see you again.
Mr. Williams: Me too.

Module 1 Business Reception

Ms. Liu: Mr. Williams, I'd like you to meet Mr. Pan. I'm very pleased to introduce our Canadian friend. This is Mr. Williams, the manager of Master Technology Corporation. Mr. Williams, this is Mr. Pan. He is the general manager of SIM.

Mr. Pan: How do you do, Mr. Williams? I'm so glad to meet you. On behalf of our company, we warmly welcome you and are obliged to your firm for the friendly cooperation in recent years.

Mr. Williams: Thank you for your kind words, Mr. Pan. You know, we do value our long association with SIM.

Mr. Pan: Well, Mr. Williams, what's your initial impression of Guangzhou? I heard that you'd been away for quite a while.

Mr. Williams: Yes, a lot of changes have taken place here.

Mr. Pan: That's right. This is a good time of the year for coming to Guangzhou. It is not too hot yet, the best season of the year.

Ms. Liu: What's the weather like back in your hometown?

Mr. Williams: The best time of the year, too. Flowers everywhere, warm days.

Mr. Pan: Here comes our first course. Please help yourself to it.

Mr. Williams: It looks pretty good to me!

Mr. Pan: Well, we Chinese have one rule about feast, that is you all must enjoy yourselves.

Mr. Williams: I should say that the rule will not cause me any difficulty.

(*All laugh.*)

Mr. Pan: (*Standing up and holding a small glass*) OK, may I propose a toast to the success of our negotiations and also to our friendship and cooperation.

All: (*Standing up and holding small glasses*) To our friendship and cooperation.

The next day Sally Liu and Mr. Williams are having dinner in a Western food restaurant.

Ms. Liu: Mr. Williams, I've reserved a seat in a restaurant nearby which serves fresh steak and sea food as well.

Mr. Williams: Really? It is great. I have not eaten the natural Western food for several weeks.

Ms. Liu: Ha-ha. Shall we go now?

Mr. Williams: Great! I can't wait for that.

Ms. Liu: What appetizer would you like? Jelly or caviar?
Mr. Williams: Jelly, please.
Ms. Liu: And a full-course meal?
Mr. Williams: Yea. And the dessert after the meal.

A few minutes later, the waiter serves the dishes.

Ms. Liu: It tastes so good. But excuse me, Mr. Williams, I am always confused with the Western tableware.
Mr. Williams: Never mind. We are quite free. For me the chopsticks are really a hard nut to crack.
Ms. Liu: Are you interested in Chinese food?
Mr. Williams: Very much. I hope I have the chance to know more about Chinese food.
Ms. Liu: Really? Do you like spicy food?
Mr. Williams: I'm afraid not.
Ms. Liu: Well, I know of a good restaurant nearby specializing in Cantonese cuisine. Let's go to have a seat there tomorrow.

■ Dialogue 2

Sightseeing is arranged during foreign clients' stay in China if time permits. It is never easy to be a good guide. Good preparation makes the first step. Information collection about the scenic spots and travel arrangements will help you as a good tour guide. The work flow of serving as a tour guide is as follows.

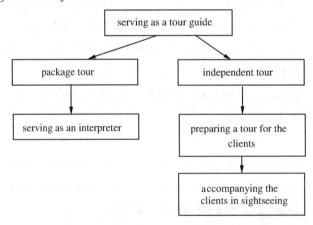

Mr. Richards and Fang Jia are talking about the tour arrangement.

Mr. Richards: Where are we going to visit next?
Fang Jia: According to the itinerary, we are going to visit the Great Wall next,

Module 1 Business Reception

	Mr. Richards.
Mr. Richards:	That's wonderful.
Fang Jia:	We set off at 12:00 and go to Badaling first, the most visited section of the Great Wall, where we can enjoy a panorama of the Wall. Then we go back from Badaling at 2:30 p.m.
Mr. Richards:	I've heard of the Great Wall for a long time. Could you give me a brief introduction to the Wall?
Fang Jia:	The Wall was designed to defense alien tribes' invasion. It can accommodate six horses to run abreast. And the top surface of the Wall was paved with three or four layers of large bricks. Some of the rock slabs were as long as two meters.
Mr. Richards:	Oh, Miss Fang, it's a miracle. I can't wait to go there.
Fang Jia:	We'll be there soon.

Mr. Richards and Miss Fang are mounting the steps to get to the top of Badaling.

Fang Jia:	Do you find it tiring to climb up all these steps?
Mr. Richards:	No, not at all. I find it most refreshing. Look! What a magnificent sight! I wonder how long the Wall actually is. It seems endless.
Fang jia:	From its starting point in Gansu Province, to Shanhai Pass, the eastern end near the sea, it's more than 12,000 li that is about 4,500 miles long.
Mr. Richards:	It certainly is a great great wall.
Fang Jia:	We Chinese call it "Changcheng", which means "long wall".
Mr. Richards:	It is truly one of wonders! How long did it take to build a great wall like this?
Fang Jia:	The project began over 2,500 years ago in the latter part of the Zhou Dynasty. At that time, China was not unified but divided into a number of small states. They often fought against each other, and some built walls to protect themselves. So, at the beginning, the walls were disconnected.
Mr. Richards:	But when were they connected as one wall?
Fang Jia:	The Great Wall first took shape in the reign of the Qin Dynasty. Then throughout the years till the Ming Dynasty, the strengthening and renovation of the Wall went on.
Mr. Richards:	The Chinese are certainly great people. Standing here at the top of the

	Great Wall, I see the Wall winding like a huge serpent up and down endless mountains! What a grand view this is! It's a most rewarding trip.
Fang Jia:	Absolutely. The Great Wall is a must-see that no visitors to China should miss seeing.
Mr. Richards:	That's true.
Fang Jia:	Mr. Richards, you can take some pictures if you like.
Mr. Richards:	Yes, you have reminded me. I'd love to.

Fang Jia and Mr. Richards are back to the hotel. Now they are at the lobby talking bout the tour.

Fang Jia:	I hope you had a wonderful time.
Mr. Richards:	That's for sure! Look at these photos, Miss Fang. They are terrific.
Fang Jia:	I couldn't agree more.
Mr. Richards:	I enjoyed the scenic spots we visited very much. The Forbidden City, the Summer Palace, the Great Wall. I've really fed my eyes this time.
Fang Jia:	I'm so glad to hear that. No tourist would deny they are worth visiting.
Mr. Richards:	Absolutely.
Fang Jia:	I'm so happy you enjoyed the sightseeing.
Mr. Richards:	I love the wonderful scenery. I love China. I wish I could stay longer, but I have to be back tomorrow. Thank you for what you've done for me.
Fang Jia:	It's my pleasure to be your guide. I hope to see you again soon.

Section 2 Creating your own

■ **Task 1 Pair work: Make a conversation according to the given information.**

Tips for you (A)

You are in charge of entertaining a new client of your company to dinner. The tips are for you to prepare a conversation.

- You are

    from China

    the assistant manager of Xiamen Time Trade Co., Ltd., China

---

Module 1 Business Reception

- You

  invite your client to have a business dinner in a local restaurant

  introduce some delicious local food

  toast a successful cooperation

Tips for you (B)

You are invited to have a dinner while you are visiting a company in China. The tips are for you to prepare a conversation.

- You are

  from Dubai

  the head of the Import Dept. of the ABC Imp./Exp. Corp., Dubai

- You

  accept A's invitation for a dinner

  show your interest in Chinese food

  toast a successful cooperation

Task 2 Pair work: Make a conversation according to the given information.

Tips for you (A)

You are telling your foreign client about tomorrow's schedule of sightseeing in your local area. The tips are for you to prepare a conversation.

- You are

  from China

  the foreign affairs secretary of MDA Company

- You

  tell your client the route of a tour

  tell your client the basic information of the places you will visit

  tell your client the time needed to visit these places

Tips for you (B)

You come to MDA Company for a visit. They arrange a tour for you after business negotiation. Now the secretary Luo Lan is telling you about the tour arrangement. The tips are for you to prepare a conversation.

> - You are
>   from New Zealand
>   the manager of a New Zealand-registered company
>   ask about tomorrow's arrangement for a tour
>   ask about the basic information of the places you will visit
>   ask about the time needed to visit these places

Part V Writing

You are a manager of a small export company. Peter Watson, an important client, is visiting your company for three days from October 22.

Write a note of 40~50 words to your secretary Mary:

- asking her to book a hotel room;
- saying where the hotel should be;
- giving her the dates.

Part VI Follow-up reading

Passage 1

Read the passage with five statements attached to it, and identify the paragraph from which the information is derived. You may not choose a paragraph more than once.

A. Entertaining current and potential clients is an integral part of business. Clients' breakfasts, lunches, dinners, coffee meetings, seminars, conferences or weekend retreats are an opportunity to get to know each other. Face-to-face meetings are crucial for establishing trust between any two or group of business professionals. Mastering a few skills and social graces will put you years ahead in building lasting client relationships.

B. Before inviting your clients, think about how the event will play out. What possible worst-case scenarios can you take a proactive approach to solving? How will your clients arrive at the venue? Are there issues with parking? Will there be lines? Do your clients have mobility issues? Will there be any language or cultural barriers?

Module 1 Business Reception

C. Whether you're at a networking event, business meeting or just enjoying a few drinks with colleagues, the handshake may be the single most important action for you to master when entertaining clients. It's the first point of contact, and you want to make sure you nail it. Give a firm shake that shows you mean business, yet at the same time says that you're easy going and friendly.

D. A trendy new restaurant that everyone is raving about might not sound like a perfect choice to impress clients, since you're not the only one with this bright idea. Service might be slow, and the noise may not be suitable for conversation. Impress your clients with a restaurant where you know the location, menu, and staff.

E. To alleviate the stress of the unknown, you can make recommendations as to the chef's specialties or bartender's drinks. This is probably the easiest skill to master, especially in a crowded bar. Keep a few things in mind. First, you should know your clients' drink of choice by this point. Whether it's a whiskey neat, top-shelf gin or just a tall pint of Guinness, the goal here is to get your drinks as quickly as possible and get down to business.

F. To get your drinks fast, the first and most important thing to do is just to stare at the bartender. Keep your gaze fixed on them until they acknowledge your presence. This shows them you know exactly what you want and are not going to waste their time with endless questions.

G. Be direct, speak up and then remain patient as your bartender crafts your drinks. You can set your cash down on the table, but make sure not to wave it in their face and distract them from pouring your beverages. This will likely result in sub-par drink, and you want your clients to be happy and enjoy the meeting.

H. Keep the toast short and sweet: You've already proven yourself, and now it's time to speak confidently and give your thanks for the flourishing partnership. Make sure you get right to the point and try to keep your toast within 2 minutes.

I. Be careful with jokes and humor: Unless you have shared a joke or other humorous experience with your clients in the past. It is best to stay away from controversy.

(From: https://www.firmex.com/thedealroom)

(　) (1) You may stare down the bartender if you want your drinks to be served fast.
(　) (2) One needs to be thoughtful when planning to invite clients.
(　) (3) It is not always a good idea to entertain clients in a trendy new restaurant.
(　) (4) It is advisable for you to give your clients a firm shake in a serious but friendly way.
(　) (5) It is recommended to give thanks for the thriving partnership when proposing a toast.

Passage 2

Read the passage carefully, and fill in the blanks.

Some foreign clients would like to go shopping and buy some souvenirs for their family members or friends when they are not involved in business activities. If the clients show their intention of shopping, it is necessary for you to show that you, as the host, are ready and enthusiastic to accompany them in shopping and it is also important to show your zeal at any time. Only in this way can you win your clients' trust. Besides, it is the efficient channel of establishing communication relationship and narrowing the gap between each other.

Before going shopping, be aware of what the clients want to buy or you can offer some local specialties initiatively, which is up to your clients' decision. With certain inclination of the clients, you should make for them some plans as to what can be bought in certain shops and what is more economical. Then, it is time for you to introduce some places where people can buy better quality products at reasonable prices. At last, your clients can determine the destination and set off. In this way, the clients waste no time and enjoy the shopping with your help.

The best commodity is one with low price and high quality, so bargaining becomes one important link in accompanied shopping. When accompanying clients in shopping, you can inform the clients of the approximate price of what the clients want to buy, as it can better their understanding about the market information of the goods. In shops where prices of goods could be bargained, you can inform the clients of the approximate discount and help to bargain with them. The escorts should show respect for the clients' shopping inclination and offer some suggestions in due time so as to make the purchase as economical as possible. If the shopping time lasts for a long time and the clients seem to be a little tired, you can show concern for the clients and ask them whether they are tired or not or whether it is necessary to find a place for rest. You can also help to carry the shopping goods the clients have bought. If what they buy is too heavy or too large, you can suggest mailing the goods for them. It is significant to be attentive to such a small case as going shopping, because it can not only enhance the emotion between your clients and you, but also convince the clients that you are a good business partner.

(Form: JI Shujun, 2010: 106)

(1) It is crucial to show your _____ when your clients show their interest in shopping.

(2) You'd better introduce places where better quality products with _____ prices are available.

(3) _____ is important as the best goods are those with relatively low price and superior quality.

(4) When accompanying clients in shopping, you are supposed to show _____ for their shopping preferences.

(5) If your clients' shopping goods are too heavy or large, you could suggest _____ them.

Training Assessment

Part I Self-study

Complete the following dialogue.

A: Sir, how will the meals this afternoon be served, (1) _____? (点菜还是自助餐?)

B: Buffet will be served for three meals. You may choose the Western food, Chinese food or Moslem food as you like.

A: (2) _____? (用餐时凭身份卡还是用餐券?)

B: ID card.

A: (3) _____? (能告诉我就餐时间吗?)

B: Please read the timetable on the wall outside the restaurant.

A: (4) _____? (请问本酒店有中餐厅吗?) We want to arrange some Chinese food for our foreign business clients.

B: (5) _____. (我们酒店的14层设有中餐厅,那里的广东菜很地道,你们客户会喜欢的。)

A: Thank you for your advice.

B: You're welcome.

Part II BEC exam focus

Listening Test

Questions 1 – 12

You will hear three telephone conversations or messages.

Write **one or two words or a number** in the numbered spaces on the notes or forms below.

You will hear each recording twice.

Conversation 1（Questions 1 – 4）

- Look at the form below.
- You will hear a message about a magazine subscription on a telephone answering machine.

Subscriptions form

NAME: Ms. Cynthia (1) _____

COMPANY: (2) _____ solutions.

ADDRESS: On record

SUBCRIPTION NO: (3) _____

REQUEST: Send (4) _____ edition of the magazine.

Conversation 2（Questions 5 – 8）

- Look at the notes below.
- You will hear a man calling about changes to a project.

Notes

Tom Yishan called about the (5) _____ we're making on the 11th.

They want to delay the filming in the (6) _____ by ten days.

I've asked to put it back by (7) _____.

Tom will (8) _____ that with me when he had spoken to the manager.

Conversation 3（Questions 9 – 12）

- Look at the notes below.
- You will hear a woman telephoning another department in her company about a job applicant.

MESSAGE

Message for: Michael

From: Rachel Robins, IT

RE: Job application of Rufus Nichols

Problems:

The applicant hasn't filled in all the sections of the (9) _____.

She needs the (10) _____ for his college tutor to get reference.

Please confirm with Rachel when you have (11) _____ the interview and she wants to know (12) _____ the interview will last.

Module 2 Business Travel

Business today is international

 ## Into the Module

Business travel is the travel undertaken for work or business purposes, as opposed to other types of travel such as for leisure purposes or regularly commuting between one's home and workplace. The reasons to conduct business travel might include:
- visiting customers or suppliers;
- meetings at other company locations;
- professional development and attending a congress;
- marketing or promoting a new or existing product;
- visiting a project site for evaluation;
- strengthening the relationships with customers;
- strengthening employees' loyalty to the business;
- building new partnerships;
- networking;
- identifying trends and new markets.

 ## Training Objectives

By the end of this module, you are expected to:
- master how to make a reservation before a trip;
- deal with issues on your journey;
- know how to have a comfortable stay in hotel.

To know what people really think, pay regard to what they do rather than what they say.

—Rene Decartes, Philosopher

Module 2 Business Travel

Unit 4 Making Reservations

Minimize stress and maximize enjoyment

 **Training Objectives**

> By the end of this unit, you are expected to know:
> - how to make a reservation of tickets by telephone;
> - how to book hotel rooms;
> - how to arrange your trip in an economic way.

 **Training Portfolio**

Part I Starting up

Section 1 To discuss

Have you ever logged on to (viewing) a website for Hotel Reservation? Try to book a hotel room through Internet next time you go for a trip.

Section 2 To read

Read the following passage and then report the idea that you remember to your classmates and tell what impresses you most.

How to prepare for a business trip

Business trips are essential to keep a business thriving. Traveling to different locations to attend meetings and conferences or even just to meet old and new clients is just some of the reasons why people embark on business trips. To have a successful business trip, it is important to plan wisely.

Items you will need:

- Datebook or journal
- Contact list or address book
- Laptop
- PDA
- Cell phone
- Flash drive, compact discs or floppy disks
- Conference and meeting venues

Plan ahead. Once you have determined the dates of your business trip, it is necessary to plan ahead. Often, a business trip is done in a location farther than your local hub. Reserve your travel accommodations which can include air travel, hotel, and car reservations way in advance. If you are planning on attending big conferences that will surely be attended by a lot of people from different parts of the globe, ensure that you do this months in advance so that you can still get a confirmation for the travel accommodations as well as the conferences themselves.

Set goals before you leave for your business trip. What would you like to accomplish when you arrive at your destination? You want to be as productive as possible for a very short amount of time. Time management is the key to making sure that you meet your goals.

Set up appointments. Business trips cost companies money to pay for the travel accommodations as well as food. Make it worthwhile by hitting more than one bird with one stone. Try to schedule some appointments to meet with your clients, vendors and other key business contacts. If you have staff members that report to you in the same location you are attending a conference, try to meet with them personally.

Set up tasks and deliverables before you travel. For example, if you are running a conference yourself, ensure that the equipment you will be using such as projection screen, projectors and microphones have been reserved together with the meeting room. Contact the local admin in the branch you are visiting or the technical support personnel to ensure that you have a spot to do your work with proper network and phone connections. If there are certain tasks to be completed before your arrival by some people who are attending your meeting, set them up weeks in advance to allow them enough time to prepare or complete such tasks.

Send information ahead. If you have agenda or PowerPoint presentations for the meetings, send them via email ahead of time. Preparing your attendees on what needs to be discussed will allow them enough time to review the materials and prepare questions for you to answer. Doing this gives you also an opportunity to review your own materials and make necessary corrections prior to the meeting if needed.

Get ready for your business trip by packing your luggage with essential items. Do not forget to bring enough outfits to use, especially if you anticipate attending formal dinners; bring an outfit that fits the occasion. Bring your personal effects and toiletries that you can use while away from home.

Bring tools. Don't forget to bring your laptop, PDA, address books, journals, cell phones, flash drives, disks, or anything that you would anticipate needing for you to be able to work. Be prepared by bringing files saved in a flash drive, CD or floppy disks. Even if your laptop gets damaged or lost, you still have your documents safe to use on other people's computers.

Update contacts. Business trips is also an opportunity to update your contact list. Add new contacts of people you meet while traveling and attending conferences. The person seated next to you on the plane may have something in common with you. Build your networking list for more future opportunities for your business and for you.

(From: http://bizfluent.com/how-2160827-prepare-business-trip.html)

Part II Listening in

Task 1 Listen to the following passage and fill in the blanks.

Airline credit cards offer some of the most lucrative rewards available and perk for (1)_____. Though annual fees can make airline credit cards some of the most expensive rewards cards to carry, (2)_____ who take advantage of their airline benefits can recoup more than that fee. The (3)_____ can be worth it for cardholders who travel frequently and pay their credit card balance each month.

There are two types of credit cards for earning (4)_____:

Airline cobranded cards that let you earn and redeem rewards for a specific airline.

Travel rewards cards that can be used for a wide selection of (5)_____.

Best airline credit cards of 2018

U. S. News researched leading cobranded airline credit cards and credit cards

(6)_____ to identify the best cards available for air travel. The value of each card's rewards rate for flights was evaluated, along with the amount and minimum spending requirement of (7)_____. The card's annual fee and cardholder benefits, including free checked bags, priority boarding, travel credits and (8)_____, were factored in to each card's overall value.

Airline loyalty, (9)_____ and other preferences are different for every traveler, so the best airline card for you may not be the same as another traveler's. A cobranded airline card may offer excellent rewards value, but it's not valuable to you unless you (10)_____ with that airline, or a sign-up bonus may be enticing but out of reach for your spending habits. U. S. News' top choices for airline travel rewards credit cards offer the best value for (11)_____, whether you want to maximize your rewards with a particular airline or earn rewards for flights you can redeem with flexibility.

■ **Task 2　Listen and decide whether the following statements are true (T) or false (F).**

Mr. Clinton, the CFO of ABC company, is discussing his business travel arrangement with his secretary Miss Yang.

(　　) (1) Mr. Clinton is leaving Beijing for Madrid at 9 a. m. on the 18th of June.

(　　) (2) Mr. Clinton will stay in Sheraton Hotel for 4 nights.

(　　) (3) Miss Yang booked Mr. Clinton in Sheraton Hotel in Copenhagen.

(　　) (4) It takes about three and a half hours by train to Stockholm.

(　　) (5) Mr. Clinton planned to fly straight back to Beijing on 26th 3:30 in the morning.

Part Ⅲ　Language focus

■ **Reserving a room**

1. We'd like to book a twin bed-room, with queen size beds next Sunday.
2. What is the rate, please?
3. Do you require a deposit?
4. Please reserve a single room with bath.
5. I'd like to book a double room from this Thursday for three days, please.
6. Have you got any vacancies for tonight?
7. I'd like a room away from the street.
8. Can I have a smoking room, please?

9. Do you have any discount if we stay longer?

■ **Booking a ticket**

1. Could I make a reservation for Flight 10 to Tokyo?
2. There are not window seats left, but a few entrance seats are open.
3. I want an economy ticket to Beijing, please.
4. Sorry, we are all booked up for that flight.
5. May I reconfirm my flight?
6. I'd like to change my reservation.
7. Is it a direct flight?
8. I prefer the direct flight. Are there any seats available?

Part IV Speaking out

Section 1 Sample dialogues

Dialogue 1

The receptionist is receiving a call from one guest.

Receptionist: Hello, Marriott Hotel, may I help you?

Nancy: Hi. I'd like to make a reservation of a single room with a king bed.

Receptionist: Just a moment. OK, for what date?

Nancy: July 25th.

Receptionist: How many nights will you be staying?

Nancy: Two nights. What's the room rate?

Receptionist: A single room with a front view is 175 dollars a night plus tax, one with a rear view is 115 dollars. Would you like me to reserve a room for you?

Nancy: Yes, I think I'll take the one with a front view then.

Receptionist: OK, your name, please.

Nancy: Nancy Anderson.

Receptionist: Miss Anderson, how will you be paying?

Nancy: Visa.

Receptionist: Card number, please.

Nancy: 4198 2289 3388 228.

Receptionist: Expiration date?

Nancy: September 1, 2012.

Receptionist: OK. You're all set. We'll see you on the 25th.

Dialogue 2

A: Good morning. What can I do for you?

B: Yes, I'd like to make a reservation to Boston next week.

A: When do you want to fly?

B: Monday, September 12.

A: We have Flight 802 on Monday. Just a moment, please. Let me check whether there're seats available. I'm sorry we are all booked up for Flight 802 on that day.

B: Then, any alternatives?

A: The next available flight leaves at 9:30 Tuesday morning, September 13. Shall I book you a seat?

B: Err … it is a direct flight, isn't it?

A: Yes, it is. You want to go first class or coach?

B: I prefer first class, what's the fare?

A: One way is $176.

B: OK, I will take the 9:30 flight on Tuesday.

A: A seat on Flight 807 to Boston 9:30 Tuesday morning. Is it all right, sir?

B: Right. Can you also put me on the waiting list for the 12th?

A: Certainly. May I have your name and telephone number?

B: My name is Lorus Anderson. You can reach me at 52378651.

A: I will notify you if there is cancellation.

B: Thank you very much.

A: My pleasure.

Section 2   Creating your own

Task 1   Role-play in pairs according to the situation below.

Student A is the Export Manager of Shanghai Cosmetics Ltd. and is now planning a trip to Los Angeles in US. Student B is the booking-office clerk and is answering Student A's telephone call about buying a flight ticket.

Task 2 Role-play in pairs according to the situation below.

After the ticket-booking, Student A is now making a reservation of a hotel room. Student B becomes a clerk at Hotel Reservation Department answering the phone call from Student A.

Part V Writing

Invitation letter

You are one of the organizers of the International Auto Fair, which will be held in Switzerland. please write an invitation letter to the director of China Industrial Association asking for the attendance of China delegation. All the following details should be included in your letter:

—date

—location (name of the city)

—duration

—all the related expenses are paid by attendants themselves

(Tips: If you know the recipient's name, use "Dear Mr. ×××" or "Dear Ms. ×××" to start and "Yours sincerely" to end; if you do not know, use "Dear Sir" or "Dear Madam" to start and "Yours faithfully" to end.)

Part VI Follow-up reading

Passage 1

Read the following passage and answer the questions.

11 easy ways to slash travel costs

Traveling on a budget doesn't mean you have to compromise on comfortable accommodations and decent flight times. In fact, savvy travelers already know how to maximize their travel budget and take advantage of low prices on travel packages, airline tickets, and other travel-related expenses. Planning ahead will usually give you the upper hand when it comes to playing the vacation-booking game, and there are several tricks and tactics you can use to slash those costs even further. Whether you're dreaming of a trip to the

Bahamas or looking to book an overseas adventure, make sure you're aware of all of the different deals, discounts, and specials available to your destination of choice.

Here are 11 tips to help you slash travel costs with ease:

- **Fly into alternate airports**

Don't overlook the opportunity to fly into an alternate airport when you are heading to a major city or other hub with multiple airports. Flights to alternate airports can end up being slightly less expensive than flying into a larger international airport in the same city. In some cases, you might also be closer to your final destination and be able to skirt traffic. Just make sure to calculate taxi fares from all airports, so you aren't paying extra for ground transportation when flying into an alternate airport.

- **Book and fly on the right day of the week**

Shop for airfare on Tuesdays and Wednesdays, says Travelzoo's Senior Editor Gabe Saglie. Most airlines publish their sale fares on Tuesday—this is when competition to match those fares begins each week. You're also likely to find a better deal when you fly on a Tuesday, Wednesday or Saturday. This might mean you have to wait a few days to secure that vacation package, but you could end up saving a significant amount of money on those airline tickets.

- **Book group travel with a rewards card**

Earn bonus miles when booking a group trip by paying for travel expenses using a travel rewards credit card. The best travel rewards card program will allow you to earn extra miles under your own account, and you can have the group members pay you directly in cash for their portion of the trip. Buying airline tickets with a rewards credit card is a smart move for most—especially if you travel frequently and are planning on taking another trip in the near future.

- **Plan ahead for holiday weekends**

Holiday weekends will be among the priciest times to fly, so unless you're heading to a destination specifically to celebrate the holiday, steer clear of those long weekend trips to save some money. The weekend before or after a major holiday weekend usually commands lower rates and fares.

- **Seek out off-peak deals**

Do your homework to find out which destinations are currently in their off-peak season. You'll find that many destinations around Europe have very attractive package deals during the spring and early summer months. Traveling during the off-peak season could save you up to 50 percent or more of your entire vacation package.

- **Keep your passport up-to-date**

Don't wait until the last minute to update your passport information if it's expired. The application process can take up to six weeks and you'll need to pay a set of fees for the service. If you're an avid traveler, make sure your passport never gets too close to the expiry date before you request a renewal.

- **Subscribe to deal sites**

Groupon Getaways, Travelzoo and LivingSocial Escapes are just three of the leading travel deal sites that will keep you in the knowledge about the latest deals and discounts. You can also sign up for free membership-only sites like Jetsetter or Spire to get exclusive, pre-negotiated rates at many luxury hotels and travel packages around the country.

- **Learn to pack properly**

Overpacking can lead to extra checked baggage fees, so make sure you're packing only what you really need. If you're planning an extended stay trip, get quotes from shipping service providers that will be able to ship and pick up your items at your destination of choice. In some cases, shipping your belongings instead of carrying them in a suitcase will end up being less expensive.

- **Negotiate hotel rates**

If you can't find a great deal on a hotel and flight package through a third-party travel site, consider calling the hotel or resort directly and inquiring about the best available deals. Sometimes the rates extended by the hotel end up being lower than rates published online. Hotels may need to fill rooms at the last minute and some will be open to negotiating a rate or package deal.

- **Research ground transportation options**

Don't wait until you arrive at the airport to figure out how you are going to get from the airport to your hotel or resort. Research taxi service providers and rental car companies before you leave so you can negotiate a rate or book a great deal. Waiting until you arrive won't give you any time to compare prices, so you'll end up just paying any price as you go.

- **Look for freebies and deals at your final destination**

Search like a local for free attractions in the area, free events you could participate in, and free guided tours that may be available at different venues throughout the town or city you're visiting. Keeping activity costs low means you can spend more on a great meal and splurge on other travel expenses if you want to. You could also check out the daily deal sites at the city you're visiting to see what types of discounts may be available for local activities, events and dining destinations. Consider buying a "city pass" or similar activity card that lets you visit several attractions for one low price. Save even more with a discount that reduces the ticket prices of some of the most popular attractions in the city.

(From: http://money.usnews.com/money/blogs/my-money/2012/05/29/11-easy-ways-to-slash-travel-costs)

(1) How do you save money in the proceeding of booking tickets?

(2) Which day in a week can you check sales fares of most airlines?

(3) What is a rewards credit card for?

(4) Is it economical to travel at a destination around Europe in early summer months?

(5) Why is it better to call a hotel directly about deals than make a reservation online?

Passage 2

Read the following passage and decide whether each of the following statements is true (T) or false (F).

Ten business etiquette tips

A workplace with rude, dismissive or careless employees is one that is unproductive, unpleasant and ripe for litigation. This sort of behavior internally spills over to customers eventually, and an insulted customer can easily find someone else to replace your services. Good business etiquette practices start from the top, but employees at every level can help promote good business etiquette.

Everyone has a role

When dealing with your own employees, remember that every person in the company, from the CEO to the mail clerk, can affect every other person. All employees' jobs are interconnected, and the person you may be dismissive of today could have information that is relevant to you tomorrow.

Make meetings useful

When a meeting is necessary, be mindful of other attendees' schedules, and ensure that you are prepared with any materials or information needed for the meeting topic. Thank attendees for their contributions, and send out a written record of what was discussed with action items. A meeting that requires no action to be taken is a meeting that wasn't necessary in the first place.

Prompt communication

When you receive a phone call or email, whether internally or from a client, be sure to respond to it in a timely manner. Even if the inquiry will take longer, a quick email or phone call to let the sender know that you're looking into the subject is going to be appreciated.

Email use

The instant gratification of email can lead to careless use and unprofessional appearance. Take the same care in crafting email that you would for any published work, including spelling, punctuation, grammar and capitalization. Be specific, avoiding unclear questions or one-word answers. If you have to send an email asking for clarification and receive one back, you've doubled the amount of emails sent on what could have otherwise been a simple exchange.

Respect others' time

When you need to interrupt someone, try to do it unobtrusively. Be polite and get to the point quickly, to allow him to get back to his work in progress. Avoid interrupting meetings unless time is of importance.

Dress for success

Even in a casual environment, one should err on the side of caution. A slovenly appearance can imply to clients and coworkers that the situation, company or people involved aren't worth the effort to present yourself respectably. If the dress code is uncertain, it is always safer to be overdressed than underdressed.

Keep your boss informed

Don't overdo compliments and agreements regarding your boss. Primarily, you should treat all your coworkers with respect, but also behaving differently towards a superior can easily appear to be brown-nosing. You should, however, provide your boss with more information, since he is ultimately responsible for your performance. Keep him informed of any delays, setbacks, new developments or concerns.

Respect other cultures

If your company does work internationally, always respect the other cultures. While you needn't be fluent in every language you do business in, an attempt to learn at least a portion of a language can demonstrate a strong desire for cooperation and respect. Other cultural differences such as holidays and table manners should be studied before any international meeting.

Timeliness

When there is a time factor in anything business related, from a deadline for a project or a meeting set to begin, don't be late. It implies that you have things more pressing than your coworkers or clients, and more worthy of your attention.

Remember the basics

Above all else, remember the simplest manners you were taught as a child. "Please", "thank you" and "you're welcome" are some of the most basic spoken manners, and yet some of the most forgotten. Avoid raising your voice and offensive language.

(From: https://smallbusiness.chron.com/ten-business-etiquette-tips-176.html)

(   ) (1) If the inquiry from a client will take longer to deal with, then you don't need to give a quick response of confirmation (like a phone call) to the client.

(   ) (2) Be specific and avoid one-word answers when you are emailing in work.

(   ) (3) You should give equal treatment to your boss and all your coworkers.

(   ) (4) It is helpful to learn different cultures such as holidays and table manners before an international meeting.

(   ) (5) Always use polite expression, but never mind if you raise your voice to make a point.

Training Assessment

Part I Self-study

Translate the following dialogue and then practice with your partner.

A: Hey, Jane, the boss is sending me to Shanghai for a marketing seminar next week.

B: Aha, you must be happy. You've been itching to go on a business trip for months.

A: (1)_____? (能给我详细说说出差需要做哪些准备吗?)

B: Sure, no problem. First, go and see the secretary and tell her where you're going and when. (2)_____. (她会通过我们的旅行代理,为你安排交通和酒店,并在几天内给你旅程表。) At the same time, ask her for an application form for the card.

A: Will I use the card for everything?

B: No. The fact is that we have company credit arrangements with some major airlines and hotels. For this trip, you'll probably only use it for food. (3)_____. (但并不是所有的饭店都接受这种信用卡。你也许要付现金。)

A: Do I pay out of my own pocket?

B: I am afraid so. We used to have cash advances, but the company stopped that when they slotted to use credit cards.

A: Will the company reimburse everything?

B: No, there is a maximum every day. I'll give you a list. Of course, personal items aren't covered. (4) _____. (记得必须保留所有收据。) You'll have to attach them to your expense account when you get back.

A: Anything else?

B: That is it so far. _____. (如果你有什么其他问题的话，可以随时联系我。)

A: Great. Thank you very much.

B: That is OK.

Part II BEC exam focus

Reading Test

Questions 1 – 6

- Read the advice below about producing a company brochure and the questions on the next page.
- For each question (1 – 6), mark one letter (A, B, C or D) on your Answer Sheet.

The art of persuasion

"Let me send you our brochure" is probably the most commonly used phrase in business. But all too often, it can spell the end of a customer enquiry because many brochures appear to be produced not to clarify and to excite but to confuse. So what goes wrong and how can it be put right? Too often, businesses fail to ask themselves critical questions like "Who will the brochure be sent to?" "What do we want to achieve with it?" The truth is that a brochure has usually been produced for no other reason than that the competition has one.

However, with a little research, it often transpires that what the client wants is a mixture: part mail shot, part glossy corporate brochure and part product catalogue—a combination rarely found. Having said that, the budget is likely to be finite. There may not be enough money to meet all three marketing needs, so the first task is to plan the brochure, taking into account the most significant of these. The other requirements will have to be met in a different way. After all, introducing the company's product range to new customers by mail is a different task from selling a new season's collection to existing customers.

The second task is to get the content right. In 95 percent of cases, a company will hire a designer to oversee the layout, so the final product looks stylish, interesting and professional; but they don't get a copywriter or someone with the right expertise to produce the text, or at least tidy it up—and this shows. A bigger failing is to produce a brochure that is not what a customer focuses on. Your brochure should cover the areas of interest to the customer, concentrating on the benefits of buying from you.

Instead, thousands of brochures start with a history lesson, "Founded in 1987, we have been selling our products …". I can assure you that customers are never going to say to themselves, "They've been around for 20 years—I'll buy from them." It's not how long you've been in business that counts, it's what you've done in that time. The important point to get across at the beginning is that you have a good track record. Once this has been established, the rest of the brochure should aim to convince customers that your products are the best on the market.

It is helpful with content to get inside the customer's head. If your audience is young and trendy, be creative and colorful. As always, create a list of the benefits that potential customers would gain from doing business with you, for example, product quality, breadth of range, expertise of staff and so on. But remember that it is not enough just to state these; in order to persuade, they need to be spelt out. One possibility is to quote recommendations from existing customers. This also makes the brochure personal to you, rather than it simply being a set of suppliers' photographs with your name on the front.

At the design stage, there are many production features that can distinguish your brochure from the run of the mill. You may think that things like cutouts or pop-ups will do this for you and thus make you stand out, or you may think they just look like designer whims that add cost. Go through all the options in detail. One of them might be that all-important magical ingredient.

( )(1) What point does the writer make about brochures in the first paragraph?

    A. Customers' expectations of them are too high.

    B. They ought to be more straightforward in design.

    C. Insufficient thought tends to go into producing them.

    D. Companies should ensure they use them more widely.

( )(2) The writer's advice to companies in the second paragraph is to _____.

    A. produce a brochure to advertise new product lines

    B. use a brochure to extend the customer base

    C. accept that a brochure cannot fulfill every objective

    D. aim to get a bigger budget allocation for producing brochures

( )(3) In the third paragraph, which of the following does the writer say would improve the majority of brochures?

A. Better language and expression.

B. Better overall appearance.

C. More up-to-date content.

D. More product information.

( ) (4) In the introduction to a brochure, the writer advises companies to focus on _____.

A. their understanding of the business environment

B. the range of products they offer

C. their unique market position

D. the reputation they have built up

( ) (5) When discussing brochure content in the fifth paragraph, the writer reminds companies to _____.

A. consider old customers as well as new ones

B. provide support for the claims they make

C. avoid using their own photographs

D. include details of quality certification

( ) (6) What does "run of the mill" in the last paragraph mean?

A. Eye-catching.

B. Complicated.

C. Stylish.

D. Ordinary.

Unit 5　On the Journey

Safe and sound

 Training Objectives

By the end of this unit, you are expected to:
- master the basic process of boarding;
- learn how to go through the customs;
- know how to ask for directions;
- know how to take public transportation.

 Training Portfolio

Part I　Starting up

Section 1　To discuss

(1) Do you know the precautions for each step?
(2) Have you experienced any bewildered or awkward moment when you went through the procedure?
(3) Please predict what kind of problems will happen in each step.
- Queue at the check-in
- Go through security

- Watch an in-flight movie (Ask the stewardess for blankets and drinks)
- Collect their luggage
- Go through the Customs
- Take a bus or taxi to a hotel

Section 2 To read

Read the following passage and then report the idea that you remember to your classmates and tell what impresses you most.

15 tips for surviving a long flight

Long flights: Do you love them or hate them? They're a necessity to get to the most far-flung destinations on the planet and some people love them, while others loathe them. But long flights don't have to be something to be dreaded—they can actually be enjoyed if you plan ahead and arm yourself with things that will help to pass the time and help you sleep.

Here are my top 15 tips for surviving a long flight:

- **Power up**

Make sure you have all your chargers with you so that you can keep all your gadgets powered up throughout your flight. Alternatively, bring extra batteries or an external charging device in case your plane doesn't have electrical outlets. Tip: Keep your chargers organized with a portable carrying case.

- **Load up your devices**

Before you board your flight, make sure that your devices (tablet, laptop, smartphone, e-reader) are loaded up with games, movies, television shows, music, books and the airline's app just in case that is how they stream their entertainment.

- **Pack a pillow (and a blanket)**

There are tons of different pillows on the market. Find out which one works for you and go with it. I like these ones from Passage Pillows. Also, not all airlines provide blankets so you might want to bring your own ... or at least a cozy sweater. For the ladies, my wife swears by the blanket scarf.

- **Wear comfortable clothes**

The temperature on a plane is rarely comfortable for everyone. You might be freezing, while the person a few rows away finds it too warm. You just never know so it is best to be prepared. Wear comfortable clothes on a long flight and pack some layers so that you can adjust as the temperature changes on the plane. Pack some cozy socks too, but don't go into the bathroom in just your sock feet—put your shoes on!

- **About sleeping pills**

The key to surviving a long flight is being able to get some shut-eye. I personally don't take any kind of pills (including melatonin) since I want to be fully aware in case of an emergency. But I know many people who swear by them. Usually, the drug of choice is Ambien but consult your doctor first before taking anything and test it out before getting on the plane.

- **Don't forget your eye mask**

Eye masks help you create an ideal sleeping environment by blocking out all the light. Instead of using the cheap, scratchy eye masks that the airlines sometimes pass out on long flights, I bring my own fluffy one. I might look silly in it but it feels so good and does the trick. Mine is made by Lewis & Clarke and is $10 on Amazon.com.

- **Bring earplugs**

Bringing earplugs is self-explanatory and is essential for a good night's sleep. If you forget them, the flight attendant will have an extra pair.

- **About noise-cancellation headphones and soft music**

If there's a screaming baby near you or people speaking loudly, earplugs aren't necessarily going to do the trick. In that case, pop on your noise-cancellation headphones or earbuds and play soft music, an audio book or meditation music to drown out the noise and help put you to sleep.

- **Pack anti-bacterial wipes**

We all know that planes are dirty and germy so minimize your risk of picking up and spreading germs by using anti-bacterial wipes to wipe down your arm rests, seat belt, seat back tray, etc. A somewhat sanitized area should help you relax and rest a little bit easier, especially on a long flight.

- **Bring games and something to read**

If you are old school and traveling with someone, bring a deck of cards or a portable game. My favorite game is Travel Scrabble. But you had better bring the Scrabble Dictionary for challenges or use the in-flight WiFi if available to check the Scrabble Dictionary online. If you're not into tech gadgets, travel armed with magazines, newspapers and books. Everyone needs something good to read to pass the time.

- **Bring snacks/water**

On a long flight, you want to be able to eat and drink according to your own schedule, not the flight crew's, so pack some snacks and bring water (purchased or filled-up in the terminal after you've gone through security). At some major U.S. airports (JFK, LGA, EWR) taxi time can be up to an hour and once you are in the air, it's usually 40 minutes before the crew brings out the food and drinks.

- **Choose your seat wisely**

If you plan to sleep for most of the flight, the best seat is usually next to a window for you have something to lean against and you don't have to worry about your seatmates waking you up so they can use the toilet. But if you think you'll be awake, then get an aisle seat so you can get up and stretch your legs easily. Consult SeatGuru.com or SeatExpert.com for your best options.

- **Buckle up**

If you're planning to sleep, make sure your fastened seat belt is visible over your clothing or blanket. That way, the flight attendants won't have to wake you up when they do their safety checks if the seat belt sign goes on. If your seat belt is visibly fastened, they won't disturb you.

- **Bring sleep assistants**

Bring a device that works for you like the First Class Sleeper, which provides neck and lumbar support and can help to make a long flight more comfortable. Also try the Travel Rest Pillow, which attaches to the seat back of a plane and provides comfort and support for your head and neck.

- **Be nice**

Last but definitely not least: Be nice. You're all on this long flight together so be pleasant to everyone, from the gate agents to your fellow passengers. Put on a smile and bring three boxes of chocolates. One for the gate agents, one for the flight attendants and one for yourself! The flight attendants can really make or break your flight and they'll be sure to appreciate this simple acknowledgment of their hard work.

Did I miss anything? Do you agree or disagree with these 15 tips? What do you do to survive a long flight?

(From: http://www.google.com/amp/s/www.johnnyiet.com/15-tips-surviving-long-flight/amp/)

Part II Listening in

■ **Task 1 Listen to the following passage and fill in the blanks.**

How to go through U. S. customs

Before gaining entry to the U. S., all passengers must first clear (1)_____ maintained by the United States Customs and (2)_____ (CBP). Many people feel a little intimidated by the thought of this experience, but it is really simple and straightforward. Follow CBP's instructions to pass through it without issue. The officers will (3)_____ your passport and customs form, ask you some simple questions, and then send you on your way.

- **Filling out a (4)_____**

(1) Pack your passport and carry it with you.

(2) Get a customs form from staff on the plane or boat.

(3) Fill the form out with your basic (5)_____ information.

(4) Estimate the value of all the items you need to (6)_____.

(5) Write a list of declared items on the back of the form.

- **Going through (7)_____**

(1) Walk to the passport control line for U. S. or foreign citizens.

(2) Give your passport and customs form to (8)_____.

(3) Answer any question about your trip the agent asks you.

(4) Provide your (9)_____ and photograph if you are a visitor.

- **Passing through baggage and customs**

(1) Move to the (10)_____ to retrieve your luggage.

(2) Take your bags to the correct line in customs.

(3) Hand the officer your customs form.

(4) Listen to the officers if you are chosen for a (11)_____.

(5) Continue your trip or leave the facility.

(From: http://www.wikihow.com/Go-Through-U. S. -Customs)

■ **Task 2 Listen and answer the following questions.**

Joyce is talking about his baggage with someone on his journey of business.

(1) Where did this conversation take place?

(2) What is Joyce going to do with his baggage?

(3) How many items are allowed to be carried on with the passage?

(4) What's the problem of Joyce's camera tripod?

(5) Who may help Joyce store his tripod in a suitable position on plane?

Part III Language focus

■ Check luggage

1. I want to check these three pieces.
2. Are those inside the free allowance?
3. How many carry-on bags can I have?
4. Where is the baggage claim area?
5. My baggage didn't come out of the baggage claim.

■ Go on board

1. Is this the right counter to check in my flight?
2. Which gate does my flight leave from?
3. The entire overhead compartment seems to be full. Is there anywhere else I can put my bag?
4. Can I use the lavatory now?
5. May I have a vegetarian meal instead?

■ Go through customs

1. Where do I have to go through the customs?
2. Should I go through the green line?
3. I only need to declare one or two things, right?
4. Your passport and customs declaration form, please.
5. How long are you planning to be here?
6. What's the purpose of your visit?

■ Ask for direction

1. Excuse me. Do you know how to get to the shopping mall from here?
2. Excuse me. I'm looking for the Bank of America. I thought it was around here. Do you know where it is?
3. Go along the street until you come to the traffic lights.
4. Turn right/left at the second crossing. (Take the second turning on the right/left.)
5. Take a Number 46 bus, and get off at the square.

Part IV Speaking out

Section 1 Sample dialogues

Dialogue 1

A: Good afternoon, Sir. May I see your passport, please?

B: Of course. Here you are.

A: What is the purpose of your visit? Business or pleasure?

B: Business. I have a number of meetings to go to.

A: I see. How long will you be staying in the USA?

B: Two weeks.

A: Where do you intend to visit while in the country?

B: Seattle first, and then I'll be heading on to the east coast.

A: Do you have a return ticket to China?

B: Yes. However, I'll be returning via Japan—not going back to China directly.

A: Your passport and visa seem to be in order. Do you have anything to declare?

B: No, Sir.

A: Any whiskey or cigarettes?

B: Nothing at all. I'm just bringing in personal effects. Shall I open my bags now?

A: It won't be necessary. Have a nice stay in the United States, Sir.

B: Thank you. I'm sure I will.

Dialogue 2

A: Excuse me, can you help me figure out how to get to the Wudaokou Subway Station from here?

B: Sure. First you're going to have to buy a ticket to ride on the subway. The Wudaokou Station is on the lightrail, so you'll have to transfer. Be sure you buy a combination ticket for the regular subway and the lightrail. It should cost you 5 yuan.

A: And after I buy the ticket, where should I go?

B: You can take the red line train from here, but you'll have to transfer to the blue line at Fuxingmen Transfer Station. After you transfer, take the blue line that is heading north towards Fuchengmen.

A: So I transfer from red to blue, and then how long do I ride the blue?

B: You'll take the blue line until you reach Xizhimen. That's a big station, so there will likely be a lot of people getting off at that stop. You can transfer to the lightrail there, you'll have to exit the subway and present the unused portion of your combination ticket to the ticket master, they'll give you a new ticket to use on the lightrail system.

A: It sounds so complicated!

B: No, not really. Don't worry about it. Like I said there'll be a lot of people there doing the same thing that you are doing, so just follow the crowd. There's only one direction to go, so you won't get on the wrong train. Head north on the yellow line, and you'll see Wudaokou in just a couple of stops.

A: Thanks.

Section 2 Creating your own

Task 1

Student A is departing from an airport in Australia and is stopped by Student B, a security officer, who thinks there is something unusual with Student A and asks some questions:

- What is the purpose of your visit?
- Where have you been staying?
- Who have you been in contact with in Australia?
- What is inside your case?

Task 2

Student A is a traveler in Beijing and gets lost around Jintailu Subway Station (Line 6) in the city. Student B, a citizen here, will help Student A use subway lines to go to Shahe (Changping Line).

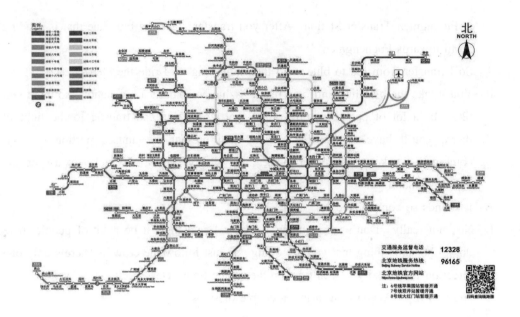

Part V Writing

Itinerary (Travel schedule)

The winter vacation is approaching, and you are going to make a 10-day travel schedule for your family and plan 3 stops at least. Organize your itinerary according to the format of the following example and make sure that you actually search on the booking websites for real information.

Example:

From December 21, 2018 to January 4, 2019

Date	Location	Activity
Dec. 21, 2018 – Dec. 22, 2018	From Hong Kong to New York	At Airplane CX830 (09:35 – 12:10)
Dec. 22, 2018 – Dec. 26, 2018	New York (Hotel Howard Johnson Flushing New York, 135-33 38th Avenue, Flushing New York, New York 11354)	Sight-seeing in New York.
Dec. 27, 2018 – Dec. 27, 2018	From New York to Los Angeles.	At Airplane UA1693 (09:00 – 11:55)
Dec. 27, 2018 – Jan. 02, 2019	Los Angeles (the Historic Mayfair Hotel, 1256 West 7th Street, Los Angeles)	Sight-seeing in Los Angeles.
Jan. 03, 2019 – Jan. 04, 2019	From Los Angeles to Hong Kong	At Airplane CX885 (11:25 – 19:05)

Part VI Follow-up reading

Passage 1

Read the following passage and answer the questions.

Transportation at Hong Kong International Airport

A wide variety of public transport services operate to and from Hong Kong International Airport. Discover the options below to determine which service best suits your needs.

- **Airport express**

Travel comfortably between the airport and Central in just 24 minutes on the airport express. Trains depart at 10-minute intervals from 05:54 to 23:28 and approximately 12-minute intervals from 23:28 to 00:48 daily. (For a detailed schedule of the airport express, please click here.) You may also download the MTR "Next Train" app to keep track of real-time train schedules.

- **Public buses**

Hong Kong International Airport is well served by public bus routes. The buses provide a convenient but relatively inexpensive transport option.

- **Taxis**

Taxis offer a door-to-door service to and from Hong Kong International Airport. Arriving passengers can catch a taxi at the Taxi Station, located near the left-hand ramp outside the Arrivals Hall.

Hong Kong taxis are colour-coded according to their operating areas. Separate rows are designated for different taxi types:

— Urban taxis (red) operate in most areas in Hong Kong (except partial of Tung Chung Road and roads in south Lantau).

— New Territories taxis (green) mainly operate in the north-eastern part (i.e. north of Sha Tin) and north-western part (i.e. north of Tsuen Wan) of the New Territories.

— Lantau taxis (blue) operate only on Lantau Island and Chek Lap Kok.

— All taxis are allowed to provide services at the passenger terminals of Hong Kong International Airport.

- **Hotel coaches**

If you are staying at a major hotel, the hotel coach will deliver you directly to your hotel. You can book a seat on a hotel coach by approaching the following Commercial

Services Counter in Arrivals Hall B, Terminal 1.

Vigor Airport Shuttle Services Limited

—Reservation/Enquiry: +852 2738 9500

—Service Counter: +852 2186 6883

—Email: general@ vigorholding. com

—Website: www. vigorholding. com

—Location: Counter B18, Arrivals Hall B, Arrivals Level (L6), Terminal 1

—Boarding Point: Coach Station, Arrivals Level (L3), Terminal 2

- **Transport for special needs**

Passengers with mobility difficulties can also consider a variety of flexible and personalized transport services through advance booking.

Coach

Rehabus

Telephone: +852 8100 8655 (Overseas visitors)

+852 2817 8154 (Hong Kong residents)

Easy-Access Bus

Telephone: +852 2772 7301

Limousine

Telephone: +852 8106 6616

Taxi

Telephone: +852 2760 8771 (Quotation & Booking)

+852 3484 3582 (Enquiry)

- **Residents' coaches**

If you are travelling to Discovery Bay and Park Island, you can use the residents' coaches.

(From: http://www. hongkongairport. com/en/transport/to-from-airport)

---

(1) How many different kinds of public transport services may travellers enjoy at Hong Kong International Airport?

(2) Could you take Airport Press if you arrive at 02:30 a. m.?

(3) Could you go into the north-eastern part of HK if you take the blue taxis?

(4) What number you dial could offer you a Taxis-help if you travel with a disabled person?

Passage 2

Read the following passage and answer the questions.

8 air travel rights you didn't know you have

With disputes between the airlines and the passengers that fly with them increasing, it's always good to understand your rights as a traveler. Airlines are not inclined to share policies that favor the customers they serve, but there are myriad rules and regulations from the U. S. Department of Transportation they must follow. Below are eight rights that passengers have—but might not know about when things go wrong.

1. Voluntary bumping/overbooking

The 2017 United Airlines dragging incident brought this issue to the forefront, forcing the carrier to revise how this routine situation is handled. U. S. airlines fly nearly 24,000 flights a day. The odds of passengers being on an oversold flight are pretty slim. But when it happens, the airlines prefer to first seek volunteers to take a later flight for vouchers that can be used on future travel. Not only do you get compensation (up to $10,000 on United and Delta Air Lines), but you get priority seating on the next available flight. Depending on the airline (and how desperate they are for the seat), you can ask for perks like first/business class seats, access to a premium lounge and food vouchers.

2. Involuntary bumping/overbooking

If the bumping is involuntary, travelers are entitled to receive boarding compensation by check or cash, depending on the price of their ticket and the length of the delay. The key here is that the airlines can't give you vouchers, which tend to expire after a year. They must give you cash or a check.

If the airline gets you to your final destination within an hour of the original scheduled arrival time, a traveler will not be compensated. If the substitute transportation arrives between one and two hours after the original arrival time (between one and four hours on international flights), an airline must pay an amount equal to 200 percent of the original one-way fare, with a maximum of $675. If you arrive more than two hours later (four hours internationally), or if the airline does not make any substitute travel arrangements for you, the compensation hits 400 percent of the one-way fare, with a maximum of $1,350.

Those using frequent-flyer award tickets or a ticket issued by a consolidator will be compensated based on the lowest cash, check or credit card payment charged for a ticket in the same class of service on the flight. And travelers can keep the original ticket and either use it on another flight or ask for an involuntary refund for the ticket for the flight you were bumped from. Finally, airlines must also refund payments for services on the original flight, including seat selection and checked baggage.

3. Flight delay or cancellation

Compensation for a delay or cancellation depends on the reason and the airline in question. If there's a weather delay, there's not much that the airline can do. But if the delay is for manmade reasons, including mechanical, compensation depends on the airline you're flying. All airlines have a contract of carriage that outlines what they will do. Travelers can ask for things including meals, phone calls or a hotel stay. They can also ask an airline to endorse the ticket over to a new carrier that has seat availability, and legacy carriers can rebook you on their first flight to your destination on which space is available without charge if you ask.

4. Air fares

You've found what looks to be a great fare. DOT regulations allow travelers who have booked a flight at least seven days in advance to make changes or even cancel the reservations within 24 hours without being hit with a high cancellation fee. Or if an airline refuses to carry a passenger for any reason, they can apply for a refund, even if they bought a nonrefundable ticket.

5. Ticket changes/cancellations

Airlines sometimes have schedule or aircraft changes that force them to re-accommodate travelers on a different flight. If the change does not work, travelers have the right to propose a schedule that works better for them. It's better to call the airline directly to make the change. Let them know you're calling about a flight change so you're not charged to speak with an agent. If the change is significant (like a major time change, a longer layover or even an overnight stay), you can request a refund.

6. Lost baggage

The basic rule is that if an airline loses your luggage, you will be reimbursed, depending on the type of flight. The maximum reimbursement for domestic flights is $2,500. For international travel, the Warsaw Convention applies, which limits liability to approximately $9.07 per pound up to $640.00 per bag for checked baggage and $400.00 per customer for unchecked baggage. Most airlines will also provide basic necessities, like toothpaste and other personal items, to hold you over. You also have the right to ask for reimbursement to buy replacement clothes in case you were traveling for an event.

7. Damaged baggage

If your luggage is damaged, go immediately to the airline's office in the baggage claim area and file a report and document any issues. It helps if you can submit photos of the luggage before the flight. If the airline is at fault, you can negotiate a settlement to either repair the damage or replace the bag if it can't be fixed.

8. Stuck on the tarmac

On Jan. 16, 1999, thousands of passengers were trapped for up to 10 hours on

Northwest Airlines jets stranded after a major snowstorm at Detroit Metro Airport. That led to a $7.1 million settlement to those travelers and the creation DOT regulations on how long passengers can be forced to stay on a delayed plane. A similar incident happened to JetBlue at its JFK Airport hub on Valentine's Day, 2007. The CEO announced a $30 million initiative to rewrite its procedures for handling flight disruptions and create a customer bill of rights.

DOT rules don't allow U.S. airline domestic flights to stay on a tarmac for more than three hours, but there are exceptions. One: the pilot feels there is a safety or security reason why the aircraft can't go back to the gate and deplane passengers. Two: air traffic control feels that moving an aircraft to a gate would significantly disrupt airport operations. International flights operated by U.S. carriers are required by DOT to establish and comply with their own limit on the length of tarmac delays. But passengers on both types of flights must be given food and water no later than two hours after the delay begins. Lavatories must remain operable and medical attention must be available if needed.

(From: http://www.tripsavvy.com/air-travel-rights-you-didn't-know-you-have-4139838)

---

(1) Can you ask for business-class seats if you volunteer to take the next available flight due to overbook?

(2) What can you ask for if the flight is delayed for manmade reasons?

(3) Can you apply for a refund if an airline refuses to carry you for any reason?

(4) How much would you ask for reimbursement if an airline loses your luggage?

(5) What would you do if your luggage is damaged?

Training Assessment

Part I Self-study

Translate the following dialogues and then practice with your partner.

■ Dialogue 1

L = Lucy   A = Airport staff

L: Excuse me, I'm going to take Flight SH307 to Shanghai, but the board shows it'll be delayed. (1) _____? (你知道新的起飞时

间吗?)

A: The flight has been pushed back by about an hour but please keep checking the board just in case.

L: Is it OK for me to go out to have something to eat?

A: You'd better stay at the airport. (2) _____.
(随时都有可能广播航班起飞。)

L: (3) _____? (出了什么问题导致飞机延误呢?)

A: Sorry, I'm not sure.

Dialogue 2

A: (4) _____? (第一次坐飞机感觉怎么样?)

B: Couldn't be worse. I spent almost the same time in the airport as I spent on the plane.

A: What happened?

B: The flight was delayed, and we waited in the airport for eight whole hours.

A: (5) _____. (哦,真够倒霉的,下次估计会顺利点儿。)

B: Hope so.

Part Ⅱ BEC exam focus

Reading Test

Questions 1–15

- Read the article below about a company's results.
- Choose the best word to fill each gap from A, B, C or D on the next page.
- For each question (1–15), mark one letter (A, B, C or D) on your Answer Sheet.
- There is an example at the beginning (0).

Another successful year

The UK-based agricultural and garden equipment group PLT has had another successful year and is looking forward to the future with (0) __B__. The group, which also has distribution and fuel (1) _____, has enjoyed record profits for the fifth year in a (2) _____. Pre-tax profits for the year (3) _____ March 31 rose by 24 per cent to £4.2 million.

Total group sales (4) _____ by five per cent to £155 million, with the agricultural business delivering yet another record (5) _____, despite the somewhat difficult trading (6) _____ in the industry. Sales in the garden equipment (7) _____ were slow in the early months of the year, but increased dramatically in the final quarter.

Chairman Suresh Kumar said, "It is my (8) _____ that we have continued to grow by (9) _____ our customers well. I am delighted to (10) _____ the continued development of our customer (11) _____ and I would like to thank all our customers for their (12) _____. As well as an increase in customers, our staff numbers also continue to grow. During the year, we have taken (13) _____ 58 new employees, so that our total workforce now numbers in excess of 700. All of the staff deserve my praise for their dedication and continued efforts in (14) _____ these excellent results."

The group has proposed a final (15) _____ of £9.4 per share, bringing the total to £13 for the year.

---

(0) A. promise   B. confidence   C. trust   D. security
(1) A. commitments   B. interests   C. responsibilities D. benefits
(2) A. row   B. series   C. line   D. sequence
(3) A. completing   B. closing   C. finalizing   D. ending
(4) A. extended   B. lifted   C. expanded   D. climbed
(5) A. display   B. production   C. performance   D. demonstration
(6) A. conditions   B. features   C. states   D. aspects
(7) A. part   B. division   C. component   D. side
(8) A. certainty   B. thought   C. belief   D. idea
(9) A. caring   B. dealing   C. providing   D. treating
(10) A. inform   B. notify   C. comment   D. report
(11) A. source   B. base   C. foundation   D. origin
(12) A. support   B. favor   C. assistance   D. service
(13) A. up   B. back   C. on   D. over
(14) A. winning   B. gaining   C. achieving   D. earning
(15) A. dividend   B. recompense   C. return   D. interest

Unit 6 Hotel Accommodation

Affordable and comfortable

Training Objectives

> By the end of this unit, you are expected to:
> - learn how to check in and check out in a hotel;
> - know how to ask for room services and other information;
> - know how to deal with problems that may happen during your stay in hotel.

Training Portfolio

Part I Starting up

Section 1 Brainstorm

Are you satisfied with the hotels you have stayed in? Did you have any wonderful or terrible experiences when you were there? What kind of hotel do you prefer to stay in if you are on a business trip in terms of atmosphere, location, facilities and services?

Section 2 To read

Read the following passage and then report the idea that you remember to your classmates and tell what impresses you most.

Avoid extra hidden fees

Checking out of some hotel rooms can give a serious case of sticker shock. With taxes, room service, phone charges and other "hidden" fees, that $199 deal you booked online can turn into a $379 bill, literally overnight. Keep these tips in mind on your next stay to keep your hotel bill within your budget.

- **Telephone charges**

Check what the phone charges are at each hotel you stay in. Many hotels charge as much as $1.50 (or more) for local phone calls.

Long distance rates can be unconscionably high. Even 800 numbers (such as the one you probably use for your calling card) can come with a high price tag. Before you make a call, check the rates. They should be posted somewhere in the room. If you don't see them, call the front desk and ask. Use your cell phone for all calls, even local.

- **Room service**

Room service is expensive. At the last hotel I stayed in, an "American Breakfast" (two eggs, bacon, toast, coffee, and juice) cost upwards of $30. Avoid ordering it if possible. Walk down to the hotel restaurant to order, or better yet, walk down the street.

When you do order room service, pay close attention to the fees tacked on to the bill. Many hotels charge a "delivery charge" of several dollars added to the already steep prices. Plus, most room service bills automatically add a 15 ~ 18 percent gratuity, often called a "service charge". Overlooking this can cause you to overtip, so beware.

- **Internet access**

Many hotels are adding high-speed Internet access to their amenities. This is a great service if you are doing a lot of work online while on the road. Be aware that there is usually a charge for this service (generally $10 per day). If you have the time, it's cheaper to stop in at a nearby coffee shop that offers free wi-fi.

Many hotels that charge for Internet access in the rooms also offer it free of charge in the lobby.

- **Mini bar**

If you have late-night food cravings, plan ahead and pack accordingly. Otherwise, that 3 a.m. Snickers bar may cost you five bucks. The honor bar tempts you by stocking tasty snacks, alcohol and other luxuries right in your room for convenience, but you are definitely paying for it.

If you don't prepare, you may not have a choice but to pay the premium. Last time I was sick, and I had to shell out $11 for two Pepto-Bismals and a couple of Advils. To avoid that situation, pack an emergency kit with first-aid supplies, common medications and perhaps a sewing kit for loose buttons.

- **Bellman**

I hate to be unsympathetic to the situation of others, but I have to say, in the case of some hotels, the bellman situation is getting out of control. On a recent trip to San Francisco, I had a total of three bellmen help me with my luggage—one to take it out of the cab, one to bring it to the bell stand, and one to take it to my room. That's a lot of tipping. Save yourself the aggravation and buy a "Bellman Buster"—a suitcase on wheels—and wheel it to your room yourself.

- **Resort fees**

Resort fees are daily charges hotels add to your bill for things you might expect to be complimentary, like access to the fitness center or swimming pool and daily newspaper delivery.

The fees can range from ten dollars a day upwards of thirty or forty dollars, impacting your bill quite a bit. You should be informed of resort fees when you check in. If you don't plan to use the facilities included in the resort fee, the best time to protest the fee is when you are checking in. Ask to speak to a manager and make your case. (Once, I checked into a hotel for a 12-hour overnight layover and knew I wouldn't be using anything outside of my room; I successfully had the front desk waive the resort fee.)

If the resort fee includes tips to bell staff, you should understand that no additional tips are necessary. Pay attention when you are checking in to what you are signing; better yet, ask about a resort fee at the time you book your room at any resort.

- **Early check-in fees**

If you arrive at a hotel slightly before the official check-in time, some hotels might charge you an early check-in fee.

- **Early check-out fees**

Some hotels are extending the 24-hour cancellation limit to three days or more.

- **Unattended-parking fees**

Look out for hotels that add parking fees for unattended lots.

(From: http://www.tripsavvy.com/avoid-extra-hidden-fees-1895648)

Module 2 Business Travel

Part II Listening in

Task 1 Listen to the following passage and fill in the blanks.

The Loews Universal Aventura Hotel in Orlando, Fla., Universal theme park's newest hotel, marks the U. S. debut of Digi Valet's (1)_____. For guests at the resort, Digi Valet provides its standard luxury connectivity, allowing guests to control their entire in-room environment with (2)_____ and it also connects all guests to the park seamlessly (3)_____.

From looking up park information to gaining information and looking at menus from any of the park's 60 + restaurants, and even (4)_____ and transportation services, guests can become (5)_____ their Universal experience all from the comfort of their room. Additionally, guests can unwind after a long day at the park by taking advantage of Netflix and personal content streaming through the television, ordering in-room dining and more, all while planning their (6)_____ for the following day through the iPad.

For hotel management, the DigiValet platform provides a scalable solution for continuously (7)_____ to the theme park, hotel information, direct guest messaging and more. Its direct integration with the property's guest-request platform replaces a manual system with an automatic solution, further (8)_____ by reducing workloads and streamlining back-end processes.

Task 2 Listen to the following dialogue and fill in the blanks.

A: Hello, welcome to Prescott Hotel. May I help you?

B: Hi, yes, (1)_____. My secretary called and booked the room a couple weeks ago. The reservation should be for (2)_____, non-smoking room.

A: And what name was the reservation made under?

B: It should be under Steve Johnson.

A: Hmm ... Let me see ... It seems there's no Johnson (3)_____ for tonight, is there any other name that your reservation may be listed under.

B: No ... here is the (4)_____, will that help? It's H98007. I had the room booked with a VISA gold card.

A: Oh, yes, here it is ... You have a standard double room, non-smoking, on the third floor. I just need to (5)_____, and the credit card you booked the room with, if you don't mind.

B: Sure, here it is ... Would it be possible to check out and (6)_____ in the morning? Also, what time is breakfast served?

A: There's a continental breakfast buffet from 6 am to 10 am, it's (7)_____. Also, you can settle your bill in the morning, but we require a twenty percent (8)_____, but I can just keep a record of your credit card on file. Okay, I've got you (9)_____, if you could just sign here, and initial here ... Here's your room key. Anything else I can do for you?

B: Yes. Could you call me a taxi, please?

Part III Language focus

■ **Check-in**

1. I have a reservation under the name Gregory.

2. I would like to check in.

3. Do you need a deposit?

4. What type of room did you reserve?

5. Please fill out this registration form.

6. How do I get to my room?

■ **Check-out**

1. What's your check-out time?

2. Would it be possible to check out and pay the bill in the morning?

3. Excuse me, here is your bill. Please check it.

4. How would you like to pay the bill, by credit or cash?

■ **Room-service**

1. Housekeeping, may I come in?

2. When would you like me to clean your room?

3. Would you tidy up a bit in the bathroom?

4. Could you come back in three hours?

5. Could you send someone up for my laundry?

Part IV Speaking out

Section 1 Sample dialogues

Dialogue 1

- **Check-in**

R: Good afternoon, Sir. Can I help you?

T: Yes. I have a double-room reserved in your hotel.

R: What's your name, please?

T: My name is Neil Brown.

R: Okay, just a second, please. Yes. A double-room for three nights.

T: That's right. Is the room ready?

R: Yes, it's ready. How will you be paying for the room, Sir?

T: With my credit card.

R: Very good, Sir. If I could have your card for a moment? (*After the credit card transaction is approved*). Here's the key. Your room number is 309.

T: Thank you. Where's the elevator?

R: The elevator is on your left. Have a nice stay.

T: Thanks.

- **Check-out**

A: Check out, please.

B: Your room number, please?

A: Oh, the room number is 666 and here is the key.

B: Thank you. Did you enjoy your stay with us here?

A: Very much. The room was comfy and the service was great.

B: Thank you. Our pleasure. Here is your check. The total is three hundred and forty-five dollars, tax included. How would you like to pay?

A: Can I pay by traveler's check?

B: Of course. Can I have your passport, please?

A: Here you are.

Dialogue 2

A: Excuse me, can you help me? I would like to change rooms if possible. I couldn't sleep at all last night because the people in the room next to mine were making a lot of noise. Also, if at all possible, I'd like a room that doesn't overlook the street. Between the noisy neighbors and the highway outside, I didn't sleep a wink!

B: I'm so sorry to hear that, Sir. Let me check and see what is available. What room are you in now?

A: I'm on the sixth floor, Room 698. I've had so many problems with that room. Just this morning I called someone up to fix the light fixture in the bathroom, it didn't work, and it still doesn't work.

B: Oh dear ... Well, it looks like we have a few rooms available. Can I put you into a room on the 17th floor, it has a balcony and it doesn't face the highway.

A: Okay, that would be very nice. What do I need to do to transfer?

B: Let me check you out of your old room. You'll have to sign here, and acknowledge these charges and also the charges to your previous room. Then I can hook you right up for Room 1780.

A: Hmm ... I don't think these charges are right. Can you explain them, please?

Section 2   Creating your own

Task 1

At reservation in Hilton Hotel, Student A is checking in and Student B, a front desk staff, is receiving this guest. However, there is an error occurred in reservation. Act this story like a show and try to solve the problem. Here are some problems you can use:

- wrong date
- room type (front view or rear view)
- Room charge doesn't include breakfast.
- ...

Task 2

Student A, a guest living in Marriott Hotel, is asking for room service. Student B, a clerk at housekeeping department, is answering the phone call. Here are some kinds of room service Student A would like to enjoy:

- book meals
- change sheets, pillows, towels ...
- ask for morning-call service
- laundry service

  ...

Part V Writing

You are the Manager of Maintenance Department in Hilton Hotel. Due to the equipment failure, the hotel has to turn the hot water system down for 3 hours from 2 a.m. to 5 a.m. December 2, 2018 (contact number: 76693765). Now you need to give a NOTICE to all the guests in your hotel. Make sure you give all the details the guests need to know and indicate that you will appreciate their understanding, and also you would like to help with any further problems.

NOTICE

Please note that ...

Part VI Follow-up reading

Passage 1

Read the following passage and answer the questions.

When you arrive too early for check-in

Everyone wants to get the most out of their vacation. Unfortunately, yours may become stalled if you arrive too early before the hotel check-in time. At most places, check-in doesn't officially begin until the afternoon. That can be more than an inconvenience for those who have traveled many hours and/or through many time zones and arrive exhausted.

When you present yourself at hotel check-in tired and in need of a shower and hear,

"Sorry, your room is not ready yet," there are steps you can take. Not all of them will get you into your room sooner, but they can make the wait more productive and comfortable.

Suggest a room upgrade or offer to accept a downgrade

If the hotel or resort has pre-assigned a specific room to you that is not available when you arrive, it's possible that other rooms are clean and vacant. Take a chance, as a honeymoon couple, and nicely suggest that the hotel might want to upgrade you (without charge) to a more expensive room. Or if you're about to fall asleep on your feet, tell the reservations clerk you are willing to accept a room-level downgrade.

Stash your luggage

Regardless of whether or not you leave the premises before your room is ready, ask the bellman, concierge or front-desk clerk to store your luggage. Remove all valuables beforehand, and be sure to get a receipt. Not having to drag a week's worth of clothing around while you wait will provide immediate relief. Before you depart, freshen up in the hotel bathroom. And If you've packed an extra outfit in your carry-on, change into it before you go outside.

Request early check-in when you make a reservation

While there's no guarantee your hotel or resort will honor this, if you make hotel reservations in advance, the request is in the system and rooms are available early—and you good-naturedly mention to the front desk that this is your honeymoon—there's a chance you can fly into your love nest that much earlier.

Use the hotel spa

If the property has a spa, ask permission to use the facilities before check-in. If the answer is yes, you can shower, have a snack, and perhaps even snooze there while your room is readied. Some hotel spas offer "jetlag" treatments, and one might help you to start your trip off feeling perkier.

Access the hotel business center

Log on to free wi-fi. Check your email. Surf the Web. Call or text home, and tell them you arrived safely. Draft thank-you notes to wedding guests. How much longer before can you lie down? Not yet? Play video games. Time will fly. If there's no business center at your hotel, ask at the front desk for the wi-fi password and use the lobby.

Explore the area and get something to eat

With your baggage safely stored, take a walk. Before leaving the reception area, ask for a map and have someone circle the street where your hotel is. Check out the neighborhood, and stop in for coffee, tea, or something stronger while you wait.

Locate the guest lounge or lobby

Hotels are public spaces, and you may have an area with comfortable couches where you can await your ready room. Alternately, ask if the hotel has a concierge floor. A fee is charged for access to these special areas. Inside, drinks and snacks are served, so you can spread out and read newspapers and magazines and perhaps watch TV until they hand you a key.

Exchange currency and buy stamps

If you haven't gotten the local currency at your port of entry, need more, or hope to find a better rate, head for a local bank with an ATM to exchange currency. On your way, stop at a post office and buy some distinctive stamps to use for sending postcards.

Go to the park

If your hotel is in an urban area, there may be a park nearby. Ask the concierge for directions, get a map, and pick up snacks along the way for an impromptu picnic. Find a park bench or velvety green patch and start unwinding from your travels.

Get a recommendation

The hotel staff knows the neighborhood best: Ask the concierge or front desk clerk where he or she would go if there were a couple of hours to kill. You might be near a world-class museum, a don't-miss restaurant, or the coolest shop in town. So get a recommendation, allow your body to reset itself to the local time, and do some discovering before you dive under your duvet.

(From: http://tripsavvy.com/when-you-arrive-before-check-in-1863579)

---

(1) What would help you recover from "jetlag" at a hotel if you arrive early?
(2) What if you check-in early and there is no business center at your hotel for time killing?
(3) What is the "concierge floor" for at some hotels?
(4) What could you do if you prefer to kill a couple of hours around your hotel?

Passage 2

Read the following passage and answer the questions.

10 things a hotel guest should never ask a concierge to do

What is a hotel concierge supposed to do? Everything and anything for a guest? Not really, because a hotel concierge is neither a butler nor a personal assistant. A hotel concierge's job is to enhance guests' stay at the hotel and help them discover the destination.

If a guest's request to the hotel concierge is not strictly related to their stay, it's the wrong question to ask. A luxury traveler does not ask a hotel concierge ...

- **To help you procure anything illegal**

It's easy to laugh at outrageous behavior. But ... sadly, every day, every concierge in the business endures at least one outrageous request for something dicey …? For an escort, for prescription drugs like Ambien and fentanyl, or for marijuana. In places where these vices are legal, it's OK for a concierge to refer you to a source, but not to do the procuring for you. Keep it classy. Your concierge is not a Mafia fixer.

- **Where to eat (really!)**

Even though the local restaurant advice is an aspect of hotel concierges' official role, you won't get inspired advice from them. So if you're looking for an interesting dining experience, you're unlikely to get it from your concierge.

Why? It's the rare concierge who doesn't play it safe by recommending well-known, middle-of-the-road restaurants. They'd rather err on the side of tame.

Another reason not to rely on concierges' dining recommendations: concierges are comped (or otherwise gifted) by restaurateurs in the expectation they will funnel streams of hotel guests to their eateries. And restaurants that go the concierge route are typically hurting for business: they're obscure, or over the hill, or just-plain-awful tourist traps.

- **The way to get a righteous restaurant rec at your hotel**

Simply ask the bartender instead of the concierge. Why? He or she is the true insider in the local restaurant scene, and unlike the concierge, has nothing to gain from referring you.

- **To do anything that goes beyond the job**

Hotel guest, please act like the classy person you are. Do not ask your concierge to be your personal organizer or guinea pig. Refrain from requesting that he or she: take your dog for a walk outside your pet-friendly hotel; to be your personal shopper or messenger; to save you a trip to your room by stashing your shopping bags or other stuff while you dine, shop, or gamble; to try on a gift you just bought; to introduce you to another guest, or to divulge a name or room number.

- **To act as your personal assistant**

Running late to your business meeting? Send the text yourself. Your hotel concierge is connected in the destination, not in your contacts list. Please do not ask him or her to do anything unrelated to your stay at their hotel.

Here's the exception. If you've upgraded to your hotel club floor, the dedicated concierges in the club lounge can and do help guests with business communications.

- **To act as your travel agent**

Finessing your vacation or business trip's logistics is not a concierge's job either. The right choice for a guest is to refrain from asking the hotel concierge to make or change travel plans.

The only exception: getting you from the hotel to the airport. (Again, a club-floor concierge will be more involved with a guest's travel arrangements.)

- **To act as your therapist**

Don't ask your hotel concierge for personal advice. Yes, your concierge is a friendly character with a caring disposition. That's in the job description. But listening to your sob story is not. Your concierge has a job to do, and it's not to hear about your relationship with your partner, your ex, your kids, your parents, your siblings, your boss, and your neighbor. And it's certainly not a hotel concierge's business to give you personal advice. Save the therapy session for your bartender at home.

- **To negotiate a price for something at the hotel**

The price isn't going to change for you just because you asked (or begged) your concierge. This kind of request is very nervy. It's not a concierge's role to haggle on your behalf for anything, whether it's the $8 Milky Way from your minibar, the cover charge in the hotel's nightclub, or the $10,000 Tahitian black pearl necklace in the lobby boutique.

- **To wrangle your hotel bill**

As the song goes, "It's too late, baby, now it's too late." Take it from a travel editor: The time to request a hotel freebie or discount is before check-in. Not before checkout.

Please do not ask your kind concierge to save you money. He or she cannot misrepresent your VIP status or room category; "put in a good word" to management; or finagle a hotel freebie, from the $6 Fiji water to the $600 third night.

If you seek a room change or upgrade for a good reason (hating your room is one), go to the front desk and ask for a manager.

- **To get you tickets to sold-out concerts, shows or games**

Your concierge has influence, not a magic wand. And he or she certainly zero desire to debase himself or herself by begging. "I'm sorry, ma'am" (or "sir") means I am unable to do this, and "sold out" means "there are no tickets to be had anyway". What the concierge can do: get you onto a waitlist for a cancellation at a hot restaurant.

- **To name celebrity guests**

A concierge is a discreet hotel staffer, not a brazen gossip columnist or Twitter tattler. Thanks to the gossips, the hotel's celebrity guests' names are already on the Internet.

OK, so suppose you've Googled all these and you already know who hotel's boldface guests are. But if you want to know more, you won't get anywhere by asking your concierge for the dirt on them. Why? Concierges are under contract not to spill. So it's not going to happen.

An exception: often, minor celebrities like reality-show contestants do want their names dropped, and have given permission to the hotel to mention them.

(From: http://www.tripsavvy.com/things-to-never-ask-hotel-concierge-2251187)

(1) What is usually a hotel concierge's job?

(2) Who would give you the best answer if you want to enjoy a great meal outside the hotel?

(3) Is it appropriate to ask the concierge to take your dog for a walk outside your pet-friendly hotel?

(4) Is the hotel concierge never your helper in business communications?

(5) Who will take the responsibility of getting you from the hotel to the airport?

(6) What is the best time to request hotel freebies or discount?

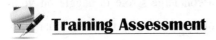

Training Assessment

Part I Self-study

Translate the following dialogue and then practice with your partner.

A: (1) _____? (你能告诉我餐厅在哪儿吗?)

B: Yes, on the first floor. We serve both Chinese and Western food.

A: (2) _____? (餐厅几点开餐?)

B: Breakfast is served from six to nine. Lunch is from eleven to two and supper is from six to eight at night.

A: (3) _____? (有提供房间用餐服务吗?)

B: Yes, you just dial 101 to have it sent up.

A: That's great, thank you. (4) _____? (如果我想打电话该怎么办?)

B: Dial "0" first, and then the number you want.

A: Oh, yes, another thing. (5) _____? (我可以兑换钱吗?)

B: Of course. There is a bank counter on the first floor.

A: Thank you very much.

Module 2 Business Travel

Part II BEC exam focus

Listening Test

Questions 1 – 8

- You will hear an interview on a radio program with Dede McGee about becoming a manager.
- For each question 1 – 8, mark one letter (A, B or C) for the correct answer.
- You will hear the recording twice.

1. What is the first problem that Dede McGee points out?

    A. That too many people want to become managers.

    B. That many people aren't serious about being a manager.

    C. That many people take a management job without thinking it through.

2. The transition to manager can be difficult because _____.

    A. you don't solve problems any more

    B. your old colleagues want to spend time with you

    C. you might be in charge of your old colleagues

3. New managers should avoid _____.

    A. socializing with old colleagues

    B. criticizing the company

    C. pleasing employees

4. To become a manager, Dede thinks you _____.

    A. should talk to your current manager

    B. shouldn't talk to your manager because you might be seen as a threat

    C. should apply to a new company

5. Whenever they have the opportunity, potential managers need to _____.

    A. take on new responsibilities and attend courses

    B. tell other staff what to do

    C. try and take over their boss's job

6. Dede McGee says that the main reason for networking is to get _____.

    A. a better job   B. ideas   C. friends

7. New managers can become frustrated because _____.

    A. they don't have time to get their work done

B. they spend less time working at a practical level

C. they spend too much time complaining

8. Her final piece of advice is to _____.

A. model yourself on your old boss

B. identify and build on what you are good at

C. show staff that you will make changes

Module 3 — Business Communication

Effective communication—the lifeblood of successful organizations

 Into the Module

> We live in an information age that revolves around communication. Effective communication is the lifeblood of every organization and also a key to success in your business career as well as in your personal life.
>
> When communication stops, organized activity ceases to exist. Communication for an organization, therefore, is viewed as vital as blood for life. Moreover, communication to persons outside the company, such as customers, inquirers and suppliers, can have a far-reaching influence on the reputation and ultimate success of the company.
>
> Furthermore, the globalization of business is accelerating as more companies cross national borders in search of new customers, new sources of materials and money thanks to technological advances in communication and transportation. This rise of international business has increased international business communication by increasing exports, relaxing trade barriers, and increasing foreign competition in domestic markets.
>
> Developing excellent communication skills, therefore, is extremely important to your future career. Surveys of employers often show that communication skills are critical to the effective job placement, performance, career advancement and organizational success. In making hiring decisions, employers often rank business

communication skills among the most requested competencies. Many job advertisements specifically ask for excellent oral and written communication skills. In a poll of recruiters, oral and written communication skills were by a large margin the top skills sought in applicants. Another survey of managers and executives ranked the oral skills most lacking in job candidates, and writing skills topped that list.

 Training Objectives

By the end of this module, you are expected to learn how to:
- prepare and attend an interview and answer questions at the interview about personal details, education, work experience, etc.;
- describe jobs and responsibilities and express likes and dislikes about jobs;
- deal with problems through phone calls.

If I went back to college again, I'd concentrate on two areas: learning to write and to speak before an audience. Nothing in life is more important than the ability to communicate effectively.

—Gerald R. Ford, 38th President of the United States

Module 3 Business Communication

Unit 7 Job Interview

Well-prepared and confident

 Training Objectives

> By the end of this unit, you are expected to learn:
> - what the interview procedure is like;
> - how to prepare for an interview;
> - how to answer questions about personal details, education, work experience, etc.

 Training Portfolio

Part I Starting up

Section 1 To discuss

(1) Do you have a career plan? Where do you want to be in 5 years' time?

(2) Which of the following areas do you work in (or would you like to work in)? Why?

a. Management   b. Finance
c. Sales and marketing   d. Administration and personnel
e. Production   f. Research and development (R&D)

(3) Which of the following would you prefer to do?

a. work for a large state-owned corporation or a multinational company

105

b. work for a small private company

c. work for several different companies

d. work for yourself

(4) Study the list of things which are important in a job.
- opportunities for promotion
- a good salary and holidays
- comfortable working conditions
- status and respect
- colleagues I like
- a fair and reasonable boss
- interesting and satisfying work
- training opportunities
- fringe benefits (e.g. company car, private health insurance)
- job security

a. Choose the three which are most and least important for you.

b. Compare your answer with a partner and agree on the same list.

c. As a class, decide the three most and least important.

(5) You are going to hear a psychologist being questioned about the following test.

a. Make notes about what a "yes" answer means for each of the questions.

b. What do your answers say about you?

c. How far do you believe in this kind of test?

	No	Yes	Interpretation
① I often feel I chose the wrong career/studies.	☐	☐	
② People should keep their cars clean.	☐	☐	
③ I enjoy science fiction films and stories.	☐	☐	
④ I would like to make a model from Matchsticks.	☐	☐	
⑤ Poor people are often happier than rich people.	☐	☐	
⑥ I prefer baths to showers.	☐	☐	
⑦ I am terrified of snakes.	☐	☐	
⑧ I have had at least one vision or a supernatural experience.	☐	☐	

Section 2　To read

A CV or job application form should always be accompanied by a short covering letter. Its purpose is to draw the prospective employer's attention to the key points in your CV and to highlight your suitability for the job.

Read the following covering letter and decide whether the statements below are true (T) or false (F).

Dear Mrs. Proctor

Re: Vacancies for Trainee Consultants

　　I am writing in response to your advertisement in the September edition of *Telemarketing Magazine* and would like to be considered for one of the posts mentioned.

　　As you will see from my enclosed CV, I have recently completed a degree in International Marketing at Clifton University. A six-month company placement in France gave me the opportunity to put some of the theories learned on my course into practice, and to acquire a good working knowledge of French. The post involved helps with the development of telemarketing scripts for salespeople. Since then, I have had several months' experience of working in the international section of the Automobile Club's call center. This means I have had direct experience of the day-to-day realities of communicating with the public.

　　From your corporate website, it appears that working for your organization would offer a stimulating and challenging career within a highly competitive field. I am extremely attracted by this opportunity and feel that I have already acquired some of the skills and awareness necessary to make an effective contribution to the company.

　　I am currently available for interview and would welcome the opportunity to discuss the post in more detail. I look forward to hearing from you.

Yours sincerely
Russel Fleming

(　　)(1) The applicant heard about the job from a TV commercial.

(　　)(2) The applicant ever worked in France for six months.

(　　)(3) The applicant has no experience of communicating with the public.

(　　)(4) The applicant knew nothing about the organization he wants to work for.

(　　)(5) The applicant is quite confident that his qualifications would fit the position.

Part II Listening in

Task 1 Apply for the position of Sales Manager.

Listen to the conversation and decide whether the following statements are true (T) or false (F).

(   ) (1) Kate got to know the company from a TV commercial.

(   ) (2) Kate passed IELTS test at college, and she is good at oral English.

(   ) (3) Kate has worked for ZARA for two years since she graduated from college.

(   ) (4) Kate will be in charge of the marketing activities in southeast China.

(   ) (5) Kate will receive the final notification by the end of this month.

Listen to the conversation again, note down the key information about Kate Wiley and construct the following resume for her.

Curriculum Vitae

Name: Kate Wiley
Nationality: Chinese
Address: 256 Huixindong Street Beijing
Telephone: (010) 16801327767
Email: katewiley@hotmail.com

OBJECTIVE

A position of (6) _____

SUMMARY OF QUALIFICATIONS

- (7) _____ year's successful experience at ZARA.
- Motivated and enthusiastic about developing good relations with clients.
- Effectively working alone or as a team member.

EMPLOYMENT HISTORY

2003 – present Working at ZARA, being the (8) _____ for two years, responsible for (9) _____ for new products.

EDUCATION

1999 – 2003 Peking University, Beijing, Bachelor of (10) _____.

Module 3　Business Communication

> SKILLS
> · Computer skills: Windows, MS Office, Excel, Lotus 123, Microsoft FrontPage.
> · Language skills: Passed IELTS at college; being good at (11) _____.
>
> INTERESTS
> Bowling, travelling, yoga

Task 2　Listen to the interview and try to answer the questions.

An unemployed man is talking to an adviser in an employment agency.

(1) Before you listen to the interview, expand the prompts a – g to form the adviser's questions. Then listen and check.

　　a. How long—you be—out of work?

　　b. What exactly—you do—before?

　　c. How long—you work—there?

　　d. What—you do—before that?

　　e. What—you do—since you lose—your job?

　　f. How many jobs—you apply—for?

　　g. You ever think—about working in a call center?

(2) Listen again. What are Greg's answers to the questions a – g above?

Part Ⅲ　Language focus

■ **Opening**

　1. Good morning, Sir. I'm Chris Wiley. I have come for an interview as requested.

　2. Good morning, Miss Wiley. I am Kate Carter, the HR Manager. Take a seat, please.

　3. Nice to meet you, Ms. Carter.

　4. Nice to meet you, too. I've gone through your resume and would like to know more about you.

■ **Education**

　1. I am graduating in June from ABC University and my major is hotel management.

　2. I have obtained/received a BA/an MA degree.

　3. I major in Business Administration.

4. I received honors in several school-wide English and computer contests.

5. I won the university scholarship for four years on end.

■ Work experience

1. I've been working for a large cosmetics company as a Sales Manager for three years.

2. I am now working for AT&T Company as a medical representative.

3. At the beginning of this year, during the probationary period, I was involved in a new product launch in a car company. I really learned a lot from that experience, especially how to work effectively and cooperatively in a team.

4. During my internship at the Shangri-La Hotel, I worked as a receptionist. My duties included offering friendly and efficient check-in and check-out service to guests, answering phone calls, taking and passing on messages to guests.

■ Qualifications & skills

1. I possess excellent interpersonal skills and a very positive attitude.

2. I passed IELTS test (My score was 7.5) at college, and I am good at oral English. I think I can communicate quite well with people from other countries.

3. I have very good computer skills.

4. I enjoy working with people from different backgrounds. I am good at communicating, organizing and coordinating.

■ Reasons for application

1. As far as I know, your company is one of several leading international consultant corporations which came to China after China entered WTO.

2. I think working here would give me the best chance to use what I've learned at university.

3. Interest is the best motivation. I love the fashion industry, so I will definitely devote to it.

4. Moreover, high job satisfaction can be attained when the job is what I am interested in.

5. I'm keen on communicating with different kinds of people, so that's why I decide to move into sales.

6. My major in the university and my past experience are closely related to this position. So I will definitely contribute to the company.

■ Questions about money

1. I'm sure when the time comes, we'll be able to work out a fair compensation package. Right now, I'd rather focus on whether we have a match.

2. Well, I would leave it to you to decide after you consider my abilities.

3. My current annual income at ABC Bank is $150 thousand.

■ **Questions to ask**

1. Are there any opportunities for Chinese employees to be transferred to the head office in London or other branch offices around the world?
2. Are there any training opportunities for new employees?
3. I'd like to know if there would be any chance to work abroad in the future.
4. Would I be able to work abroad in one of your overseas branches?
5. Could you tell me a little bit more about what the job entails?
6. I wonder when I can have the decision.

Part IV Speaking out

Section 1 Sample dialogues

Dialogue 1

I = Interviewer   A = Almudena Ribera

I: So, Ms. Ribera, I'd like to ask you a few questions about your professional experience and qualifications, if I may.

A: Sure.

I: Now your CV says that you have experience of dealing with clients from different countries. Could you tell me which countries you've dealt with?

A: My department publishes translations of foreign books. Most of them are English language books so I deal with America a lot and Britain. And sometimes Italy, too.

I: So, America, Britain and Italy. So your English is obviously very good and you speak Italian too. Could you tell me how good your French is?

A: It's OK. I did French as part of my degree but it isn't as good as my English or Italian.

I: So, that's reasonable French. Now, on your CV you say you have good keyboard skills. Could you tell me how many words you can type in one minute?

A: About 50. I learned to type as part of my studies but I need to practice a bit more.

I: You're not the only one. I still use two fingers! And what about computers? Could you tell me a bit about which programs you use?

A: At the moment I use Microsoft Word as I only need the computer for correspondence. In my last job I also used PowerPoint for our presentations.

I: You used PowerPoint? Did you design the presentations yourself?

A: The Training Director planned them but I had to do the actual computer work and make sure it worked properly during the presentations.

I: So that was at Informatica. But it says here in your CV that you left in 2015. Could you tell me why you left?

A: I think the main reason was languages. I liked my job at Informatica but all our clients were Spanish so I never got to use my languages. Then one day I saw the advertisement for the job at Ediciones Gomez and I'd always been interested in publishing, so I applied.

I: So why do you want to change jobs now?

A: Well, I still feel that I don't get enough practice with my languages …

Dialogue 2

Mr. Bell: Good morning, Ms. Tucker.

Ms. Tucker: Good morning. Sit down, please.

Mr. Bell: Thank you.

Ms. Tucker: I am Cathy Tucker, Director of the HR Department.

Mr. Bell: I am John Bell. Nice to meet you, Ms. Tucker.

Ms. Tucker: Nice to meet you, too. I've gone through your resume and would like to know more about you. So would you please introduce yourself?

Mr. Bell: Thank you for your interest in me. I'm a senior student at the University of International Business & Economy in Beijing. I'm graduating this July. My major is international finance.

Ms. Tucker: So, why did you choose our company?

Mr. Bell: As far as I know, your company is one of several leading international consultant corporations which has started to do business in China for many years. I think working here would give me the best chance to use what I've learned at university.

Ms. Tucker: As a major in international finance, what do you think you can do in a consultancy?

Mr. Bell: Well, I know how to tackle problems. For example, I know I must first analyze the problem and work out its major cause. Then I will be able to search for ways to solve it.

Ms. Tucker: Have you got any relevant experience in this field?

Mr. Bell: Last year, during the probationary period, I was involved in a new product launch with a textile export company. I really learned a lot from that experience, especially how to assess people's strengths and abilities, and how to work together with other people in a team.

Ms. Tucker: So that means you enjoy working in a team?

Mr. Bell: Definitely, I enjoy teamwork very much. As part of my degree program, I needed to finish different projects with my teammates. I possess excellent interpersonal skills and a very positive attitude.

Ms. Tucker: Right. Can you cope with hard work under pressure and in a tough environment?

Mr. Bell: No problem. I don't care about pressure or the environment as long as I enjoy the work.

Ms. Tucker: Good. Now, do you have any questions to ask?

Mr. Bell: Yes, I've got one. Are there any opportunities for Chinese employees to be transferred to the head office in London or other branch offices around the world?

Ms. Tucker: Um, probably. I think you are likely to be sent to work in an overseas branch to get experience later on once you've proved your worth.

Mr. Bell: Oh, great. If I'm accepted, I will do my best for the company.

Ms. Tucker: All right, we'll notify you of our final decision by Friday.

Mr. Bell: Thank you, Ms. Tucker. Goodbye.

Ms. Tucker: Goodbye.

Section 2 Creating your own

Task 1 Role-play in pairs according to the situations below.

Three people are writing in response to a job advertisement of Curtis Publishing. Read the job advertisement and the three covering letters. Then work in groups of four. Students A and B are interviewers, working together to decide on four or five questions that you would like to ask the candidates at their interviews. Student C is the first applicant your group chose to interview and Student D is the second. Students C and D should use the information in the corresponding letters. Role-play the interviews.

CURTIS PUBLISHING

Curtis Publishing is recruiting enthusiastic salespeople to promote its range of beautifully produced reference books, video cassettes, and DVDs. These are flexible part-time posts. Working from home, you will be expected to generate new business contacts, visit schools, and organize events where people can inspect our publications. In return, you will receive excellent sales training and support, good commission, and a generous car allowance.

Write to Julia Summers, enclosing a CV, at:
Curtis Publishing, Rowan House, Harlan Road,
Bristol B45 7FL

Covering letter A

Dear Ms. Summers,

I am writing in reply to your advertisement for salespeople in *Strike Out* magazine.

I am a fully qualified primary school teacher with eight years' experience. Six years ago, I gave up my teaching post to become a full-time mother and housewife. Now that my children are both in full-time education, I am keen to return to the job market.

I am very excited by this opportunity, as it will give me the chance to work with teaching professionals once more, as well as allowing me to fit my career around the needs of my family. I have a very wide network of friends and former colleagues and am active in the community. I am confident that these would all be highly useful contacts. I have enjoyed using your materials with my children and I feel I could communicate their advantages to other parents and teachers.

Covering letter B

Dear Julia,

I was really pleased to see your ad in last month's *Strike Out* magazine. This is exactly the kind of opportunity I have been looking for! I think I am the kind of person who would soon become a key member of your team.

I don't have much of a formal education and learnt most of what I know in the "university of life". One thing I can promise you is that I can sell anything. I have sold holidays at a travel agency, kitchen equipment at exhibitions all over the country and imported toys from the Far East.

I've had a look at some of your publications, and I have got to agree with you that they are really beautifully produced—like little works of art.

I'm sure you can tell from this letter that I am full of energy and enthusiasm and that I'm an excellent communicator. There is nothing I love more than travelling around and getting to know new people.

Covering letter C

Dear Madam,

I was most interested to see your advertisement in *Strike Out*. I should like to put my application forward for your consideration.

After serving as an officer in the Navy for seven years, I took up my current position as a naval training officer. I specialize in navigation and radio training at the Negus Training College in Soharma. I have spent four happy and productive years here but would now like to return to the UK for personal reasons.

Consequently, I am seeking suitable employment using our large family home as a base. I have a number of your publications in my possession and have certainly enjoyed using them with my students.

Task 2 Pair work: Make a conversation according to the given information.

You are the Managing Director of a large consultancy. You need a bilingual PA (English-Spanish) to work with you. Your partner has sent you a copy of his/her resume. You both agreed to meet for an interview on a certain date. Make a dialogue for the interview. The conversation should include the following points:

—Self-introduction
—Personality
—Strengths and weaknesses
—Relevant work experience
—Qualifications
—Reasons for choosing the job
—Questions asked by the candidate about the job

Part V Writing

Using Russell's letter as a guide (see Section 2 in Part Ⅰ), write a letter of application in reply to the following job advertisement. Remember to keep it short—use only one side of page. Make sure that the page isn't too full and that the layout is clear.

An international hotel group is looking for young graduates with good interpersonal skills to train as managers to work in various branches of its international hotel chain.

Graduates of any discipline are welcome to apply although preference may be shown to those with at least one foreign language.

Write to: Joelle Baker, Silver Service Appointments, 23 Regent Square, London SW1

Part Ⅵ Follow-up reading

Read the article "On Employment Interviewing" and discuss the following questions.

(1) Is it normal about fearing an employment interview, and what can be done to overcome this fear?

(2) What can you do to make sure the first contact on the phone before the interview will be impressive?

(3) Why is it essential to research the target company before the interview?

(4) Why is it important to avoid discussing salary early in an interview?

(5) Do you think it necessary for a candidate to ask some questions at the end of an interview? Why or why not? If the answer is yes, what kind of questions would be appropriate?

Job interviews, for most of us, are intimidating. No one enjoys being judged and, possibly rejected. Should you expect to be nervous about an upcoming job interview? Of course! Everyone is uneasy about being scrutinized and questioned.

Yes, you can expect to be nervous during the interview process. But you can also expect to ace an interview when you know what's coming and when you prepare thoroughly. Remember, it's often the degree of preparation that determines who gets the job. You can become a more skillful player in the interview game if you know what to do before, during and after the interview.

BEFORE THE INTERVIEW

Once you've sent out at least one resume or filled out at least one job application, you must consider yourself an active job seeker. Being active in the job market means that you must be prepared to be contacted by potential employers. Here are tips for sounding and acting professionally once an interview is scheduled.

- **Ensuring professional phone contact**

Even with the popularity of e-mail, most employers will contact job applicants by phone to set up interviews. Therefore, once you're actively looking for a job, any time the phone rings, it could be a potential employer. Don't make the mistake of letting an unprofessional voice mail message or a lazy roommate ruin your chances.

- **Making the first conversation impressive**

When you answer the phone directly or return an employer's call, make sure you're prepared for the conversation. Remember that this is the first time the employer has heard your voice. Here are the tips to make that first impression a positive one:

- Keep a list near the telephone of positions for which you have applied.
- Treat any call from an employer just like an interview. Use a professional tone and businesslike language. Be polite and enthusiastic, and sell your qualifications.
- Have a copy of your resume available so that you can answer any question that comes up. Also have your list of references, a calendar, and a notepad handy.
- Take good notes during the phone conversation. Obtain accurate directions, and verify the spelling of your interviewer's name. If you'll be interviewed by more than one person, get all of their names.
- Ask the employer to send you a copy of the job description and other company information, which you can use to prepare for the interview.
- Before you hang up, reconfirm the date and time of your interview. You could say something like *I look forward to meeting with you next Wednesday at 2 p. m.*

- **Researching the target company**

Once you've scheduled an interview, it's time to start preparing for it. One of the most important steps in effective interview is gathering detailed information about a prospective employer. Recruiters are impressed by candidates who have done their homework.

Visit the library or search the Web for information and the articles about the target company or its field, service or product. Visit the company's Web site and read everything. Call the company to request annual reports, catalogues or brochures. Ask about the organization and possibly the interviewer. Learn something about the company's mission and goals, size, number of employees, customers, competitors, culture, management structure and names of leaders, reputation in the community, financial condition, future plans, strengths and weaknesses.

In learning about a company, you may uncover information that convinces you that this is not the company for you. It's always better to learn about negatives early in the process. More likely, though, the information you collect will help you tailor your application and interview responses to the organization's needs. You know how flattered you feel when an employer knows about your background. That feeling works both ways. Employers are pleased when job candidates take an interest in them. Be ready to put in plenty of efforts in investigating a target employer because this effort really pays off at interview time.

DURING THE INTERVIEW

During the interview you'll be answering questions and asking your own questions. The interviewer will be trying to learn more about you, and you should learn more about the job and the organization. Although you may be asked some unique questions, many interviewers ask standard, time-proven questions, which means that you can prepare your answers ahead of time.

The way you answer questions can be almost as important as what you say. Use the interviewer's name and title from time to time when you answer. *Ms. Lyon, I would be pleased to tell you about* ... People like to hear their own names. Be sure you are pronouncing the name correctly, and don't overuse this technique. Avoid answering questions with a simple *yes* or *no*; elaborate on your answers to better sell yourself.

Occasionally it may be necessary to refocus and clarify vague questions. Some interviewers are inexperienced. You may even have to ask your own question to understand what was asked *Do you mean _____?*. Consider closing out some of your responses with *Does that answer your question?* Or *Would you like me to elaborate on any particular experience?*

Always aim your answers at the key characteristics interviewers seek: expertise and competence, motivation, interpersonal skills, decision-making skills, enthusiasm for the job and a pleasing personality. Remember to stay focused on your strengths. Don't reveal weaknesses, even if you think they make you look human. You won't be hired for your weaknesses, only for your strengths.

Use good English, and enunciate clearly. Remember, you will definitely be judged by how well you communicate. Avoid slurred words such as *gonna* and *din't* as well as slangy expressions such as *yeah*, *like*, and *ya know*. As you practice answering expected interview question, it's always a good idea to make a tape recording. Is your speech filled with verbal static?

- **Ways to answer FAQs**

Employment interviews are all about questions, and many of the questions interviewers ask are not new. You can actually anticipate a large percentage of all questions that will be asked before you ever walk into an interview room.

- **Questions to get acquainted with**

After opening introductions, recruiters generally try to start the interview with personal questions that put you at ease. They are also striving to gain an overview to see whether you will fit into the organization's culture. When answering these questions, keep the employer's needs in mind and try to incorporate success stories. For example,

* Tell me about yourself.

Experts agree that you must keep this answer short (one-to-two-minute tops) but on target. Use this chance to promote yourself. Stick to educational, professional or business-related strengths; avoid personal or humorous references. Be ready with at least three success stories illustrating characteristics important to this job. Demonstrate responsibility you have been given; describe how you contributed as a team player. Try practicing this formula:

I have completed _____ degree with a major in _____. Recently I worked for _____ as a _____. Before that I worked for _____ as a _____. My strengths are _____ (interpersonal) and _____ (technical).

Try rehearsing your response in 30-second segments devoted to your education, your work experience, and your qualities/skills.

* What are your greatest strengths?

Stress your strengths that are related to the position, such as *I am well organized, thorough, and attentive to detail.* Tell success stories and give examples that illustrate these qualities: *My supervisor says that my research is exceptionally thorough. For example, I recently worked on a research project in which I ...*

* Do you prefer to work by yourself or with others? Why?

This question can be tricky. Provide a middle-of-the-road answer that not only suggests your interpersonal qualities but also reflects an ability to make independent decisions and work without supervision.

- **Questions to measure your interest**

Interviewers want to understand your motivation for applying for a position. Although they'll realize that you are probably interviewing for other positions, they still want to know why you're interested in this particular position with this organization. These types of questions help them determine your level of interest.

· Why do you want to work for (name of company)?

Questions like this illustrate why you must research an organization thoroughly before the interview. The answer to this question must prove that you understand the company and its culture. This is the perfect place to bring up the company research you did before the interview. Show what you know about the company, and discuss why you desire to become a part of this organization. Describe your desire to work for this organization not only from your perspective but also from its point of view.

- Why are you interested in this position?
- What do you know about our company?
- Why do you want to work in the _____ industry?
- What interests you about our products (services)?

- **Questions about your experience and accomplishments**

After questions about your background and education and questions that measure your interest, the interview generally becomes more specific with questions about your experience and accomplishments. Remember to show confidence when you answer these questions. If you're not confident in your abilities, why should an employer be?

- Why should we hire you when we have applicants with more experience or better credentials?

In answering this question, remember that employers often hire people who present themselves well instead of others with better credentials. Emphasize your personal strengths that could be an advantage with this employer. Tell success stories. Emphasize that you are open to new ideas and learn quickly. Above all, show that you're confident in your abilities.

- Describe the most rewarding experience of your career so far.
- What were your major accomplishments in each of your past jobs?
- What were your major achievements in college?
- How do your education and professional experiences prepare for this position?

- **Questions about the future**

Questions that look into the future tend to stump some candidates, especially those who have not prepared adequately. Employers ask these questions to see whether you are goal-oriented and to determine whether your goals are realistic.

- Where do you expect to be five (or ten) years from now?

Formulate a realistic plan with respect to your present age and situation. The important thing is to be prepared for this question. It's a sure kiss of death to respond that you'd like to have the interviewer's job! Instead, show an interest in the current job and in making a contribution to the organization. Talk about the levels of responsibility you'd like to achieve. One employment counselor suggests showing ambition but not committing to a specific job title. Suggest that you hope to have learned enough to have progressed to a position where you will continue to grow. Keep your answer focused on educational and professional goals, not personal goals.

- If you got this position, what would you do to make sure you fit in?
- Do you plan to continue your education?
- How do you think you can make your contribution to this company?
- What would you most like to accomplish if you get this position?

- **Challenging questions**

The following questions may make you uncomfortable, but the important thing to remember is to answer truthfully without dwelling on your weaknesses. As quickly as possible, convert any negative response into a discussion of your strengths.

- What is your greatest weakness?

It's amazing that how many candidates knock themselves out of the competition by answering this question poorly. Actually, you have many choices. You can present a strength as a weakness. (Some people complain that I'm a workaholic or too attentive to details.) You can mention a corrected weakness. (I found that I really needed to learn about conducting Web research, so I took a course.). You could cite an unrelated skill. (I really need to brush up on my Spanish.). You can cite a learning objective. (One of my long-term goals is to learn more about international management. Does your company have any plans to expand overseas?)

- What type of people do you have no patience for?

Avoid letting yourself fall into the trap of sounding overly critical. One possible response is, *I've always got along well with others. But I confess that I can be irritated by complainers who don't accept responsibility.*

- How would your former (or current) supervisor describe you as an employee?
- What do you want the most from your job? Money? Security? Power? Advancement?

- **Questions about money**

Remember that nearly all salaries are negotiable, depending on your qualifications. Knowing the typical salary ranges for the target position helps. The recruiter can tell you the salary ranges—but you will have to ask. If you've had little experience, you will probably be offered a salary somewhere between the low point and the midpoint in the range. With more experience, you can negotiate for a higher figure. A word of caution, though. One personnel manager warns that candidates who emphasize money are suspect because they may leave if offered a few thousand dollars more elsewhere. Here are some typical money questions:

- How much money are you looking for?

One way to handle salary questions is to ask politely to defer the discussion until it's clear that a job well be offered to you. *I'm sure when the time comes, we'll be able to work out a fair compensation package. Right now, I'd rather focus on whether we have a match.* Be sure to do research before the interview so that you know how much similar jobs are paid for in your geographic region.

- How much are you presently earning?
- How much do you think you're worth?
- How much money do you expect to earn within the next ten years?

CLOSING THE INTERVIEW

At some point in the interview, usually near the end, you will be asked whether you have any questions. The worst thing you can do is to say "No", which suggests that you're not interested in the position. Instead, ask questions that will help you gain information and will impress the interviewer with your thoughtfulness and interest in the position. Remember, though, that this interview is a two-way street. You must be happy with the prospect of working for this organization. You want a position for which your skills and personality are matched. Use this opportunity to find out whether this job is right for you. Also remember that you don't have to wait for the interviewer to ask you for questions. You can ask your own questions throughout the interview to learn more about the company and position.

- What training programs are available from this organization? What specific training will be given for this position?
- Is travel required in this position?
- How is job performance evaluated?
- What are the major challenges for a person in this position?
- What do you see in the future of this organization?
- When do you expect to make a decision?

After you have asked your questions, the interviewer will signal the end of the interview, usually by standing up or by expressing appreciation that you came. If not addressed earlier, you should at this time find out what action will follow. Demonstrate your interest in the position by asking when it will be filled or what the next step will be.

Before you leave, summarize your strongest qualifications, show your enthusiasm for obtaining this position, and thank the interviewer for a constructive interview and for considering you for the position. Ask the interviewer for a business card, which will provide the information you need to write a thank-you letter.

AFTER THE INTERVIEW

After leaving the interview, immediately make notes of what was said in case you are called back for a second interview. Write down key points that were discussed, the names of people you spoke with, and other details of the interview. Note your strengths and weaknesses during the interview so that you can work to improve in future interviews. Next, write down your follow-up plans. To whom should you send thank-you letters? Will you contact the employer by phone? If so, when?

A thank-you letter, also called a follow-up letter, is always necessarily sent to thank your interviewer. This courtesy sets you apart from other applicants, most of whom will not bother. Your letter also reminds the interviewer of your visit as well as suggesting your good manners and genuine enthusiasm for the job. Follow-up letters are most effective if sent immediately after the interview.

(From: Mary Ellen Guffey, 2012: 422 – 436)

Training Assessment

Part I Self-study

1. **Complete the sentences below, using the words in the box.**

challenge   persevering   fascinating   depressing   good at   environment

   (1) Our office is quite a noisy _____ to work in, because it's too busy.
   (2) If you are _____, you will get the results you want in the end.
   (3) It is very _____ when the computer crashes and you lose work.
   (4) It's a pity Sonia is leaving, because she's very _____ her job.
   (5) I was offered a job with more responsibility, and I was keen to take up the _____.
   (6) Your work sounds really _____—I wish my job was as interesting as yours!

2. **Re-arrange the following words to make phrases from a letter of application.**

   (1) please/copy/my/CV/a/find/enclosed/of

   _____

   (2) I/because/position/am/in/the/interested/very

   _____

   (3) since/as/been/have/2016/I/working

   _____

(4) I/reference/am/advertisement/writing/with/to/your

3. **Choose the correct answers after reading.**
   - Read the text below which advises candidates how to answer difficult interview questions.
   - Are the sentences below "Right" or "Wrong"?
   - If there is not enough information to answer "Right" or "Wrong", choose "Doesn't say".
   - For each question, mark the correct letter A, B or C.

FAQs for interviews

Interviewers normally go through candidates' application and CV very carefully and prepare their questions in advance. Candidates therefore need to be fully prepared. Here are some useful suggestions on answering interview questions.

What are your dislikes about your current position?

Take a positive attitude. Be honest but don't give a list of complaints. The important thing is to talk positively about how you deal with problems at work.

What are your career objectives?

Your objectives should be relevant to the job you have applied for and achievable. The interviewer will think you probably won't stay with the company very long if the new job can't offer you everything you want.

How do you reply if your employer ask you where you are today?

Be honest. If you lie to your current employer, you'll lie to your next employer. Don't phone in sick on the day of the interview. Take a day's holiday but don't say why.

What are your weaknesses?

You must be very clear no one is perfect. Think about this before the interview and give a very careful answer. Pick out one that will not disqualify you from the job and show your determination to correct it. This is far more important than the weakness itself.

(　　)1. Interviewers normally read through candidates' CV very quickly before interviews.

   A. Right　　　　B. Wrong　　　　C. Doesn't say

(　　)2. You can mention problems with your current job.

   A. Right　　　　B. Wrong　　　　C. Doesn't say

(　　)3. You'd better lie to your boss by asking for a sick leave for the interview.

   A. Right　　　　B. Wrong　　　　C. Doesn't say

(　　)4. You should give realistic and feasible objectives.

A. Right   B. Wrong   C. Doesn't say

( )5. Your objectives need not be related necessarily to the position you apply for.

A. Right   B. Wrong   C. Doesn't say

( )6. You should practice your answers at home over and over again.

A. Right   B. Wrong   C. Doesn't say

( )7. You'd better talk about how you deal with a weakness.

A. Right   B. Wrong   C. Doesn't say

Part II BEC exam focus

Listening Test

Section 1 (Questions 1 – 5)

- You will hear five short recordings.
- For each recording, decide which training course the speaker is referring to.
- Write one letter (A – H) next to the number of the recording.
- Do not use any letter more than once.
- You will hear the recordings twice.

1. _____
2. _____
3. _____
4. _____
5. _____

A. Managing teams
B. Using PowerPoint
C. Sales on the telephone
D. Effective presentations
E. Doing business with other cultures
F. Report writing
G. Marketing on the web
H. Interviewing and staff selection

Section 2 (Question 6 – 10)

- You will hear another five short recordings.
- Each speaker is on the phone.
- For each recording, decide what the main reason for the call is.
- Write one letter (A – H) next to the number of recording.
- Do not use any letter more than once.

· You will hear the recordings twice.

6. _____

7. _____

8. _____

9. _____

10. _____

A. To complain
B. To explain a delay
C. To ask for information
D. To confirm arrangement
E. To report on plans
F. To ask for confirmation
G. To request help
H. To speak to someone else

Module 3 Business Communication

Unit 8 Job Description

Presenting skills and professionalism lead to good image

 **Training Objectives**

> By the end of this unit, you are expected to be able to:
> - describe positions or departments in a company;
> - describe jobs and responsibilities;
> - express likes and dislikes about jobs.

 **Training Portfolio**

Part I Starting up

Section 1 To discuss

(1) · What do you think are the main causes of stress at work?
  · Work in pairs. Talk about the advantages and disadvantages of being self-employed.
(2) Rank the following situations from the first one (most stressful) to the last one (least stressful). Then discuss your choices.
  · Writing a report with a tight deadline
  · Asking your boss for a pay rise
  · Dealing with a customer who has a major complaint

- Meeting important visitors from abroad for the first time
- Telephoning in English
- Making a presentation to senior executives
- Leading a formal meeting
- Negotiating a very valuable contract

(3) What should you do to get ahead in your career? Choose the four most important tips from the list below. Compare your ideas in a group and try to agree on a final choice.

- Change companies often
- Use charm and sex appeal with your superiors
- Attend all meetings
- Go to your company's social functions
- Be energetic and enthusiastic at all times
- Be the last to leave work every day
- Find an experienced person to give you help and advice
- Study for extra qualifications in your free time

Section 2　To read

Read the following article about the changes in employment in Europe and decide whether the statements below are true (T) or false (F).

Changes in employment in Europe

From the 1750s to the middle of the nineteenth century, Britain led an industrial revolution that changed manufacturing for ever. With other Western countries, it produced consumer goods for the rest of the world well into the 1960s. Generations of workers spent their entire careers in the same workplace. Yet, nowadays, most of the consumer goods we buy have been made in the East. If, by magic, our shoes could return to where they were made, most would march all the way back to China or Vietnam—and the jobs have gone with them.

Manufacturing gravitates to countries with lower labor costs or more efficient production methods. Since the US economy started to recover in 2003, unemployment has remained high. This is because two million manufacturing jobs have gone elsewhere.

China is undoubtedly the latest big success story. As well as making 90% of the world's toys, the country is now responsible for a quarter of global steel production. By contrast, much of the US's industrial heartland has been a "rust-belt" for years. In Western Europe

Module 3 Business Communication

too, industry has been declining for decades. Europe's shipyards have been closing one by one ever since South Korean rivals learnt how to build more efficiently and cheaply. Nearly all Britain's coal mines have ceased production since it became cheaper to ship coal all the way from Australia. Since the 1980s, tens of thousands of British workers have lost their jobs in these sectors.

Some workers may have retrained and found jobs in hi-tech industries; however, most have ended up working in services. In the UK, more people are now employed in making sandwiches than in making steel. Even jobs in knowledge-based services are threatened by globalization. Improvements in telecommunications have allowed firms to outsource work thousands of miles away. Bangalore, with its workforce of highly skilled computer programmers and engineers, has transformed itself into India's answer to Silicon Valley. Many UK businesses have relocated their call centers there too—an Anglophone Indian worker will work for a fraction of his British counterpart's salary. This all proves that even though employment in hi-tech sectors such as pharmaceuticals and aeronautics remains strong, for most of us the idea of a job for life—or at least a safe job—has been untrue for years.

(   ) (1) The majority of people have always remained in the traditional manufacturing areas.

(   ) (2) During the 1960s, generations of workers spent their entire careers in the same workplace.

(   ) (3) Many people in European countries are forced to turn to service sectors for jobs.

(   ) (4) It's still possible to find a job for life.

(   ) (5) Jobs in services are safe from globalization.

Part II Listening in

Task 1 Two people are talking about the results of a survey into young people's attitudes towards work.

(1) Listen to Part A and decide if the statements are true (T) or false (F).

a. _____ 2,500 people were questioned.

b. _____ They were under twenty-five.

c. _____ More young people are working in the traditional jobs.

d. _____ There are fewer secure jobs now.

(2) Listen to Part B and answer the following questions.

a. What are young people doing instead of going into the traditional employment?

b. What kinds of business are they going into?

c. What effects are changing attitudes among young people having upon established companies?

Task 2   Listen to three department managers describing their job responsibilities and complete the notes below.

Helen:

Developing sales strategies; achieving (1) _____; recruiting and training sales stuff; supervising and motivating (2) _____; expanding the (3) _____ and ensuring high levels of (4) _____.

Robin Seaton:

Writing (5) _____ and then I have to choose which applicants I want to interview; interviewing the applicants with the head of the department where (6) _____ is; dealing with employees' problems; informing employees if (7) _____ isn't satisfied with their work, (8) _____.

Chris:

Managing all aspects of the product development process, including resource allocation, budget requirements and (9) _____; analyzing the needs of the (10) _____ and directing the work accordingly; creating and managing the R&D teams and being responsible for the overall (11) _____, (12) _____, and success of the projects.

Part III   Language focus

■ **Jobs**

1. What do you do?

2. I'm the Head of the Sales Department.

3. What's your job?

4. What job do you have?

5. I work as a software engineer for IBM.

6. I work as a marketing manager for a large pharmaceuticals company.

7. I'm the manager of the Research & Development Department.

■ **Responsibilities**

1. What are you in charge of?

2. What are your duties?

3. What are you responsible for?

4. Who do you report to?

5. I'm responsible for employing most of the people in the company.

6. I write the job advertisements and then I have to choose which applicants I want to interview.

7. I'm in charge of establishing and maintaining good relationships with customers.

8. I'm responsible for creating and managing the R&D teams.

9. I'm also responsible for identifying the training needs of our staff.

10. My job involves a lot of travelling.

11. It's my job to organize a conference for the medical press so that they can ask us questions about it.

■ **Likes and dislikes about jobs**

1. I don't like my current job.

2. I enjoy my job because it involves a lot of challenges.

3. I get fed up with travelling. Nowadays, I want to spend more time with my family.

4. The salary and benefits are OK, but I don't have time to go anywhere. I have to stay in my office all the time.

5. I hate my job because I can't stand my boss.

Part IV   Speaking out

Section 1   Sample dialogues

Dialogue 1

There is a vacancy for Senior Marketing Assistant at Goldsmiths. Two HR managers are discussing the vacancy.

R = Rick   P = Patricia

R: So Patricia, have you given any more thought to taking on an assistant in marketing?

P: Yes, and I'm still not sure about it. If we decided to take someone on, where would we advertise the vacancy?

R: Well, I guess we'd advertise the position internally as we always do.

P: But if we advertised the job internally, we'd have the same old problem—not enough applicants and lots of internal political problems. Couldn't we advertise the job outside the company for once?

R: Well, I suppose we could. But if we did, a lot of people wouldn't be very happy about it.

P: So? Would that be a problem?

R: Well, yes. I mean, the company always talks about how we like to promote our own people and how you can develop a career with us. So it'd look a bit funny if we didn't advertise it internally first.

P: But even if we promoted one of our own people, the other internal applicants wouldn't be happy anyway. So what's the difference? Why couldn't we just advertise it in the national papers?

R: But it's company policy. You know that. We always advertise internally first.

P: Yes, I know. But why can't we try something different for a change? If we took someone on from outside the company, we'd bring some new ideas into the department. It's what we need, Rick.

R: Look, why don't we just advertise it internally as we always do, right? That'll keep everyone happy and then, after a couple of weeks, we can put an advert in the paper as well. What do you say?

P: Oh, all right. But I'm not going to do the interviews. You can. I had to do the interviews last time and the people who didn't get the job didn't speak to me for weeks afterwards.

Dialogue 2

At the former classmates' party, five people are getting together and talking about their jobs.

Robin: What's your job now, Jerome? Do you still work for that wholly funded American company?

Jerome: No, I left it three years ago. I have my own business now.

Frank: Gee, that's great! How do you feel as a self-employed entrepreneur?

Module 3　Business Communication

Jerome: I feel good. I can make a lot more money than before and I have a lot of independence in doing things. But, sometimes I get tired. As you know, it's not very easy to run a business on your own. What about you, Frank? What are you doing now?

Frank: I've worked for several companies. After graduation, I went to a private company. Then a year later, I changed to a Sino-Japanese joint-venture enterprise and worked as a sales assistant. Two years later, I moved on to a computer company and worked in export sales. And now, I'm an advertising executive.

Colin: Oh, you are a real job-hopper. Why have you changed jobs so often?

Frank: I'm always interested in new challenges. I know changing jobs frequently can be a waste of a company's human resources, but I'm gaining a lot of experience! How is your job, Colin?

Colin: I've been working for the PMC Textile Plant since I graduated. Two years ago, I was promoted to Line Supervisor.

Frank: Do you like your job?

Colin: The salary and benefits are OK, but I don't like the work environment. You know, the workshops are very noisy sometimes. Also, I don't often get an opportunity to go anywhere, I hate staying in the same place all the time. You often travel on business, right, Robin?

Robin: Yes. As a buyer, I must travel to purchase stock. I've been to a lot of places.

Colin: Maybe I should think becoming a buyer ...

Robin: Mm ... everything has two sides. I get fed up with travelling. Nowadays, I want to spend more time with my family.

Janet: Hi, guys, may I join you?

Everybody: Sure. Have a seat.

Janet: You enjoy getting together, don't you? What are you talking about?

Robin: Jobs. What kind of job do you have, Janet?

Janet: I'm the Public Relations Manager in a holding company.

Colin: Do you enjoy it?

Janet: Yes. What I like about it is that I can meet a lot of new and interesting people.

Robin: How about your working hours?

Janet: That's the trouble. I usually have to work overtime, because I often have dinner parties in the evening. I don't get enough time with my family and baby.

Section 2   Creating your own

■ Task 1   Pair work: Role-play in pairs according to the following situations.

Student A is the Director of Sales Department at a computer company and Student B is a self-employed entrepreneur, running a small computer business. Make up a dialogue to talk about each other's responsibilities, likes and dislikes.

■ Task 2   Pair work: Role-play in pairs according to the following situations.

Student A and Student B are friends. They haven't seen each other for years. One day, they come across each other occasionally and talk about their jobs. Student A is an engineer in a large international car corporation, working in the R&D Department while Student B is an HR Manager. Imagine what they will say and make up a dialogue.

Part V   Writing

Elizabeth Spencer is going to be the new Human Resources Manager at your company. She is going to visit your office to learn more about the company.

1. Write a memo to all staff, using the format given below:
   - Explaining who she is
   - Saying when she will be in the office
   - Asking staff to introduce themselves to her.
2. Write 30~40 words.

MEMORANDUM

To:
From:
Subject:
Date:

Part VI Follow-up reading

Terrain Ltd., a leisurewear manufacturer, is investigating staff motivation. Read five employees' talking to the HR Manager. Which grievance does each speaker refer to?

A. too much responsibility
B. uninteresting work
D. uncooperative colleagues
E. lack of recognition
F. unsatisfactory pay
G. inflexible working hours
H. lack of clear objectives

- **Speaker 1**

Well, I've only been here for a few months but I feel as if I've fitted in quite well so far. Everyone seems to have time to talk to me when I need help, which I really appreciate. The work's beginning to get interesting too. It's just that by now, I feel I should really be getting up to speed. Only it's a relatively new position and nobody's really spelt out what the exact scope of the job is or what my responsibilities and priorities should be. I think my line manager needs to give me a more concrete idea of what she expects me to achieve. She's back from holiday next week so maybe we could sit down together then.

- **Speaker 2**

Well, I get the feeling that we're starting to fall a bit behind other companies. I mean, when you look in the papers, you can't help noticing there's a bit of a gap between ourselves and the current going rate. I mean, it's not that I'm unhappy here or anything. I really like my job—it's interesting work and I think it's great that the job's so flexible. It's just that, at the end of the day, nobody likes to feel undervalued, do they? And in my position, it's not just myself I've got to think about. I've got responsibilities outside work as well.

- **Speaker 3**

Well, it's great to be part of a successful team. I don't think you could wish for harder-working or more dedicated colleagues, but I just sometimes think that our efforts aren't always rewarded. I know different managers have different styles but, well, everyone likes to feel appreciated, don't they? I mean, in my last job, managers always made a point of praising us when we beat our targets. One manager even used to encourage us to clap and cheer each other. And I must admit, I do miss that at times. I find praise here is sometimes a bit, shall we say, limited. It's like there's a "That's what you're paid for" type of attitude.

- **Speaker 4**

I suppose, on the whole, I've got very little to complain about really. I get on with the rest of the team and that kind of thing. But there's one thing that's been on my mind for a while now. I just feel that, well, I've reached a stage where I'm capable of dealing with a lot more responsibility than I do at present. I just don't feel stretched any more. I don't feel as though I'm contributing as much as I could. It's almost as if I'm on autopilot. Things are beginning to feel a bit stale. What I need is a bit of variety, something to get my teeth into a challenge.

- **Speaker 5**

Well, you're probably already aware of the fact that things aren't functioning too smoothly in production at the moment. I don't know what other people have said but personally I think it's down to our procedures. There's no formal system for putting our ideas forward and in the past suggestions have just been ignored. I think management has to accept a lot of the responsibility. What we need to do is to schedule regular meetings, which will improve the flow of information in both directions. I mean, at the moment I get more information through the shop floor grapevine than from my line manager.

Training Assessment

Part I Self-study

1. **Match the sentence halves about Beth Lambert.**

   (1) I work as   a. questions people have about their accounts.
   (2) I'm responsible for   b. an accountant with RTLP.
   (3) My job also involves   c. produce financial reports.
   (4) I deal with   d. checking companies' accounts.
   (5) As part of my job I have to e. Reading, not far from London.
   (6) I am based in   f. giving financial advice.

2. **Complete the following sentences with the correct form of the words in the box.**

   | discuss | product | sell | organize | interview | apply | advertise |

   (1) We're going to _____ ten applicants for the position of accountant.
   (2) Could you _____ the room for the meeting tomorrow?
   (3) Are we going to _____ our new sports shoes on the radio or only on television?
   (4) There were forty _____ for the job but we short-listed only five of them.

(5) My company sells financial _____.

(6) We had a very interesting _____ about increasing output at the factory.

(7) Peter works in the _____ department. His job involves a lot of travelling to visit clients.

Part II BEC exam focus

Reading Test

- Read the article below about the need for language training in the international marketplace and the questions.
- For each question (1-6), mark one letter (A, B, C or D) on your Answer Sheet.

Speaking your customers' language

Modern international trading practices are highlighting the growing importance of language training.

Modern-day business really does transcend national barriers. Thanks to sophisticate IT and communications systems, businesses can now market their products on a truly global scale. The world is indisputably becoming a smaller place, as service and manufacturing companies search the international marketplace for new suppliers and clients. Businesses must, however, be aware that once they expand the area in which they operate, they face increased competition. The standard and quality of their goods become increasingly important in keeping up with competitors. But most of all, it is the service element accompanying the goods which is crucial to a company's success in a particular market. This new philosophy has led to many companies, some of which have even offered products of a lesser quality, gaining success overseas.

Although globalization may, in some senses, have brought national economies closer together, societies around the world still have radically different expectations, processes and standards. These are not a function of economic change, but are more deep-rooted and difficult to alter. They can be a major problem for businesses expanding abroad, with the greatest obstacle of all being the language barrier. If you have to deal with clients, suppliers and distributors in a range of countries, you will not only need the skills to communicate with them, you will also need to reconcile any national biases you have with the diverse ways of doing business that exist around the globe.

The value of effective communication is not to be underestimated. New technology such as videoconferencing and email has played a part in making the communication process easier, and it may also be possible that the introduction of language interpretation software will help with some global communications problems. But, of course, it is the human element of the communication process that is so vital in business, especially in negotiations, presentations and team-building. It is essential for managers to meet regularly with staff, customers and partners, so that issues can be discussed, messages communicated and feedback obtained.

The value of well-organized language training is immense, and can bring benefits to all levels and departments within a multinational organization. Unfortunately, however, many organizations have a very narrow view when it comes to the training of any kind. Often, an urgent requirement has to be identified before training is authorized. Then, a training company is employed or a program is developed in-house, the team is trained, and that is seen as the end of the matter. However, the fact remains that training programs are effective only if they are relevant to a company's broader, long-term needs. They should be regarded as an investment rather than a cost.

Changes in expectations and attitudes are certain to continue for companies that trade globally. Although such companies are not yet faced with their international partners and clients demanding that business be conducted in their mother tongue, they realize that overseas competition is increasing fast. If these companies want to continue to achieve success on the international trading circuit, they must be prepared to adapt to situations and speak the local language. If not, someone else will.

(　　)1. According to the first paragraph, improved communications have enabled companies to _____.

　　A. offer a wider variety of products and services

　　B. expand beyond their domestic markets

　　C. perform better than their international competitors

　　D. open more manufacturing facilities abroad

(　　)2. Some companies have succeeded at an international level even though they have _____.

　　A. produced inferior goods

　　B. failed to adapt products for local markets

　　C. ignored the standards set by their competitors

　　D. reduced the standard of the service they offer

(　　)3. Approaches to doing business vary between countries because of _____.

　　A. local economic considerations

B. the existence of cultural differences

C. strong wishes to remain independent

D. regulations about business practices

( )4. The writer thinks that the use of modern technology will _____.

A. speed up the process of language interpretation

B. never replace the need for face-to-face interaction

C. help solve the problems involved in maintaining strong teams

D. not lead to greater communication between companies and clients

( )5. A common weakness of training courses is that they _____.

A. are developed by the wrong team

B. do not give good value for money

C. are provided only if there is an immediate need

D. do not deal with a company's specific requirements

( )6. Why should companies do business in the language of the countries they are operating in?

A. To prevent other companies taking their business.

B. To help them find new international partners.

C. To meet clients' current expectations.

D. To become more aware of their competitors' activities.

Unit 9 Business Calls

Ensure a professional phone contact

 Training Objectives

By the end of this unit, you are expected to:
- answer the phone;
- ask to be connected;
- put someone through;
- leave messages;
- deal with problems by telephone.

Training Portfolio

Section 1 To discuss

A. Among the new types of communication, such as QQ, WeChat, mobile phone call, Skype, etc., which one do you use most frequently in your daily life?

B. Compared with other types of communication, what advantages do you think telephone communication has?

C. With the development of the Internet and communications technology, do you think the telephone will be completely replaced by other types of communication? Why or Why not?

Section 2 To read

Read the following article about using English for international business and decide whether the statements below are true (T) or false (F).

Is your English too English?

English may be the language of international business but, as Alison Thomas reports, it's not only non-native speakers who need to learn how to use it effectively.

Ask a Swedish Ericsson executive "Talar du Svenska?" and he may well reply, "Yes, but only at home. At work I speak English." Ericsson is one of a growing number of European companies that use English as their official corporate language. These companies recognize and, at the same time, increase the dominance of English as the language of international communication. Soon the number of speakers of English as a second language will exceed that of native English speakers.

Although a company might use English as its official language, its employees are unlikely to be bilingual. Language trainer Jacquie Reid thinks we consistently over-estimate the fluency of non-native speakers. "We always assume that because their language skills are better than ours, they understand everything we say."

So how should we adapt our use of language and what are the common problems? "Simplify it" is Reid's advice. "Don't over-complicate the message. Reduce what you're saying to manageable chunks." Reid always tells people to limit themselves to one idea per sentence. "It's also important to slow down and not raise your voice."

Dr. Jasmine Patel, a language consultant at Europhone, says different languages also have their own approach to dialogue. "The British start with idiomatic expressions such as *so, should we get down to it?* And understate important issues with phrases such as *There could be a slight problem*. They also say *That's a good idea, but ...* when they mean *no* and they repeatedly use the word *get* with different meanings. And worst of all, they insist on using humor which is so culture-specific that no one understands it."

The majority of English native speakers are insensitive to the stress of trying to understand a foreign language in a work environment because they rely on the business world speaking their language. At Ericsson, however, this is not the case. At the UK subsidiary, Ericsson Telecommunications, management training courses include seminars on both language and cross-cultural issues. A frequent comment made in follow-up evaluations is that increased awareness has improved communication and, more importantly, given participants a better understanding of their own language and how others might interpret it.

(Adapted from *Training Magazine*, June 1998)

(　　)(1) Ericsson uses both Swedish and English as its official corporate language.
(　　)(2) There is no need for those native English speakers to improve their language skills.
(　　)(3) Native English speakers are aware of the difficulties of listening to foreign languages.
(　　)(4) The British are likely to understate important issues with phrases such as *There could be a slight problem*.
(　　)(5) The UK subsidiary of Ericsson finally improved communication through various management training courses.

Part II Listening in

Task 1 Leave voice mails.

Eilish Gough, a manager at Sanderlin AB in Stockholm, receives five voice mails. Listen and decide what each speaker is trying to do.

(1) _____
(2) _____
(3) _____
(4) _____
(5) _____

A. decline an offer
B. ask for permission
C. give feedback
D. make an offer
E. request some information
F. change an arrangement
G. make a complaint
H. confirm arrangements

Task 2 Leave a message.

Mr. Wiley is in England. He is calling Mr. Mathews of ABC Company, which produces office furniture for export.

(1) Listen to the conversation and decide whether the following statements are true (T) or false (F).

(　　)① Mr. Wiley is calling from international Sales, England.

(　　)② Mr. Matthews has gone to Hong Kong on business for a few days.

(　　)③ Mr. Matthews won't be back until Friday afternoon.

(　　)④ Mr. Wiley thinks the price of the office furniture is too high.

(　　)⑤ The message isn't urgent. Mr. Wiley will phone again.

(2) Listen again and note down the three messages Mr. Wiley leaves.

Message 1 _____.

Message 2 _____.

Message 3 _____.

Part III Language focus

■ **Making a call and introducing yourself**

1. Hello, my name is Edward Green. I would like to speak to Mr. Smith, please.

2. This is Don Bradley. Can I talk to Phil Watson, please?

3. Good morning. Can I talk to Phil, please?

4. This is Don Bradley from Bibury Systems.

5. Would you please put me through to Extension 247?

6. Extension 471, please?

7. Hello, Anna. It's Marion again. We were cut off.

8. Can you put me through to Sharon Thomson, please?

9. My name is David Whelan from the Health and Safety Council.

■ **Answering the phone**

1. Good morning, Bibury Systems. Can I help you?

2. Good morning, RUYJ Advertising.

3. What company are you from, please?

4. May I ask who's calling, please?

■ **Putting the caller through**

1. I'll put you through.

2. Hold the line, please. I'm connecting you now.

3. Hang on a minute, please. I'll put through.

4. Hold the line, please. I'll put through to Sales.

■ **The person wanted is not available**

1. I am sorry, but Mr. Smith isn't available.

2. Well, Mr. Bradley, I'm afraid Phil's not in the office at the moment.

3. Can I take a message or would you like to ring him on his mobile phone?

4. Yes, I'll tell him that. Shall I ask him to call you back?

5. I'm sorry. He won't be free until this afternoon.

6. He should be available in about an hour.

7. I'm afraid he is in a meeting. Can I take a message?

8. I'm afraid she's out of the office at the moment. Can I take a message, or would you try his mobile phone?

■ **Making a request**

1. Okay. I'll ring again soon. Does Mr. Smith have a direct line?

2. I'm sorry. Could you repeat that?

3. Would you mind repeating that number?

4. Could you spell that name, please?

5. Yes, please. Could you tell Ms. Symes I'll have to cancel our meeting on Thursday?

6. Could you please tell me when he'll be back?

7. Yes. Can you put me through to Ellen Symes, please?

■ **Response to a request**

1. I'm sorry but the number is confidential.

2. I'm sorry, the line is still busy. Can I take a message?

3. I'll ask her to call you as soon as possible.

4. Fine, Mr. Murphy. I'll give her your message.

5. Fine. I'll tell her about that. Thank you. Bye.

6. Yes, I'll tell Ms. Lewis it's urgent. Thank you. Bye.

7. The line is busy at the moment. Would you like to hold?

■ **Reasons for calling**

1. I'm calling about the sales figures for the first half of the year.

2. I'm phoning because I want to talk about the early settlement discounts for this order.

3. I'm calling for some further details about the delivery.

4. I'm calling about the First Aid course Ms. Thomson is arranging with us. I'd like to confirm the week beginning 13 May but I'm not …

■ **Confirming**

1. Did you say "F" for Freddie or "S" for Sugar?

2. It's "S" for Sugar.

3. Did you say the thirteenth or thirtieth?

4. The thirteenth, one three.

5. I'm sorry. Could you spell your surname, please?
6. And it's the Health and Safety Council. Right. And what's the message, please?
7. So that's ...
8. Just let me repeat that.

Part IV Speaking out

Section 1 Sample dialogues

Dialogue 1

The marketing executive of Bibury Systems is trying to talk to Mr. Smith on the phone, aiming to introduce a new product to Mr. Smith.

(1)

Edward Green:	Hello, my name is Edward Green. I would like to speak to Mr. Smith, please.
Smith's secretary:	I am sorry, but Mr. Smith isn't available.
Edward Green:	Okay. I'll ring back. Does Mr. Smith have a direct line?
Smith's secretary:	I'm sorry but the number is confidential.
Edward Green:	Okay. Thank you.

(2)

Smith's secretary:	Hello, Mr. Smith's office.
Edward Green:	Hello, my name is Edward Green from Bibury Systems. I rang earlier. I would like to speak to Mr. Smith, please.
Smith's secretary:	I'm afraid Mr. Smith is not in the office at the moment. Can I ask what it is about?
Edward Green:	It is very important. I represent Bibury Systems. We've got a new product and I want Mr. Smith to see it.
Smith's secretary:	Please send the product specifications by mail, Mr. Green.
Edward Green:	I would like Mr. Smith to see the product and would like to talk to Mr. Smith direct. When is a good time to call?
Smith's secretary:	You could try ringing this afternoon.
Edward Green:	Thank you. Goodbye.

(3)

Edward Green:	Hello, this is Edward Green. I rang earlier. I would like to speak to Mr. Smith, please.
Smith's secretary:	I'm afraid that Mr. Smith is in a meeting.
Edward Green:	Is he free later this afternoon?
Smith's secretary:	I don't think so. Mr. Smith is very busy at the moment.
Edward Green:	I'll ring again tomorrow.
Smith's secretary:	I am afraid Mr. Smith isn't in the office tomorrow.
Edward Green:	Thank you. Goodbye.

It's six o'clock. Edward Green tries again, hoping that Mr. Smith's secretary isn't there, and Mr. Smith is still at work.

(4)

Edward Green:	Ah Mr. Smith? My name is Edward Green.
Mr. Smith:	Yes?
Edward Green:	You don't know me but I work in Don Bradley's office at Bibury Systems. I spoke to your secretary today.
Mr. Smith:	Yes?
Edward Green:	You publish your catalogue this month. And we have an exciting new product. I hope you could have a look at it. So I wonder if I would be able to meet you in your office.
Mr. Smith:	I'm busy all next week.
Edward Green:	Maybe the week after?
Mr. Smith:	Talk to my secretary.
Edward Green:	You print your catalogue this month, don't you?
Mr. Smith:	Yes.
Edward Green:	Could you possibly see the product this week? It won't take long.
Mr. Smith:	Okay. Be here Wednesday morning ... eight sharp! I'll give you twenty minutes.
Edward Green:	Thank you Mr. Smith. I'll see you on Wednesday morning at 8 o'clock.

Dialogue 2

Don Bradley, the chief executive at ABC Company, wants to talk to Phil Watson of RUYJ Advertising Company about a new product.

(1)

Receptionist:	Good morning, RUYJ Advertising.
Don Bradley:	Good morning. This is Don Bradley. Can I talk to Phil Watson, please?
Receptionist:	What company are you from, please?
Don Bradley:	Bibury Systems.
Receptionist:	I'll put you through.

(2)

Dave:	Phil Watson's phone.
Don Bradley:	Good morning. Can I talk to Phil, please?
Dave:	Can I ask who's calling, please?
Don Bradley:	Don Bradley from Bibury Systems.
Dave:	Well, Mr. Bradley, I'm afraid Phil's not in the office at the moment. Can I take a message or would you like to ring him on his mobile phone?
Don Bradley:	I'll try his mobile. Can I have the number, please?
Dave:	0802 54377.
Don Bradley:	Just let me check that. Zero eight zero two five four three double seven.
Dave:	That's it.
Don Bradley:	Thanks.

(3)

Phil Watson:	Hello, Phil Watson.
Don Bradley:	Hello, Phil, this is Don Bradley.
Phil Watson:	Hello, Don. Sorry to keep you waiting. How are you?
Don Bradley:	I'm fine, thanks. Can we meet? We have a new product and I want you to see it.
Phil Watson:	Brilliant! I will be available all day this Thursday in my office. Would that be fine for you?
Don Bradley:	That's fine. See you then! Bye!
Phil Watson:	See you!

Section 2 Creating your own

Work with your partner to role-play the following situations.

■ Task 1

Laura is the manager of Maplom Machinery Trading Co., Ltd. She calls Jimmy Warden, the manager of Cologne Exhibition (China) Co., Ltd. to enquire about exhibition plan in Germany next year. Mr. Warden is having a meeting, and the receptionist of Colongne Exhibition promises to tell him about this.

Task 2

You are the assistant of George Smith, Purchasing Manager of HRC Corporation. Someone calls to be connected to Mr. Smith. Find out who's calling and why. Explain that your boss is not available now.

Part V Writing

Read the letter below, and write a reply to Macro Francone:

- thanking him for his enquiry
- enclosing a brochure and price list
- telling him about a new special offer
- asking him to contact you if he has any questions

Dear Ms. Pickering,

　　I am writing to enquire about your latest photocopiers. We are currently renting a model from you. However, we would now like to purchase one.

　　I would be very grateful if you could send us a copy of your brochure and any relevant product literature. Would it also be possible for you to send us a current price list?

　　I look forward to hearing from you.

Yours sincerely
Macro Francone

Part VI Follow-up reading

Read the article below and discuss the following questions.

- What does the planning stage involve before starting to write a business letter?
- How do you make a well-organized message in a letter?
- How many steps are involved in general in writing a business letter?

General process for writing business letters

(1) Plan your message

Before starting to write, think about who you are writing to and why. What is your objective? What tone should you adopt? What is the correct or appropriate layout for your letter? What channel and medium should you choose?

During the planning phrase, you think about the fundamentals of your message: your reason for communicating, your audience, the main idea of your message, and the channel and medium that will best convey your thoughts. The stages of planning include:

Defining your purpose. When planning a business message, think about your purpose. Of course you want to maintain the goodwill of the audience and create a favorable impression for your organization, but you also have a particular goal you want to achieve. That purpose may be straightforward and obvious (like placing an order), or it may be more difficult to define. When the purpose is unclear, it pays to spend a few minutes thinking about what you hope to accomplish.

Analyzing your audience. Once you are satisfied that you have a legitimate purpose in communicating, take good look at your intended audience. Who are the members? What are their attitudes? What do they need to know? What is their probable reaction to your message? What is their relationship to you? The answers to these questions will indicate something about the material you'll cover and the way you'll cover it.

Establishing your main idea. Every business message can be boiled down to one main idea. Regardless of the issue's complexity, one central point sums up everything. This is your theme, your main idea. Everything else in the message either supports this point or demonstrates its implications. The main idea has to strike a response in the intended audience. It has to motivate people to do what you want by linking your purpose with their own.

Selecting the appropriate channel and medium. The communication media available to business people have mushroomed in the past three decades: faxes, e-mail, voice mail, teleconferences, to name a few. Your selection of channel and medium can make the difference between effective and ineffective communication. So when choosing a channel (whether oral, written or electronic) and a medium (whether face-to-face conversation, telephone conversation, e-mail, written letters, etc.), do your best to match your selections to your messages and your intentions.

(2) Organize your thoughts

Successful communicators rely on organization to make their messages meaningful. Achieving good organization can be a challenge. Nevertheless, the following four guidelines can help you recognize a well-organized message:

- Make the subject and purpose clear;
- Include only information that is related to the subject and purpose;
- Group the ideas and present them in a logical way;
- Include all the necessary information.

Each guideline not only helps you communicate clearly and logically but also helps you communicate ethically by making sure you state all information as truthfully, honestly and fairly as possible.

(3) Formulate your message

When you feel confident that your outline or organization will achieve your purpose with the intended audience, you can begin to write your first draft. As you compose the first draft, don't worry about getting everything perfect. Just put down your ideas as quickly as you can. You'll have time to revise and refine the material later. Composition is easier if you've already figured out what to say and in what order, although you may need to pause now and then to find the right word.

(4) Revise your message

Once you've completed the first draft of your message, you need to review and refine your messages before sending them. Read what you've written through quickly to evaluate its overall effectiveness. You're mainly concerned with content, organization and flow. Compare the draft with your original plan. Have you covered all points in the most logical order? Is there a good balance between the general and the specific? Do the most important ideas receive the most space, and are they placed in the most prominent positions? Have you provided enough support and double-checked the facts? Would the message be more convincing if it were arranged in another sequence? Do you need to add anything?

In addition, you should also think about what you can eliminate. In business, it's particularly important to weed out unnecessary material.

Overall, the composition process varies with the situation, the communicator, and the organization. Routine messages obviously require less planning and less revision than more complex messages. Moreover, various people approach composition in various ways; some compose quickly and then revise slowly; others revise as they go along. The composition process, therefore, is flexible, not a fixed prescription of sequenced steps.

P. S. The figure shows the main parts of a formal business letter and what they are.

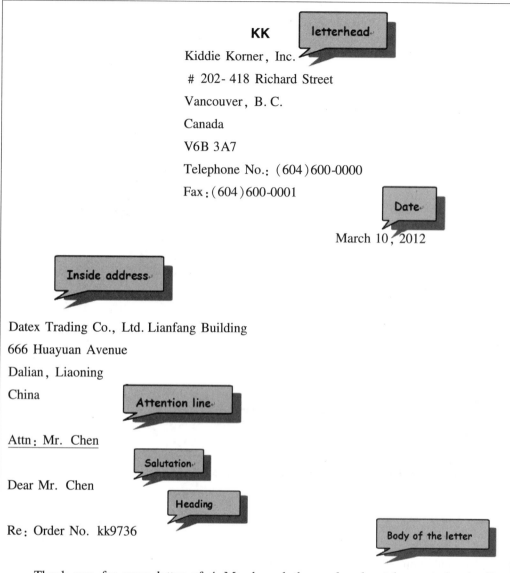

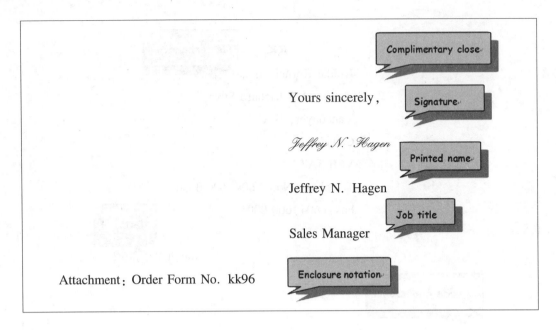

 **Training Assessment**

Part I Self-study

1. Match the telephone phrases below with the responses.

(1) I'm afraid the line's busy.　　　　　a. It's OK. I'll phone back later.

(2) Can I have Extension 236, please?　　b. It's OK. I'll hold.

(3) I'm afraid he isn't in the office.　　　c. Sorry, I'll try to reconnect you.

(4) Could you tell Sarah that I called?　　d. I'll put through.

(5) It's Dave Rogers again for Joe West.　e. OK. I'll give her your message.

2. Don Hobson applies for a job at Bibury Systems. He telephones to arrange an interview. Read the conversation and fill the gaps.

Jenny: Bibury Systems. How can I help you?

Don: Hello. I'd like to speak to Clive Harris, please.

Jenny: I'm afraid he's out of the office this morning.

　　　(1) _____

Don: Yes, please. My name's Don Hobson.

Jenny: (2) _____

Don: H-O-B-S-O-N.

Jenny: (3) _____
        B-S or P-S?
Don: B for BOOK. (4) _____ the position as sales executive.
Jenny: Yes?
Don: Mr. Harris left a message on my voice-mail asking if I could come for an interview at 2 p.m. on 18 June. (5) _____ that I'll be able to come then?
Jenny: So, that's 2 o'clock on 18 June.
Don: That's right.
Jenny: Fine. (6) _____.
Don: Thank you. Bye.

Part II BEC exam focus

Reading Test

Look at the following extracts from the Chairman's Statement in four annual reports. Which extract does each sentence below refer to?

A. Strike action and unfavorable exchange rates led to losses that were almost balanced by gains from our ongoing resource efficiency program, which delivered an impressive £100m of cost performance improvements. Another source of revenue was the recent disposal of Dennox, our wholly-owned subsidiary.

B. The company made steady progress, with profits before tax and exceptional items increasing to £596m. Careful cash management continues to be a major feature of the company's strong performance. Despite pressure from increased investment activity, the balance sheet shows net cash at £3.2bn after expenditure of £346m.

C. Trading volume increased by 4.5%, which was well up on recent years, and turnover rose by 3%. Operating margins also increased, as a result of the restructuring program that was completed at the end of last year. Although successful, the program meant a reduction in net cash to £472m.

D. Our major achievement last year was the £4.8bn acquisition of a specialty chemicals business. This investment, along with the planned sale of assets, will help streamline the company's range of businesses. Trading profit fell by 7% due to disappointments in non-core activities, confirming the logic of the actions we are taking.

(   )1. The company enjoyed a substantial increase in its sales.

(   )2. The company offset some of its poor trading results by selling assets.

(   )3. The Chairman explains why substantial investment was necessary.

(   )4. The Chairman refers to the success of previous organizational changes.

(   )5. The company's cost-cutting measures are proving very successful.

(   )6. The Chairman refers to the company's success in controlling new spending.

(   )7. The company is currently implementing a major transformation program.

Module 4 — Business Planning

An essential stepping stone to business success

 Into the Module

Planning is an essential stepping stone to business success. Just as the saying goes, "If you fail to plan, you plan to fail." Patrick Montana and Bruce Charnov outline a three-step result-oriented process for planning: choosing a destination, evaluating alternative routes, deciding the specific course of the plan. In organizations, planning can become a management process, concerned with defining goals for a future direction and determining on the missions and resources to achieve those targets. Major characteristics of planning in organizations include:

- Planning increases the efficiency of an organization;
- Planning reduces risks;
- Planning utilizes with maximum efficiency the available time and resources.

The concept of planning in organizations involves identifying what an organization wants to do by using four questions: "Where are we today in terms of our business planning? Where are we going? Where do we want to go? How are we going to get there?"

Training Objectives

By the end of this module, you are expected to:
- develop communication skills to talk about business planning;
- learn about the basic aspects involving business planning;
- get familiar with the basic vocabulary related to marketing business planning.

Plans are nothing; Planning is everything.

—Dwight D. Eisenhower

Module 4 Business Planning

Unit 10 Activity Planning

Planning increases efficiency

 **Training Objectives**

> **By the end of this unit, you are expected to:**
> - develop communication skills to talk about activity planning;
> - learn about the basic aspects involving activity planning;
> - get familiar with the basic vocabulary related to activity planning.

 **Training Portfolio**

Part I Starting up

Section 1 To discuss

In order to encourage teamwork, Blackmores Institute is to hold a team-building event. What do you think they should consider when planning this event? Discuss it with your partner.

Section 2 To read

Read the following passage and then talk with your partner about what impresses you most.

How to plan a team-building event that everyone will enjoy

The two words of "team building" produce feelings of dread in many employees and bring up images of ropes courses and awkward renditions of Kumbaya around a fire pit.

Back when I lived in San Francisco, I worked for a company that was obsessed with team building. Instead of going to a ropes course, we went to a climbing gym. Even though I found it pretty fun, many of my co-workers did not like the idea of dangling from ropes while everyone looked at their backsides. These individuals bowed out of the activity and stood in the corner pouting ... not much "team" building happened that day.

So how do you plan an event that will cater to your entire team?

According to Kate Nasser, president of CAS, Inc., a consultancy for corporations, governments and mid-sized businesses based in Summerville, New Jersey, it is important to determine an objective before diving into a team-building activity. "Team building can be fun and boost morale," she says, "It can also be designed to help address a work or communication problem."

- "Fun" team building

If you want your activity to strengthen bonds between employees, ask them what they want to do, suggests Nasser. "Expect that you will get diverse views, but know that they will be more engaged if the activity represents their definition of fun."

Nasser recommends going to a bowling alley and breaking up into teams. "It is easy and cheap—just make sure to bring small prizes to make it even more fun," she suggests, adding that books such as *Team Games for Trainers* and *The Big Book of Team Building Games* are also filled with ideas.

- "Problem-solving" team building

If there are problems within a team, first sit down with employees individually to find out what they would like to change, Nasser recommends.

"Hold conversations with the promise of confidentiality," she says, "Most teamwork problems are rooted in a lack of respect for diversity or communication problems."

If respect is the issue, Nasser recommends this exercise: Have each person bring a photo of themselves doing something they love—something that reflects who they are as a person. Then, go around the table and have each person explain why the photo makes them happy or proud. "Make sure these are not work-related photos," she says.

Play 20 questions—after someone describes their photo, give each person around the table the opportunity to ask for more information. At the end, "people will be talking to each other like human beings—this works really well."

Another option is to instruct each member of your team to take a personality indicator test. "I recommend the Keirsey Temperament tests," Nasser says, "Everyone can take the test, print off the results, and bring it to a team building meeting. Then everyone can guess each other's type. It is a very insightful exercise."

Once finished, participants then list one or two effective ways others can communicate with them. "To make it really fun, print up a sign for your desk that alerts others on how to communicate with you. For example, mine would be 'Give me the big picture and get to the point.'"

(From: https://www.americanexpress.com/)

Part II Listening in

Task 1 Listen to the following passage and fill in the blanks.

Recently we decided to open a new sales office in New York. First I arranged a meeting with the (1) _____ department to discuss the project. We prepared a budget with details of the various (2) _____ involved. Then we collected information about possible (3) _____ for the new office. We considered two options—one in Greenwich Village and the other near Central Park. After doing some more (4) _____, I wrote a report for the board of directors.

Unfortunately, we made a mistake when we (5) _____ the costs as the exchange rate changed, and so we didn't keep within our budget. We (6) _____ by almost 20 percent. We had to rearrange the (7) _____ for moving into the building because the office was not redecorated in time. The board of directors was unhappy because we didn't meet the (8) _____ for opening the office by 15 December. It (9) _____ finally in January. However, we (10) _____ sales of at least $500,000 in the first year.

Task 2 Listen to the dialogue and fill in the blanks.

A: We are going to start our promotion campaign next month. Clear your (1) _____ over the next few days because we're going to be burning the midnight oil in order to get everything ready in time.

B: OK. But it's not as bad as all that. Most everything is already set. We're going through an event (2) _____ company, so they should manage most of the details. Probably the biggest thing on our (3) _____ is to go over the event rundown with their on-site managers to make sure it all goes as planned.

A: Sounds good, but I hate to put all our eggs in one basket. What if their people drop the ball? We should be (4) _____ with a back-up plan just in case.

B: We've been working with this company to set everything up since last summer. They are very clear on all of the details for the event. Also you know, they are (5) _____. I'd say we have nothing to worry about.

A: OK.

Part III Language focus

■ **Agreeing**

1. Sounds great.
2. Exactly.
3. I agree.
4. Quite right, I couldn't agree more.
5. That's exactly what I think.
6. That's a good point.

■ **Disagreeing**

1. You are right, but …
2. Sounds good, but …
3. I see what you mean, but …
4. There is something in what you said, but …
5. That's true, but on the other hand …
6. I don't quite agree because …
7. Maybe, but don't you think …?
8. I'm afraid I have a different opinion.

■ **Giving suggestion**

1. How about …?
2. What do you think about …?
3. If I were you, I would …

4. Perhaps we could …

5. Don't you think we should …?

■ **Highlighting**

1. This is particularly important because …

2. I can't stress too much that …

3. It should be pointed out that …

4. The point I am making here is that …

5. The main thing to remember is …

Part IV Speaking out

Section 1 Sample dialogues

Dialogue 1

A: Hi, Michelle. I'd like you to follow up with the planning for our company retreat next month.

B: OK.

A: Well, we need to decide on the venue, make arrangements for speakers and door prizes, and set up all the activities and accommodations.

B: No problem. What else?

A: More importantly, we need to determine which staff members will be eligible and will be available to go. We've got to get a head count in order to make reservations.

B: What are the criteria for staff members to attend? Are we only including our management team? Or will we be extending invitations to lower level employees?

A: Lower level employees need not attend, since the purpose of this retreat is for training, specifically for our management team.

B: OK, I see.

A: Oh, there is one more thing. In order to get everyone to jell together, we've got to include some fun.

A: Yes, I agree. We can have an icebreaker to get everyone warmed up.

B: Sounds great. We can include it in the planning.

Dialogue 2

A: How much do you have budgeted for our trip to Los Angeles?

B: In total, it should be about $7,000 for the week conference. Would you like to see the breakdown?

A: Yes. I want to know exactly where the money is going. Would you please give me a detailed report?

B: OK. First we have the airline tickets, which are $400 per person; with 6 of us going, that's $2,400. For our accommodations, we are spending $100 a night, per room, for 5 days. That's another $1,500.

A: Weren't you able to find anything less expensive? We are sharing rooms, right?

B: I have two people to a room. The $100 room rate is the lowest I could find. With the conference going on that week, all the hotels have inflated their prices—they're making a killing.

A: So far we have $3,900, what else?

B: I have budgeted $30 per person per day for food expenses. That totals another $900. And for other incidentals, like taxi fees and tips, I have estimated about $500.

A: Well, that's only $5,300. Didn't you tell me your budget was $7,000? Where is the rest of the money?

B. That's my buffer. I wanted to leave a little room in the budget, just in case. It's better to be safe than sorry.

Section 2 Creating your own

Pair work: Make a dialogue with your partner about your planning for a team-building event.

Your dialogue could include:
- What's your budget?
- Who will attend the event?
- Where do you want to hold the event? (Decide on the venue)
- What kind of activities will you set up to strengthen bonds between employees?
- How about accommodations?
- What else should you consider in the planning?

■ Role play: Discuss the details of the plan with your colleagues.

The head of your department is retiring. Your department is planning to hold a farewell party for him.

- When and where will the party be?
- What kind of entertainment will you have at the party?
- Do you need to prepare a farewell speech?
- Do you need to prepare a gift? If so, what kind of gift should you prepare for him?
- What else do you need to plan?

Part V Writing

Mr. Smith, manager of the marketing department, is leaving your company to Canada. You are to prepare a farewell speech based on the given information.

- Introduction: on behalf of the company, say a few words to Mr. Smith.
- Looking back: Mr. Smith has worked in the company for ten years.
- Personal quality: open-mindedness, tolerance, thoughtfulness.
- Expressing thanks and best wishes.

■ Sample

Dear Mr. Grant,

As you prepare to return to Australia, I take the greatest possible pleasure of sending you, on behalf of all members of this company and in my own name, our good wishes for the future.

I must also express our thanks to you for everything you have done for our company over the past 7 years. We especially appreciate the close relationship with your staff. We are all deeply impressed by their diligence and patience. Without the help of your colleagues, we could not possibly have developed our company into such a large international company. We appreciate our fruitful cooperation very much.

Thank you again. We wish you good health and every success in the future.

Part VI Follow-up reading

Passage 1

Read the passage and then answer the following questions: What do you think is the most important in trade fair planning? Why?

General guidelines for trade fair planning

Participation in a trade fair takes a huge amount of planning and organizing. The following guidelines are meant to provide a general overview of the preparation involved.

- **Setting objectives**

Trade fairs as multifunctional dialog instruments make it possible to focus on communication objectives. However, it is necessary for participants to formulate objectives clearly so that success can be measured (e.g. sales, number of contacts, number of potential customers identified, number of customers acquired, level of communication achieved).

- **Getting information**

General information about trade fairs as well as exhibitions can be obtained via the Internet. First-time exhibitors should select carefully from the wide range of international trade fairs and regional exhibitions.

- **Budget planning**

Budget planning is part of the careful preparation for trade fair participation. In addition to basic costs such as stand rental and energy supply, costs may include stand construction, furnishing and design, stand service and communication, transport, as well as personnel and travel costs.

- **Schedule**

The process of participation in a trade fair breaks down into three phases: preparation, stand operations and follow-up.

Preparation should be started well ahead of time and sufficient time must be scheduled for preparation.

An action plan should be made and each stage should be broken down to individual tasks with the names of the people responsible for each task and their individual deadlines indicated. Clearly, the dates set by the organizer for erecting and dismantling stands must be adhered to.

The total time necessary prior to the trade fair is determined by that area of activity which requires the longest advanced planning (possibly the creative and conceptual aspects regarding the stand and exhibits). Other activities should include time buffers, i. e. extra time in case of unavoidable or unexpected delays.

- **Selection of exhibits**

The exhibition program should be defined in line with the aims of the trade fair. The exhibition program is derived from the answers to the following questions:

(1) Should the entire product range be shown or should only selected items be presented?

(2) What essentials are required to show the products?

(3) Which products are new, improved, or superior to the competitors?

(4) What must be specially featured?

(5) Which product corresponds to the future needs of the target group?

(6) Have current trends been taken into account (socially, economically, technically)?

(7) Are the design, colors and packaging effective?

(8) Should special trade fair models be manufactured?

(9) What has to be explained? Should this be done via text panels, displays or videos?

(10) How much space is available?

- **Registration**

Many trade fairs are booked quite quickly. An early registration is therefore advisable. Since an indication of the space required is necessary for registration, a rough design for the stand should be prepared ahead.

- **Trade fair stand**

A trade fair stand is like a company's business card. It therefore should correspond in terms of size and furnishing with the standards found in your company as well as be suitable for the products that are to be exhibited. The focus should be on a customer-friendly presentation of your exhibits.

The trade fair stand should appeal to the eyes and ears, and may also make an emotional appeal to the visitors.

- **Stand personnel**

Competent stand personnel ensure the success of a trade fair participation. The more motivated and qualified the exhibitor's stand personnel are, the greater the opportunities for good sales results and new contacts. A targeted selection and intensive training of the stand personnel is just as important as an effective presentation of the products.

- **Advertising and publicity**

Advertising and publicity are an indispensable part of participation planning. The approach to potential visitors must be planned just as carefully as the design of the stand. Through advertising and publicity, trade fair companies create a broad resonance in the media and thus reach many potential visitors. However, the organizer can only advertise the fair as a whole. Each individual exhibitor should inform, in advance of the event, his/her respective target group of the range he/she is exhibiting.

(From: https://wenku.baidu.com)

Passage 2

Mark the following statements with T (true) or F (false) according to the passage.

New product planning

The creation of new products is the lifeblood of an organization. Products do not remain economically viable for ever, so new ones must be developed to assure the survival of an organization. For many firms, new products account for a sizable part of sales and profits.

The new-product development process has the following stages.

- **Generating new product ideas**

The starting point in the new-product development process is generating ideas for new offerings. Ideas come from many sources, including customers, employees, marketing research and competitive products. The most successful ideas are directly related to satisfying customer needs.

- **Screening**

This stage deals with the elimination of ideas that do not mesh with overall company objectives or cannot be developed given the company's resources. Some firms hold open discussion of new product ideas among representatives of different functional areas in the organization during which product managers, company scientists and other managers evaluate the new product ideas.

- **Business analysis**

Further screening is done in this stage. Does the idea fit with the company's product, distribution and promotional resources? The analysis also involves assessing the new product's potential sales, profits, growth rate and competitive strengths.

- **Product development**

At this stage, an actual product is created, subjected to a series of tests, and revised. Tests measure both the product's actual features and how consumers perceive it. Inadequate testing during the development stage can doom a product and even a company to failure.

- **Test marketing**

The product is actually sold in a limited area during test marketing. The company is examining both the product and the marketing effort it is using to support it during this phase. However, some firms choose to skip test marketing and move directly from product development to commercialization.

- **Commercialization**

This is the stage at which the product is made generally available in the marketplace. Considerable planning goes into this stage, since the firm's promotion, distribution and pricing strategies must be geared to support the new product offering.

Product identification is another important aspect of marketing strategy. Products are identified by brands, brand names and trademarks. The brand name is the part of the brand that can be vocalized. Many brand names, such as Coca-Cola, McDonald's, American Express and IBM, are famous around the world. However, Chinese marketers have made several unfortunate brand name choices for products intended for sale in the United States. High on the Chinese list of "What not to name a product" is White Elephant batteries.

Good brand names are easy to pronounce, recognize and remember: Crest and Visa, for example. Global firms face a real problem in selecting brand names, since an excellent brand name in one country may prove disastrous in another. Most languages have a short "a", so Coca-Cola is pronounceable almost anywhere.

Brand name should give the right image to the buyers. Sometimes changes in the market's environment require changes to a brand name. Therefore, many firms hire professional consultants to create new product names.

(From: Kong Qingyan et al., 2002: 116 – 118)

(　　)(1) The creation of a new product is very important for manufacturing companies to survive.
(　　)(2) The failure of a new product may be caused by inadequate promotion.
(　　)(3) New product planning always starts with commercialization.
(　　)(4) In the stage of "Test Marketing", the product is sold in a very broad area.
(　　)(5) Good brand names must be easy to read and remember.

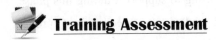

Part I Self-study

Complete the dialogue based on the Chinese given in brackets.

A: Right, I have this meeting to fix the details for the Annual Sales Conference. Basically we've got three issues to decide: firstly the date, secondly the location and finally the conference facilities. Let's start with the date. What's your view, Bob?

B: (1) _____. (我想我们得把时间定在12月份, 很可能是最后一个周末。)

C: Excuse me, Bob. Margaret, I've just been looking at your diary that last week in December you're flying out to Germany.

A: When do I get back?

C: Well, (2) _____. (你被安排乘飞机于周日晚上返回伦敦。) You hardly have time to get over to attend the conference.

A: You're right. Bob, why can't we make it the second weekend in December?

B: It'll be very difficult. The first two weekends in December are pretty busy. (3) _____. (团队的大多数人都在忙着新产品上市。)

A: Of course, I was forgetting. What about the third weekend?

B: That looks OK. (4) _____. (当然了, 我还要和亨利再确认一下。)

A: Sure. Get back to us as soon as possible. Now, what about the venue? Bob, do you have any idea?

B: Yes, I think I've found the ideal spot just outside London. It's called the Swan Hotel.

A: (5) _____? (听起来不错, 要多少钱?)

B: Well, we're working to a budget of £300 per delegate for the weekend and I reckon we can get this place for less.

A: Good. Does that include everything?

B: Yes. All is inclusive.

A: Great. Look, I have to go now. My fight leaves in a couple of hours. Can I leave you with Catherine to sort out the details?

Part II BEC exam focus

Listening Test

Questions 1 – 12

- You will hear three telephone conversations or messages.
- Write one or two words or a number in the numbered spaces on the notes or forms below.
- You will hear each recording twice.

Conversation 1

(Questions 1 – 4)

- Look at the notes below.
- You will hear a man calling his office.

Telephone message

- Martin Hayes phoned from the (1) _____. There's a problem: The (2) _____ haven't arrived! (They were sent by air last week.)
- Another thing: He needs more (3) _____. He is attaching a (4) _____ this morning, so call him back around lunchtime.

Conversation 2

(Question 5 – 8)

- Look at the notes below.
- You will hear a woman calling about a job application.

Message for Jill

- Sara (5) _____ called this morning about the post of (6) _____.
- They'd like you to attend a (7) _____ on the 28th; they'll confirm this by letter.
- In the meantime, can you send her details of your (8) _____?

Conversation 3

(Questions 9 – 12)

- Look at the notes below.

· You will hear a man phoning about some arrangements for a meeting.

While you were out

Message for: *Lauren O'Neil*

From: *Chris Darcy*

Message

Chris (HR) phoned about meeting of (9) _____ next week.

There's going to be an announcement about (10) _____.

MD wants you to make presentation on (11) _____ of the new company.

Could you also cover (12) _____ in your presentation? If any questions, call Chris directly.

Module 4 Business Planning

Unit 11 Advertising Planning

Remember your target customers

Training Objectives

> **By the end of this unit, you are expected to:**
> - develop communication skills to talk about advertising planning;
> - learn about the basic aspects involving advertising planning;
> - get familiar with the basic vocabulary related to advertising planning.

Training Portfolio

Part I Starting up

Section 1 To discuss

Work in pairs. Tell your partner which ad slogan impresses you most and why.

(1) Where there is a way, there is a Toyota. (Toyota)

(2) Good to the last drop. (Maxwell)

(3) No business too small, no problem too big. (IBM)

(4) Not all cars are created equal. (Mitsubishi)

Section 2 To read

Read the following advertising copies. Which do you like best? Why?

- **Think different.**

Here's to the crazy ones. The misfits. The rebels. The troublemakers. The round pegs in the square holes. The ones who see things differently. They're not fond of rules. And they have no respect for the status quo. You can quote them, disagree with them, glorify or vilify them. About the only thing you can't do is ignore them, because they change things. They invent. They imagine. They heal. They explore. They create. They inspire. They push the human race forward. Maybe they have to be crazy. How else can you stare at an empty canvas and see a work of art? Or sit in silence and hear a song that's never been written? Or gaze at a red planet and see a laboratory on wheels? We make tools for these kinds of people. While some see them as the crazy ones, we see genius. Because the people who are crazy enough to think they can change the world are the ones who do. (Apple)

(From: https://www.learnenglishwithwill.com)

- **It's not a journey.**

Every journey ends, but we go on. The world turns; we turn with it. Plans disappear. Dreams take over. But wherever I go, there you are. My luck. My fate. My fortune. Chanel No.5. Inevitable. (Chanel No.5)

(From: https://wenku.baidu.com)

- **Impossible is 0.**

Hi, I'm Gilbert Arenas and this is my story. When I entered the NBA, the first 40 games of my career I sat on the bench. They said I was going to play zero minutes. You know I just think they didn't see the talent that I had. They thought I was a zero. Instead of sitting there being bitter, I just practiced, practiced. If no one believes in you, anything you do is a positive. It wasn't even about basketball any more. It was about proving them wrong. Now the reason I wear No.0 is because it lets me know that I need to go out there and fight every day. (Adidas)

(From: https://wenku.baidu.com)

Part II Listening in

Task 1 Listen to the passage and fill in the blanks.

One of the most important decisions in developing an advertising (1) _____ is the media through which the ad transits the firm's message. The media the marketer selects must be (2) _____ of accomplishing the communications objectives of informing, persuading, and reminding (3) _____ customers of the products.

Market research should (4) _____ the target market and determine its size, geographic distribution and demographic characteristics, and then match the advertisement and the available media with the target audience. Finally, alternative costs should be compared to determine the best possible media (5) _____.

(6) _____ media include television and radio. Newspapers, magazines, outdoor advertising (such as posters, bulletins, etc.) represent the major types of (7) _____ media. The Internet is a new (8) _____. Nowadays, many companies jump to advertise on the Internet. The Internet advertising can assist in raising the awareness of (9) _____. It is most successful when combined with (10) _____ advertising such as TV or print.

Task 2 Listen to the dialogue and fill in the blanks.

A: Market classifieds, may I help you?

B: Yes, I would like to find out about (1) _____ an advertisement in your directory. Can you tell me a little about your rates for advertisements?

A: Sure. Our advertising rates are divided according to size, substrate and location. If you are a corporate partner with our publication, we can offer you a (2) _____. Also, our rates are different according to which publication you wish to advertise in. Our fall edition is pricier than the spring edition. When do you want to advertise?

B: We'd like to get in with the fall publication.

A: OK. Do you have a pre-determined design? You can use either your own designers, or if it is more (3) _____ for you, we have a team of graphic designers that can put something together for you.

B: That won't be necessary. We already have the image. If we run a (4) _____ page ad in your fall edition on a normal gloss paper, tri-color, what do you think that will run me?

A: It depends on the (5) _____ in the material. Are you interested in a front or back page ad? Those are more prime spots. We also have 5 tab page positions available.

B: I think a tab spot would be nice.

A: Well, for a customer supplied design, full page tab page ad, you're looking at about 6,000 RMB.

Part III Language focus

■ **Types of advertising**
1. print advertising
2. poster advertising
3. newspaper advertising
4. magazine advertising
5. yellow page advertising
6. online advertising
7. television advertising
8. broadcast advertising
9. billboard advertising
10. subway advertising
11. light box advertising
12. neon light advertising

■ **Discussing the media to use**

1. What media do you plan to use?
2. Have you ever considered other kinds of media?
3. Advertising on TV is expensive, but it reaches a mass audience.
4. Magazine advertising is relatively inexpensive, with lots of space for detailed product information and a long life span.
5. Advertising on the Internet will attract a potential mass audience, but it is difficult to control readers' attention and there are some delivery problems.

■ **Discussing advertising content**

1. What's our target audience for this campaign?
2. We have to take the target audience into account.
3. What kind of educational background does our audience have?
4. How much is our budget?

5. Which of these is most appealing?
6. We need to make some modifications on the design before we send a final copy for printing.

■ **Discussing the launch of an advertising campaign**

1. We've decided to use a variety of media for full coverage.
2. We'll run billboard and newspaper ads to help create brand recognition.
3. We'll put some ads on the Internet to attract the young generation's attention.
4. We'll take out full-page ads for three large trade magazines, and put the same full-page ads in the Sunday edition of 5 major newspapers.
5. We'll have 50-second spots on television once a day for 4 weeks.

Part IV Speaking out

Section 1 Sample dialogues

Dialogue 1

A: Have you got any ideas about the advertising of our wine?

B: I think we can start out with small newspaper ads. Then we'll see what kind of response we will get. Based on that, we'll decide whether to run full-page ads. If we don't get a positive response from the newspaper ads, we'll do some radio spots.

A: Sounds good, but I have a different idea. I plan to use the media mix to reach our target market. Our main goal is to establish brand awareness among our target audience.

B: What do you plan to use?

A: I plan to put a 20-second prime-time TV commercial.

B: Great!

A: I think we can also run billboard and print ads to help create broad brand recognition.

Dialogue 2

A: So, how is our advertising campaign going along?

B: We've come up with a good plan.

A: What media do you plan to use?

B: We've decided to use a variety of media for full coverage. First, we'll have 30-second spots on television once a day for 5 weeks. At the same time, we'll do 20-second radio commercials 4 times a day in selected cities with large populations. Finally, we'll have some outdoor ads using billboards near main entrances to big cities.

A: What style will the ads use?

B: We're focusing on a slice of life, showing how you can beat the summer heat by drinking a bottle of cooled beer.

A: Sounds good. Will we have a new slogan?

B: Yes. The advertising agency is working on it right now.

A: Good. Do you have any back-up plans?

B: Yes. If our commercials on the three kinds of media don't work out well, we will consider newspapers and magazines. We'll run newspaper and magazine ads to help create broad brand recognition. We'll take out full-page ads for two large trade magazines, and put the same full-page ad in the Sunday edition of four major newspapers.

A: Great! I'm sure our beer will soon become very popular.

Section 2 Creating your own

Task 1 Pair work: Make a dialogue with your partner according to the situation given below.

Your company has developed a new luxury lipstick. You are reporting your advertising plan to your boss.

Your dialogue should include:

(1) Who are your target customers?
- age and gender
- income
- the media they have access to

(2) What kind of media do you use to advertise your product?

(3) Do you have back-up plans?

Tips:

When an advertising campaign is planned, the first thing to consider is the age and gender of the target customers. Only when you know the age and gender of the target customers can you know their likes and dislikes, and the media they often have access to.

It is also a good idea to consider the typical income of the target customers. Their typical income can tell you the type of products or services they can afford. Your advertising campaign will fail if you are aiming at people with the wrong income group.

Task 2 Pair work: Make a dialogue with your partner according to the situation given below.

Your company wants to place an ad on TV, but TV commercials are too expensive, so you want to choose another way to advertise your product.

Your dialogue should include:
(1) What is your budget?
(2) Who are your target customers?
(3) Besides TV, are there any other options for placing your ads? Compare them with each other.
(4) What's your final decision?

Tips:

The company should decide the type of advertising according to the budget. If it is so expensive that the company cannot afford it, it will cause unnecessary burden to the company. Besides, you should consider whether it is a short-term or long-term campaign. If the type of advertisement can provide you with the long-term promotion of a product or service that can reach immense audience, it can still be cost-effective because it can reach a vast number of people at a considerable low price.

	Advantages	Disadvantages
TV commercials	combined impression (visual and acoustic)	expensive; not specified for target customers
the Internet	cheap	mainly targeted at young people
outdoor billboards	cheap; easy to reach the mass market	People might glance at them and then forget.
leaflets	cheap	Sometimes people just ignore them.
sports sponsorship	an easy way to reach the specific target customers	expensive

Part V Writing

An ad copy is a text of a print, radio or television advertising message that aims at attaching and holding the interest of the prospective buyers, and at persuading them to make a purchase all within a few short minutes or even seconds. The headline of an advertising copy is said to be the most important part, and quite often a small change in its wording brings disproportionate results.

Write an ad copy for a newly developed shampoo in P&G Company. You can use the sample for reference.

Sample

This is the Pepsi that your father drank, and his father drank before he met your grandmother.

This is the first Pepsi on the moon. What? No. Okay, fine. This might be the first Pepsi on Mars.

This is the Pepsi for this model, and his mom. Hi, Cindy. Show them how it's done.

This is the Pepsi that was right for Ray. Uh huh. And your Uncle Drew, who is still breaking ankles.

This is the Pepsi that's back from the future, and back for one last ride.

This is the Pepsi that Britney once popped. This one is for the King of Pop.

This is the Pepsi for those who are forever fun.

This is the Pepsi for every generation. (Pepsi)

Part VI Follow-up reading

Passage 1

Mark the following statements with T (true) or F (false) according to the passage.

Fundamentals of advertising

Product advertising is an important part of the marketing mix. A company can advertise in a variety of ways, depending on how much it wishes to spend and the size and type of audience it wishes to target. The different media for advertising include television, radio, newspapers, magazines, the Internet, outdoor billboards and direct mail. The choice of media for advertisements is made as a result of thorough market research, so that money is spent where it is most likely to produce results.

Corporate advertising is not directly concerned with increasing sales of a particular product or service, but more with the brand image, or company culture that a company wants to present to the public.

Advertising can pay off handsomely by increasing awareness of a business or product, developing the loyalty of current customers, generating sales and attracting new customers. You may want it to do all of these things. What's important is to prioritize the goals. Advertising works best when it's developed to meet one goal at a time.

Once you determine your goals, you can target at the right audience to receive your advertising messages. It's important to have a specific customer type or group in mind when developing the ads.

Ads should be written to communicate a message that the target audience considers important. It is important to stress the benefits of the product and to keep AIDA in mind:

- attract attention
- hold interest
- arouse desire
- motivate action

Which media will reach the right people? In addition to the "traditional" print and broadcast media, there are dozens of other options for placing your ads. Look at where your competitors advertise—and where they don't—to help focus your thinking. The important thing to remember about placement is to go where your targets will have the greatest likelihood of seeing or hearing your ads.

(From: https://wenku.baidu.com)

(   )(1) The ways that a company advertises depend on how large it is.

(   )(2) Budget is an important factor that a company should consider when advertising in different ways.

(   )(3) Corporate advertising has little to do with the brand image or company culture.

(   )(4) It's important to have a clear idea about the customer group when developing the ads.

(   )(5) According to the passage, AIDA refers to attention, interest, development, and action.

Passage 2

Read the passage and answer the following questions.

How companies advertise

Advertising informs consumers about the existence and benefits of products and services, and attempts to persuade them to buy them. The best form of advertising is probably word-of-mouth advertising, which occurs when people tell their friends about the benefits of products or services that they have purchased. Yet virtually no providers of goods or services rely on this alone, but use paid advertising instead. Indeed, many organizations also use institutional or prestige advertising, which is designed to build up their reputation rather than to sell particular products.

Although large companies could easily set up their own advertising departments, write their own advertisements, and buy media space themselves they tend to use the services of large advertising agencies. They are likely to have more resources, and more knowledge about all aspects of advertising and advertising media than a single company. The most talented advertising people generally prefer to work for agencies rather than individual companies as this gives them the chance to work on a variety of advertising accounts (contracts to advertise products or services). It is also easier for a dissatisfied company to give its account to another agency than it would be to fire its own advertising staff.

The client company generally gives the advertising agency an agreed budget: a statement of the objectives of the advertising campaign, known as a brief and an overall advertising strategy concerning the message to be communicated to the target customers. The agency creates advertisements (the word is often abbreviated to advert or ads), and develops a media plan specifying which media—newspapers, magazines, radio, television, cinema, posters, mail, etc.—will be used and in which proportions (on television and radio, ads are often known as commercials). Agencies often produce alternative ads or commercials that are pre-tested in newspapers, television stations, etc. in different parts of a country before a final choice is made prior to a national campaign.

The agency's media planners have to decide what percentage of the target market they want to reach (how many people will be exposed to the ads) and the number of times they are likely to see them. Advertising people talk about frequency or OTS (opportunities to see) and the threshold effect—the point at which advertising becomes effective. The choice of advertising media is generally strongly influenced by the comparative cost of reaching 1,000 members of the target audience, the cost per thousand (often abbreviated to CPM, using the Roman numeral for 1,000). The timing of advertising campaigns depends on factors such as purchasing frequency and buyer turnover (new buyers entering the market).

How much to spend on advertising is always problematic. Some companies simply match their competitors' spending, thereby avoiding advertising wars. Others set their ad budget at a certain percentage of current sales revenue. But both of these methods disregard the fact that increased ad spending or counter-cyclical advertising can increase current sales. On the other hand, excessive advertising is counter-productive because after too many exposures people tend to stop noticing ads, or begin to find them irritating. And once the most promising prospective customers have been reached, there are diminishing returns, i.e. an ever-smaller increase in sales in relation to increased advertising spending.

(From: Ian Mackenzie, 2006: 65 – 67)

(1) Why do large companies tend to use the services of large advertising agencies instead of writing advertisements by themselves?
(2) When it comes to how much to spend on advertising, why do some companies simply match their competitors' spending?
(3) Excessive advertising is said to be counter-productive. Do you agree?

Training Assessment

Part I Self-study

Complete the dialogue based on the Chinese given in the brackets.

A: Good morning. I'm John Howard. This is my name card.
B: Good morning. What can I do for you?
A: (1) _____. (我们想为公司新出的啤酒策划一个广告宣传活动。) We want your advice and cooperation.
B: I'm very glad to be of help to you. What do you want to know?
A: (2) _____? (您能跟我说一下在报纸上刊登广告需要多少费用吗?)
B: You just want to have your ads in a newspaper?
A: We haven't decided yet. What's your advice?
B: (3) _____? (你们的预算是多少?)

A: About 9,000 dollars per month.

B: If you only advertise in newspapers and magazines, I think that will be far from enough. (4) _____. (我建议你们在电视和电台上做广告。)

A: But this is too costly for our budget.

B: I feel this may be the best way to reach your target. Perhaps you could reevaluate the initial plan and revise the allocations of your budget. (5) _____. (此外,我认为你们可以在活动中一起采用两种或更多的媒体。)

A: I'll think about your suggestion, and discuss it with the sales department. Thank you very much.

B: You're welcome.

Part II BEC exam focus

Listening Test

Section 1

(**Questions 1–5**)

- You will hear five short recordings.
- For each recording, decide which aspect of working conditions the speaker is talking about.
- Write **one** letter (**A–H**) next to the number of the recording.
- Do not use any letter more than once.
- After you have listened once, replay the recordings.

1. _____
2. _____
3. _____
4. _____
5. _____

A. career prospects
B. health and safety
C. working hours
D. holiday allowance
E. training courses
F. discipline procedures
G. job security
H. pay increases

Section 2

(Questions 6 – 10)

- You will hear another five short recordings.
- For each recording, decide what each speaker is trying to do.
- Write **one** letter (**A – H**) next to the number of the recording.
- Do not use any letter more than once.
- After you have listened once, replay the recordings.

6. _____

7. _____

8. _____

9. _____

10. _____

A. nominate a supplier
B. present sales figures
C. support a proposal
D. refuse an increment
E. agree to expenditure
F. claim damages
G. negotiate contract
H. request a postponement

Unit 12 Marketing Planning

Reach your business objectives

 Training Objectives

By the end of this unit, you are expected to:
- talk about how to plan properly for marketing;
- learn about the basic aspects involving marketing planning;
- get familiar with the basic vocabulary related to marketing planning.

 Training Portfolio

Part I Starting up

Section 1 To do

Match up the words or expressions on the left with the definitions on the right.

(1) distribution channel
(2) market opportunities
(3) to launch a product
(4) market research
(5) packaging
(6) market segmentation
(7) product features
(8) sales representative

A. to introduce a new product onto the market
B. attributes or characteristics of a product: quality, price, reliability, etc.
C. wrappers and containers in which products are sold
D. collecting, analyzing and reporting data relevant to specific marketing situation (such as a proposed new product)
E. someone who contacts existing and potential customers, and tries to persuade them to buy goods or services
F. all the companies or individuals involved in moving a particular good or service from the producer to the consumer
G. possibilities of filling unsatisfied needs in sectors in which a company can profitably produce goods or services
H. dividing a market into distinct groups of buyers who have different requirements or buying habits

Section 2 To read

Read the following passage and then talk with your partner about what impresses you most.

7 tips for a successful product or service launch

So, it's time to launch that new service or product that you've been excited about. A launch as we used to know it as certainly changed, it's not enough to hire that PR firm and draft that press release, it's going to take more than that. Competition when it comes to press is fierce and what's "newsworthy" changes every five minutes, not to mention after that five minutes it will be tough to stay relevant with the amount of news that is pushed out to consumers on a second-by-second basis.

Encouraging news for those that want to get noticed, right? It is true that getting noticed can be a bit more difficult in today's world of constant information, but here are some tips that might help in reaching those you are targeting.

Plan early, don't wait until the last minute. You need to have a plan in place and gear up at least 8 to 12 weeks in advance. Reporters get news every day. They aren't waiting for your story. By gearing up early you can start to find the reporters that you need to target and begin building relationships with them. Tip: Relationships are key when it comes to getting in the media.

Find your influencers. You need to find the influencers that impact your target market. Introduce them to the product or service that you are getting ready to roll out. Give them the news first. Give them a trial and/or sample and encourage them to share a review or post it on their social channels. Public relations has transformed over the last few years, now we have to look at multiple sources to get our information out and one of those sources includes influencers. Online influencers have succeeded in building audiences that pay attention to them through their blog, social media channels, video, etc. and because of that their influence is often greater than that of mass media.

Use the social media platforms to plant leaks. Find those people that are interested in your product or service, brand advocates if you can and inform them of the "coming soon" information or even leaked videos or photos. This will build sizzle and interest. Not to mention everyone likes to feel like they are the "first to know".

Keep realistic expectations. Unless you are a big brand name you may not see a huge reception of your new product or service launch. Don't get discouraged, be consistent in sharing the news and try to make the launch as personable as possible. Remember, consumers love to interact with companies that they feel they have a relationship with.

Press is not one and done. As mentioned previously reporters and influencers are bombarded with news stories every day. We receive about 5 to 10 product or service launches in our inbox on any given day. We aren't always insiders on when reporters have the capacity to write an article or when influencers have the time to get to your emails, so try to be patient and stay in touch with them, don't overwhelm them, but don't let them forget your name either.

Be creative. You need to remember your objective is to get their attention. The influencers and press that you are reaching out to get several press pitches a day. What will you do to be different? Put your creative cap on. Perhaps it's a funny video, a meme, a public service announcement that will get attention. Maybe a press kit sent through the postal mail with a fun or useful chachka will grab their interest.

Make it easy for people to learn about your product. Create videos, demos, white papers and information sheets so people can easily learn about the product or service you are offering. Don't make them hunt for information. The easier you make it for them to get the word out, the better chance you will have of them sharing your information. I think sometimes we make it so difficult for the press and influencers to get the word out and then get the information that we need that they shake their head and hit the "delete" key.

(From: https://www.thebalancesmb.com)

Part II Listening in

Task 1 Listen to the following passage and fill in the blanks.

Marketers have to (1) _____ or anticipate a consumer need; (2) _____ a product or service that meets that need better than any competing products or services; (3) _____ target customers to try the product or service; and, in the long term, (4) _____ it to satisfy the changes in consumer needs or market conditions. Marketers can (5) _____ particular features, attractive packaging, and effective advertising that will (6) _____ consumers' wants. Marketing thus begins long before the product or service is put on the market; it combines market research, new product development, distribution, advertising, promotion, product improvement, and so on.

Task 2 Listen to the conversation. Decide whether the statements are true (T) or false (F) according to what you hear.

( ) (1) Since advertising can reach a large audience, it is no doubt one of the most effective promotional strategies.
( ) (2) Personal selling is of little use for promoting our product.
( ) (3) We can't afford very expensive gifts, so the gifts of high quality are not necessary.

Part III Language focus

■ **Useful sentences and structures**

1. Do you have any idea about how markets are going nowadays?
2. We can expect to see a jump in retail prices.
3. Marketing research is the study of all processes involved in getting goods from the producer to customers.
4. Market research is actually an analysis of a specific market for a particular product.
5. Salesmen have to attend refresher courses frequently.

6. A salesman must have a good understanding of the applications, design features, special advantages and almost everything of the product the company produces.
7. The primary data suggests that there be a slowdown in this market.

Part IV Speaking out

Section 1 Sample dialogues

■ **Dialogue 1**

A: Hi, John, have you found that our sales volume of detergent has dropped a lot in the recent three months?

B: Yeah. That's what worries me these days. Anything wrong with our product?

A: In my opinion, our detergent is of good quality. It seems that we can only find out the reason from consumers' preference.

B: Sounds reasonable. We should listen to our customers.

A: I agree with you. We are planning to conduct a marketing survey in order to make out why consumers accept or refuse our detergent. Then we can plan the marketing policy. That's to say, our production will be based on the demand.

B: Great. Try to get consumers' opinion about the price of our detergent as well as their preference for the smell.

A: OK. We will pay more attention to that.

■ **Dialogue 2**

A: Give these sales figures a look. It's pretty depressing. We are in the red this year. We can't afford to keep going like this for much longer.

B: You're right. We need to start making money soon, or at least manage to break even. But I think that market is slowly beginning to heat up—sales are bound to pick up anytime now.

A: Demand is dropping. The problem is our competition. They are monopolizing the market!

B: Maybe we should rethink our marketing strategy to include the possibility that our new line of cosmetics could be a big seller.

A: It's really too early to tell, but a lot is riding on the new products. If we don't do better after the product launch, we may have to go bankrupt.

B: Do you think it's that serious?

A: Look at these numbers and see for yourself. Read them and weep.

B: My goodness, I didn't realize it was that bad.

Section 2 Creating your own

■ **Task 1   Pair work: Make a dialogue based on the given situation and act it out.**

Your company has just developed a new product of toothpaste. You are asked by your manager to help develop strategies to capture a large market share for the product. Discuss the situation together, and decide:

(1) What should be the pricing strategy?

(2) What should be the promotional strategy?

■ **Task 2   Pair work: Make a dialogue based on the following situation.**

Your company has launched a new drug into market and now decides to increase sales. You have been asked for your views about how to promote the product. Discuss the situation together, and decide:

(1) What are the promotional strategies?

(2) What promotional gifts can be offered? And what are the cost and quality of promotional gifts?

Part V Writing

Section 1 Tips for sales letter writing

- The style and tone of the letter should be simple.
- There should be no confusion and no chance of errors.

- It should be a formal letter.
- Only relevant information should be provided.
- Avoid being clever and funny.
- Do not get diverted from the major point.

Section 2　Sales letter template

From,
_____

_____

Date _____ (Date of issuing letter),

To
_____

_____

_____

Subject: _____

Dear Sir/Madam,

　　We are glad to _____ (introduce your product). It is _____ (features and benefits). This product has been in the market for three months and we have got positive responses from many of our customers. We will feel glad to _____ (introduce your purpose).

　　I will be proud to _____ (reintroduce the features of the product). I would like to give a demonstration to you. We hope for a good business prospect.

　　　　　　　　　　　　　　　　　　　　From,
　　　　　　　　　　　　　　　　　　　　_____ (name, designation of the sender and the name of the firm)

　　　　　　　　　　　　　　　　　　　　_____
　　　　　　　　　　　　　　　　　　　　_____
　　　　　　　　　　　　　　　　　　　　_____

Section 3　Creating your own

　　Suppose you are working in a training company—Leishi. Your company offers a training program on creating and improving team spirit. Your boss asks you to write to a manager, Mr. Crodon, to introduce this training program to him.

Part VI Follow-up reading

Passage 1

Read the following passage and then answer the questions that follow.

The research process

The marketing research process consists of five steps: forming the research question, research design, data collection, data analysis and choosing the best solution.

Forming the research question: Marketing researchers must first define what they want to find out—the research what they want to find out—the research question. A research study should address a specific topic or problem rather than several different issues at once. Researchers need to clearly state their purpose and their plan for using the information they gather.

Research design: After defining the research question, marketers formulate a plan for collecting information essential to the study. Depending on the type and amount of information already available, the researcher will have several alternative designs.

If little is known about the question being investigated, marketers engage in exploratory research. They may look at company records and government or industry publications or talk to knowledgeable people inside or outside their organization. Focus group interviews, in which a researcher informally discusses an idea or issue with a small group of employees, consumers or others, can provide helpful insights.

Sometimes organizations conduct experimental research to determine whether one event, circumstance or situation causes another. For example, a publisher may distribute an issue of a magazine with different covers in different parts of the country. After a trial period, researchers investigate which cover resulted in the highest sales.

Marketers often want to know the age, sex, education, income, lifestyle, buying habits or buying intentions of consumers. To obtain such information, they conduct descriptive research.

Data collection: After settling on a research design, marketers accumulate the information that will answer the research question. Researchers sometimes rely on secondary data published information already available inside the organization or from government, industry or other sources. Secondary data offers tremendous advantages, being obtainable quickly and at relatively little cost, which may be especially important to small firms and non-profit organizations. Marketers generally start all research projects by looking for secondary data.

Often secondary data is unavailable or inadequate. In such cases, marketers obtain primary data—information collected for the first time and specific to the study. Researchers use experiments, observation or surveys to collect primary data.

Researchers conduct experiments either in a controlled, isolated setting (laboratory experiments) or in actual marketplace settings such as a store (field experiments). Observation involves watching a situation and recording relevant facts. A marketer may observe supermarket shoppers and record the purchases made. Through surveys, researchers question respondents to obtain needed information. Mail, telephone and in-person surveys are becoming more and more common.

Because reaching all consumers in the target market (e.g. all television viewers) is often impossible or impractical, researchers collect data from a sample. A sample is a portion of a larger group and accurately represents the characteristics of the larger group. Companies that provide ratings for television shows may survey 1,200 viewers throughout China. With a sufficient sample, the researcher can use the data collected to infer important facts about the larger group.

Data analysis: To determine what all the information means and to help find useful alternatives to specific marketing challenges, researchers analyze what they collect. Usually they enter the data into a computer and run special programs to find the frequency of responses and how different items of information are related. While extremely valuable, computer analysis is costly because of the equipment, programs and skills required. Businesses sometimes contract specialist research consultant organizations to conduct the data analysis.

Choosing the best solution: After collecting and analyzing data, market researchers determine alternative strategies and make recommendations as to which strategy may be best and why. In today's customer-driven market, ethics is important in every aspect of marketing. Companies should therefore do what's right as well as what's profitable.

The last steps in a research effort involve following up on the actions taken to see if the results were as expected. If not, corrective action can be taken and new research studies undertaken in the ongoing attempt to provide consumer satisfaction at the lowest cost.

(From: https://en.wikipedia.org)

(1) What are the five parts of the marketing research process?

(2) Conduct a very basic marketing research study that identifies a problem on your campus that needs your attention. Collect information about that problem, design the research, analyze the data, and make some suggestions.

Passage 2

*Complete the summary with the words from the passage and change the form where necessary, with **no more than three** words for each blank.*

The centrality of marketing

Most management and marketing writers now distinguish between selling and marketing. The "selling concept" assumes that resisting consumers have to be persuaded by vigorous hard-selling techniques to buy non-essential goods or services. Products are sold rather than bought. The marketing concept, on the contrary, assumes that the producer's task is to find wants and fill them. In other words, you don't sell what you make, to the opposite you make what will be bought. As well as satisfying existing needs, marketers can also anticipate and create new ones. The markets for the Walkman, video recorders, videogame consoles, CD players, personal computers, the Internet, mobile phones, mountain bikes, snowboards and genetic engineering, to choose some recent examples, were largely created rather than identified.

Marketers are consequently always looking for market opportunities—profitable possibilities of filling unsatisfied needs or creating new ones in areas in which the company is likely to enjoy a differential advantage due to its distinctive competencies (the things it does particularly well). Market opportunities are generally isolated by market segmentation. Once a target market has been identified, a company has to decide what goods or service to offer. This means that much of the work of marketing has been done before the final product or service comes into existence. It also means that the marketing concept has to be understood throughout the company, e.g. in the production department of a manufacturing company as much as in the marketing department itself. The company must also take account of the existence of competitors, who always have to be identified, monitored and defeated in the search or loyal customers.

Rather than risk launching a product or service solely on the basis of intuition or guesswork, most companies undertake market research (GB) or marketing research (US). They collect and analyze information about the size of a potential market, about consumers' reactions to particular product or service features, and so on. Sales representatives, who also talk to customers, are another important source of information.

Once the basic offer, e. g. a product concept, has been established, the company has to think about the marketing mix, i. e. all the various elements of a marketing program, their integration, and the amount of effort that a company can expend on them in order to influence the target market. The best-known classification of these elements is the Four Ps: product, place, promotion and price. Aspects to be considered in marketing products include quality, features (standard and optional) style, brand name, size, packaging, services and guarantee. Place in a marketing mix includes such factors as distribution channels, locations of points of sale, transport, inventory size, etc. Promotion groups together advertising, publicity, sales promotion and personal selling while price includes the basic list price, discounts, the length of the payment period, possible credit terms, and so on. It is the job of a product manager or a brand manager to look for ways to increase sales by changing the marketing mix. It must be remembered that quite apart from consumer markets (in which people buy products for direct consumption) there exists an enormous producer or industrial or business market, consisting of all the individuals and organizations that acquire goods and services that are used in the production of other goods, or in the supply of services to others. Few consumers realize that the producer market is actually larger than the consumer market, since it contains all the raw materials, manufactured parts and components that go into consumer goods, plus capital equipment such as buildings and machines, supplies such as energy and pens and paper, and services ranging from cleaning to management consulting, all of which have to be marketed. There is consequently more industrial than consumer marketing, even though ordinary consumers are seldom exposed to it.

(From: Ian Mackenzie, 2006: 65 - 67)

The marketing concept is that a company's choice of what goods and services to offer should be based on the goal of satisfying (1) _____. Many companies limit themselves to attempting to satisfy the needs of particular (2) _____. Their choice of action is often the result of market research. A product's features, the methods of (3) _____ it, and its price, can all be changed during the course of its life, if necessary. Quite apart from the marketing of (4) _____, which everybody is familiar with here is a great deal of marketing of (5) _____.

Module 4 Business Planning

 **Training Assessment**

Part I Self-study

Here is a definition of marketing. Complete it by inserting the following verbs in the box.

| design | develop | identify | influence |
| modify | persuade | begins | combines |

Marketers have to (1) _____ or anticipate a consumer's need; (2) _____ a product or service that meets that need better than any competing products or services; (3) _____ target customers to try the product or service; and, in the long term, (4) _____ it to satisfy changes in consumer needs or market conditions. Marketers can (5) _____ particular features, attractive packaging, and effective advertising, that will (6) _____ consumers' wants. Marketing thus (7) _____ long before the product or service is put on the market; it (8) _____ market research, new product development, distribution, advertising, promotion, product improvement and so on.

Part II BEC exam focus

Listening Test

Questions 1 – 8

You will hear a radio interview with a leading industrialist and businesses consultant, Philip Spencer.

For each question 1 – 8, make one letter (A, B or C) for the correct answer.

You will hear the recording twice.

(   ) 1. When visiting companies Philip Spencer's objective is to _____.
   A. improve staff productivity
   B. identify problem areas
   C. re-train weak management

(   ) 2. Problems at Manson's had continued after Spencer's first visit because of _____.

195

A. poor distribution systems

B. inadequate market research

C. out-dated production methods

( )3. Difficulties at Criterion Glass stemmed from lack of attention to _____.

A. competitors' designs

B. quality of merchandise

C. consumer demand

( )4. Philip Spencer blames his early business difficulties on _____.

A. inexperience with new companies

B. lack of knowledge of the financial sector

C. bad advice from established organizations

( )5. He defends his unusual personal style by saying that _____.

A. it is important in business to make a strong impression

B. his business ideas are more important than his appearance

C. most business people are too serious and traditional

( )6. He thinks he was appointed chairman of LBI because the company _____.

A. knew of his successes with failing companies

B. felt he had a positive image with the public

C. liked his fearless approach to problem-solving

( )7. According to Philip Spencer successful managers are distinguished by their _____.

A. concern for detail

B. desire to make money

C. strong leadership

( )8. His final advice to people starting in business is to _____.

A. make every effort to prevent mistakes

B. find the best sources of information

C. maintain a positive attitude at all times

Module 5 Business Meetings

Important activities in business world

 ### Into the Module

> Meetings are part of important activities in business world. If communication is the lifeblood of any organization, then meetings are the heart and mind. Despite instant communication systems like e-mail, chatting and cell phone, we still need face-to-face meetings to ensure the most effective communication and to instill a better sense of commitment from individuals towards goals and tasks. If a meeting is focused, everyone who attends will appreciate it. Whether it is a weekly staff meeting or an industry conference, planning and preparation can make a difference between a productive session and a tedious couple of hours. Business meetings can be a simple dialog, a round table meeting, or a PowerPoint presentation.

 ### Training Objectives

By the end of this module, you are expected to:
- learn about the basic aspects involving business meetings;
- learn about the key factors that lead to productive business meetings;
- get familiar with the basic vocabulary related to business meetings.

Temperate, sincere and intelligent inquiry and discussion are only to be dreaded by the advocates of error. The truth need not fear them.

—James Rush, Statesman

Unit 13 Staging a Meeting

Make full preparation

 Training Objectives

> By the end of this unit, you are expected to:
> - learn about the preparation work of business meetings and discuss some work in detail;
> - get familiar with the basic vocabulary related to business meetings;
> - learn how to write Email Invitation Letter.

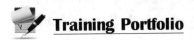 Training Portfolio

Part I Starting up

Section 1 To discuss

Discuss the following questions with your partner.
- Why is it important for a company to have regular meetings?
- Do you think meeting is a waste of time?
- Could some meetings be replaced by other forms of communication? Why or why not?

Work in pairs. Here are some characteristics of successful business meetings. First rank them in the order of importance. Then compare your list with your partner's and explain why you rank them in this way.

- A well-designed agenda
- Clear objectives which are known to everyone
- Respect for the time planning
- A good chair who ensures everything under control
- Well-prepared written materials before the meeting, if necessary
- Make sure that the laptop or any other computer devices are provided with substantial power

Section 2 To read

Read the following passage and then report the idea that you remember to your classmates and tell what impresses you most.

How to prepare for a business meeting

A well-run meeting can be used to effectively train employees, close an important sale, set business goals and keep major projects on the right track. A successful meeting starts well before everyone is gathered in a conference room. The person running the meeting needs to make arrangements, gather materials, send out invitations and coordinate the activities. Participants need to be prepared to handle any required tasks, provide feedback, make presentations or brainstorm ideas. Doing the groundwork ahead of time will keep the meeting running smoothly and help you meet your goals.

(1) Determine if you are running the meeting or expected to participate in any fashion. If you are in charge of arrangements, get ready to coordinate scheduling, materials and the pacing of the meeting.

(2) Set a goal for the meeting. Decide if you are trying to make a sale, bring an investor on board, train employees about company policies or brainstorm new product ideas.

(3) Set an agenda for the meeting. Give participants a heads up if the meeting is expected to be particularly long. Allow time for bathroom or refreshment breaks. Prepare a schedule if there will be multiple speakers or presenters.

(4) Make arrangements for a meeting room, conference call or online meeting. Book a time that works for all key participants. Call or email the group to make sure that the chosen time works for everyone.

(5) Send out time and location details to all participants. If you are dealing with

employees, let them know if attendance is mandatory or optional. Email conference call in numbers and codes if you are arranging a phone meeting.

(6) Prepare for any needed equipment. For example, if you are going to have a computer presentation, make sure that the conference room has a screen and projector. Know how to hook your laptop up to the projector so that you don't have to waste valuable meeting time dealing with technical details.

(7) Take your presentation for a test drive before you do it in front of clients. Make sure your sales or investment pitch is professional, concise and interesting. Endless charts projected on a screen don't make for compelling meetings. Understand your audience, how you can meet their needs and what goals you want to reach.

(8) Gather materials. Print off handouts. Make sure there are enough chairs for everyone. Prepare refreshments or make catering arrangements if necessary.

(9) Remind participants 24 hours ahead, or on the morning of the actual meeting. Aim to start the meeting promptly at the given time.

(From: https://smallbusiness.chron.com)

Part II Listening in

Task 1 Listen to the following passage and fill in the blanks.

Invite decision-makers. The most effective meetings involve (1) _____ to ensure decisions can be made immediately. If a key decision-maker is (2) _____, ask a subordinate to attend. Ideally, this person will be able to speak for their (3) _____, and—at the very least—take notes and report back.

Schedule strategically. If you want each meeting (4) _____ to be fully engaged, avoid Monday mornings, when everyone is (5) _____ email. Also avoid Friday afternoons, when employees are busy (6) _____ the week and looking forward to the weekend. Schedule meetings on a day and time when participants are most likely to (7) _____.

Set a time limit and (8) _____ it. Meetings that drag on for hours cause attendees to lose patience and focus. (9) _____ are short and time is valuable. The most (10) _____ meetings start on time and end on time.

Task 2 Listen to the conversation.

Decide whether the statements are true (T) or false (F) according to what you hear.

(   )(1) There are a lot of VIPs to introduce during the opening, and it should take at least an hour.

(   )(2) Before the committee reports, the minutes of the old business need to be reviewed.

(   )(3) The idea of a five-minute report followed by a three-minute Q&A sounds good for the control of meeting.

Part III Language focus

■ Meeting arrangement

1. Please ensure that those you intend to be present are properly informed.
2. All the necessary documents relevant to the meeting should be available.
3. Is the room ready for the meeting?
4. Would it be convenient for you to meet us this afternoon?
5. We will arrange the meeting on Tuesday afternoon.
6. The meeting will be held in your office.
7. The meeting is scheduled at 10 o'clock this morning.
8. Remember to take the minutes this afternoon.

■ Meeting preparation

1. Would you like to copy the EX files and pass me the copy?
2. Set up the overhead projector in the meeting room.
3. Is the conference room available today at 4:00 pm?

■ Meeting cancel

1. This meeting is called off.
2. I've told all departments of the cancellation.
3. We are going to have to cancel tomorrow's meeting.
4. Didn't you hear that the meeting was cancelled?
5. Let's cancel this meeting. I'll email everyone if something new comes.
6. I'm really sorry about cancelling the meeting at the last minute.
7. The meeting is cancelled because the A/V equipment has been damaged.

Part IV Speaking out

Section 1 Sample dialogues

Dialogue 1

The office manager is asking his assistant Cynthia to send memorandums to all the department heads of the company.

Manager: Cynthia, please send a memorandum to all department managers informing monthly meeting would be held on May 20th in the second conference room.

Cynthia: All right. Do I need to enclose the agenda?

Manager: Of course. The items in the agenda should include the general manager's approval of last meeting's minutes, department reports and new business.

Cynthia: OK, Sir. Is it necessary to put the item of next meeting, too?

Manager: Yes, it's a good idea. Could you get it ready before lunch?

Cynthia: No problem. I'll have it typed up right away.

Manager: Very good. I appreciate your attitude towards work.

Cynthia: Thank you, Sir.

Dialogue 2

The office manager is checking with his assistant Cynthia about the meeting arrangements.

Manager: The meeting is scheduled for 1:00 tomorrow afternoon. Have you made all the necessary arrangements, Cynthia?

Cynthia: Yes, Sir. We'll use Conference Room 201 for the meeting.

Manager: That's fine. The meeting is very important. Where will the guests be received before the meeting begins?

Cynthia: In the main hall downstairs. It's spacious there.

Manager: We'll have several foreign guests to attend the meeting.

Cynthia: I've arranged an interpreter to be present. But it is said these foreigners can speak a little Chinese.

Manager: All right. I'll try to speak slowly. How would you seat our guests?

Cynthia: We've prepared name cards to be put on the conference table for guests to sit by. When would you like refreshments served, Sir?

Manager: Well, after my report, there'll be an interval for rest and refreshments.

Section 2 Creating your own

Task 1 Make a dialogue based on the given situation and act it out.

Suppose Student A is the office director John, and Student B is the secretary Stella. You are talking about the meeting preparation scheduled for 2:30 this afternoon.

Task 2 Make a dialogue based on the following situation.

Suppose Student A is the manager Brian, and Student B is the secretary Julie. You are talking about the agenda for a distributor meeting next Thursday.

Part V Writing

Section 1 Tips for writing an invitation email

- Stick to the point and keep the email concise
- Maintain a strictly professional tone for all official communication
- Give complete details, including the date, time and venue for the meeting
- Double check all the facts to make sure there are no mistakes
- Ask for confirmations ahead of the meeting so you can organize everything
- Invite questions and queries before signing off
- If possible, use an official email template for the invitations

Section 2 Invitation email template

Dear [Name of invitee],

It is with great pleasure that we invite you to our (name of meeting) meeting for (purpose of meeting), hosted by (your company's name).

The venue for the meeting is (venue's name), and it is set to be held on (date) at (time). We have invited all our (valued clients/dealers/vendors), and would love to have you there as we (agenda of meeting).

Kindly acknowledge receipt of this email and reply back to confirm your spot.

If you have any questions or concerns, please feel free to contact us regarding them as well.

Looking forward to your reply.

Sincerely,
Signature
(your name)
(your designation)
(company name)

Section 3 Creating your own

Setting: Email Invitation Letter
Sender: Thomas_jiang@ healthcare. com
Recipient: John_smith@ healthcare. com
Date: Oct. 20th, 2018
Subject: A sincere invitation to participate in Chinese marketing conference of healthcare products

Part VI Follow-up reading

Passage 1

Read and decide whether the statements following the passage are true (T) or false (F).

How to arrange a successful business meeting

The business world seems to spin on an axis of meetings, but not all meetings are productive. Invest time in planning a productive session to make sure your meetings get the job done. Give careful thought to what you need to accomplish and who should participate.

- **Determine objective and audience**

Set an objective for the meeting, and make it brief and clearly stated. For example, create a short list of bullet points describing specific goals. The goal of your meeting might be to communicate important information, make decisions, resolve problems or assign actions. A concise and to-the-point objective helps the meeting organizer determine who should participate in the meeting. Build out a list of invitees by aligning each goal with team members whose presence will make it possible to actually meet the goal.

- **Set the agenda**

Set the meeting's agenda based on each goal in the objective. If a goal is to communicate the start of a project, set an agenda item that identifies who will present that information and how the information will be shared, such as by PowerPoint presentation. If the goal is to assign actions, set an agenda item that describes how assignments will be made. Every goal should have one or more agenda items aligned directly with it.

- **Select the date and time**

Select a meeting date and time based on the availability of the meeting leader and the most critical invitees. The larger the list of invitees is, the harder it is to find a day and time when everyone is available. Accept a time that fits as many schedules as possible. Before setting the time, give thought to time zones. If some invitees will participate by phone or the Internet, consider their working hours as well as your own. A 1:00 pm meeting in Eastern Standard Time is a lunch-hour meeting in Central Standard Time. That same meeting is at 2:00 a.m. in Tokyo.

- **Choose the location**

Find a conference room that will make it possible to achieve all agenda items. Choose a room large or small enough to comfortably fit the number of people expected to attend. A room that seats 40 is a poor choice for a meeting with 10 people. Likewise, you don't want a crowd squeezing in so tight it's necessary to bring in extra chairs.

- **Arrange for materials and incidentals**

If presentations are expected, make sure that the room is equipped with a projector. If not, make arrangements to bring a projector with you—also make sure you have something to project onto, such as a screen or a white wall. Don't forget to consider the availability of other incidentals, such as white boards with dry erase markers, flip charts and speaker phones for off-site participants. For multi-hour meetings, arrange for food and beverages so participants stay focused on the topic rather than their stomachs.

- **Notify invitees**

Notify invitees of the meeting objectives, date, time and location well enough in advance so they can prepare properly. In most cases, at least a week's notice is preferable. Use the workplace's calendar software to send a meeting appointment to all invitees. Many programs will alert invitees a few minutes or a few days before the meeting, or customize the alerts to your needs.

(From: https://careertrend.com)

(　　)(1) Advanced and careful planning is needed to hold a productive meeting.

(　　)(2) When you decide on the meeting time and date, you are supposed to make sure if everyone is available.

(　　)(3) A large room of 90 seats is a good choice for a meeting with 20 people because it is quite spacious.

(　　)(4) A week's notice to invitees of the meeting is proper for them to prepare well.

Passage 2

Answer the questions that immediately follow the passage.

Business meeting theme ideas

Business meetings need to be effective in conveying information, but they can also use various themes to make them more exciting and interesting for the attendees. A theme can set the proper mood or help attendees better understand the agenda.

Some business meetings take place off-site, such as sales presentations conducted by companies located out of town or simply larger meetings that need more room. When choosing an off-site meeting venue, ask the coordinator for his thoughts on a theme to help make the meeting more effective and successful. The coordinator has experience in setting the proper theme for a business meeting, and you should use that experience to your advantage.

If the meeting is a sales meeting that needs high energy to be effective, the off-site coordinator may choose a party atmosphere, including balloons and cake and possibly even party favors. If the meeting is a critical business meeting, the theme might center on relaxation, with dim lighting and neutral colors and relaxing beverages, such as tea. Creating a relaxing atmosphere in an otherwise intense business meeting can take the edge off and allow people to discuss issues in a professional and civil manner.

Sales meetings can offer the opportunity for motivational themes. Create a slogan for your meeting and build your theme off that slogan. For example, the slogan "Going for Gold" would have the Olympics as a theme. Get flags from different countries and hang them on the walls. If you will offer incentives for people who reach various sales goals, build a tri-level medal stand and put the top prize on the gold-medal stand, second prize on the silver-medal stand and third prize on the bronze-medal stand. Have company executives dress up in gear from various Olympic competitions. The more you get into a theme trying to sell it to your meeting participants, the more effective it will be.

(From: https://bizfluent.com)

(1) What role can the theme play for a business meeting?
(2) Whom can you go to for help to choose an off-site meeting venue? And why?
(3) How do you create a relaxing atmosphere for a sales meeting?

Training Assessment

Part II Self-study

Work in pairs. Complete the conversation with the help of Chinese clues in the brackets.

Tom: Good morning, Tom.

Tom: Linda, (1)_____? （拟好会议通知了吗?）

Linda: Yes, Sir.

Tom: Fine. Could you give me the main points, please?

Linda: Sure. (2)_____. （会议定于10月18日下午一点在213会议室举行。）

Tom: Who will be the chair?

Linda: Christian Gao.

Tom: Ah, good. Christian is very effective: No loose ends and always run to time. That meeting will be in a safe pair of hands!

Linda: Yes.

Tom: (3)_____? （那么,会议议程上有什么安排呢?）

Linda: The first point is to figure out the reasons for the fall in the sales of our healthcare products in South China.

Tom: I see. (4)_____. （请告诉Bill准备一份销售数据,并事先将其发送给我和董事会。）

Linda: Yes. I've already arranged that. It will be on your desk tomorrow morning.

Tom: Good. Thank you.

Linda: Then, secondly, we will discuss and determine measures to deal with the problem. (5)_____. （我们要讨论并确定解决该问题的办法。）

Tom: OK. But do remember to include Jun Ma and Lucy at the meeting.

Linda: Yes, certainly.

Tom: I think you'd better notify Christian Gao of the information, as he is the chairperson. (6)_____. (如果有任何问题，他可以直接找我。)

Part II BEC exam focus

Writing

You have to change the date of a marketing meeting that was scheduled for next Friday. Write an email to all members of the marketing team:

- giving the new date of the meeting
- explaining why the date of the meeting has been changed
- providing details of an additional point for the agenda

Write 40 ~ 50 words.

To:	Marketing team
Cc:	
Subject: New date for Next Friday's meeting	

Module 5 Business Meetings

Unit 14 Chairing a Meeting

See that everyone present is fairly treated

 Training Objectives

By the end of this unit, you are expected to:
- learn about the proper ways of chairing meetings and conferences;
- command the basic vocabulary and structures related to business meetings;
- learn how to write a meeting agenda.

Training Portfolio

Section 1 To discuss

(1) Work in groups to discuss: What should be included in a welcome speech?
(2) Work in groups to discuss: How do you make your chairing successful when you introduce a keynote speaker or a presenter as a chairman or moderator?

Section 2　To read

Read the following passage and then report the idea that you remember to your classmates and tell what impresses you most.

Business meeting etiquette

Many people cringe when they hear that they have to attend a business meeting. They're afraid that it will be a waste of time that starts late and accomplishes nothing or that it will be dominated by one or two people. These common problems can be avoided by using proper business meeting etiquette. Etiquette rules allow you to run the meeting more efficiently and to make sure it is productive.

- **Agenda**

Create an agenda before the meeting, and distribute it to everyone who has been invited to attend. This will allow people to decide whether they really need to be present at the meeting. Otherwise, someone might show up and discover that the agenda is not really relevant for him or her. The agenda is also a neutral touchstone to keep the meeting focused. If discussion starts to wander, you can say something like "According to the agenda, we should be talking about what we need for the new product introduction. Let's get back to that topic."

- **Schedule**

Schedule enough time for the meeting to allow you to accomplish the items on the agenda without asking attendees to make too large of a time commitment. Start the meeting promptly to reward the people who show up on time. If you get in the habit of starting late, this will reward people who habitually show up a few minutes past the designated start time. If you have a reputation for starting right on time, people will learn to show up at the correct time to avoid the discomfort of walking in once the meeting has already started.

End the meeting at the designated time. This shows respect for other people's schedules, since some of your attendees may have scheduled other commitments after the meeting. If there is unfinished business, schedule another meeting.

- **Participation**

Encourage participation by everyone in the room, and maintain a safe environment for input. People may be afraid to speak up if they believe that one or two dominant coworkers will immediately shoot them down. Implement a rule of "Only one person speaks at a time", and enforce it strictly. If someone tries to interrupt, say, "This is Larry's time to speak. Remember, we all agreed that no one would interrupt when someone else is speaking." If some attendees are still reluctant to give input, try a method like going around the room to get each person's feedback on the topic at hand. That way, a shy person doesn't have to worry about finding the right time to speak up.

- **Conclusion**

At the end of the meeting, summarize what was discussed and any decisions that were made. Reconfirm any action items, the people who are supposed to handle them and the deadlines. This gives the attendees a chance to speak up if they don't agree with the summary. If everyone is on the same page, use the summary to create meeting notes and send them out promptly. They shouldn't go out any later than the day after the meeting.

(From: https://bizfluent.com)

Part II Listening in

Task 1 Listen to the short passage and fill in the blanks.

When chairing a meeting, you should walk (1)_____ to the podium, stand erect, look directly at your audience, and announce the beginning of the meeting. (2)_____ a direct, friendly delivery throughout the talk. When you pronounce your name, do so slowly and (3)_____ so that everyone can catch it.

At the opening speech, you should make a short welcoming speech and a brief self-introduction. Sometimes you should introduce the (4)_____. You should also indicate the purpose of the conference, the allotted time for each (5)_____. Your introduction should stimulate interest in all the papers (6)_____ for presentation and discussion.

Besides being decisive and confident, a good chairperson also needs to be (7)_____, able to deal with all sorts of people and unexpected events in a firm but (8)_____ manner. See that everyone present is fairly and impartially treated.

When one of the (9)_____ speakers finishes his presentation, you should sum up or comment on it briefly, and then move on to the next speaker. When the last speaker finishes, (10)_____ on him and announce the session adjourned.

Task 2 Listen to the conversation and decide whether the following statements are true (T) or false (F) according to what you hear.

(   )(1) Dr. James Smith shows great interest in political research and is well-known in the field of international relations.

(   )(2) In his lecture he will talk about the present economic situation in the Middle East and how it influences the other countries.

(   )(3) In his opinion, the economies of most countries seem to become more and more unrelated.

Part III Language focus

■ **Opening remarks**

1. Distinguished guests, ladies and gentlemen, I am very honored/pleased to be here today and address such a distinguished audience. My name is ... and I'm in charge of/responsible for ...

2. Ladies and gentlemen, I feel privileged to have the opportunity to brief you on ... But before we start, let me say a few words about my own background. My name is ...

3. Good morning and thank you for making the effort to be here with us today. Some of you may know me better than others, so please allow me to briefly introduce myself. My name is ...

4. Good morning, I know I have met some of you before, but just for the benefit of those I haven't, my name is ...

5. Good morning, everyone. I'd like to start by introducing myself. My name is ...

6. I'm very pleased and proud to introduce ... who is ... He/She is known for ...

■ **Title/Subject**

1. The subject/topic/focus of my presentation/talk/speech is ...

2. I'd like to tell you something about .../introduce to you ...

3. I'm going to brief ...

4. I plan to speak about ...

5. I've been asked to give you an overview of ...

■ **Purpose/Objective**

1. We are gathered here today to discuss/agree/decide/review ...

2. The purpose/aim of this presentation is to ...

3. This talk is designed with a view to ...

4. Hopefully, my talk can serve as a catalyst/springboard for our discussion.

5. What I would like to do today is to explain/illustrate/outline/have a look at ...

6. What I want my listeners to get out of my presentation/speech is ...

■ **Length**

1. My talk will last ... minutes.

2. I plan to be brief and will only take ... minutes of your time.

3. I'll speak for 15 minutes.

■ **Outline/Main parts**

1. I am going to look at/approach this subject from the following perspectives/areas/headings: Firstly/first of all ... Secondly/then/next ... Thirdly/after that ... Finally/last but not least/lastly ...

2. I've broken down/divided my presentation into three parts/sections. Namely, they are .../They are as follows ...

3. In the first part I'll give a few basic definitions ...

4. In the next section I will explain ...

5. In Part Three, I am going to show ...

6. In the last part I would like/want to give a practical example ...

■ **Questions**

1. If you have any questions, please feel free to interrupt me as I go along.

2. I will leave ten minutes for Q&A at the end of my talk.

3. I would be glad to answer your questions at the end of my talk.

4. As it is quite a lot to cover, I would appreciate it very much if you can hold any questions until I finish my talk.

5. You may interrupt me at any moment to ask question or make comments.

6. Please stop me if you don't understand anything I say, but you could keep any specific questions until after I've finished.

Part IV Speaking out

Section 1 Sample dialogues

■ **Dialogue 1**

A = Chairman   B = Teresa   C = Taylor

A: Now that everyone is here, I'd like to call the meeting to order. Thank you all in attendance. We have a lot to cover today. Has everyone got an agenda?

B: I need a copy. Also, may I suggest something? I know we have many points to review today, but would it be possible to finish before 3 o'clock? A mountain of work is still waiting for us.

A: We should be able to finish everything before then. Let's run through the major points first, and see where we're. The first item on the agenda is to approve the minutes of the last meeting.

B: I propose we accept the minutes.

A: Good. Do I have a second?

C: I second.

A: Motion carried. Now, next on our agenda is our budget review. Teresa, can you please fill us in on where the budget review stands?

B: I gave everyone a copy of the manual last week. We've had the review board going over everything, and they have come up with a final review. Here's a copy for everyone, and if you have any questions, you can talk to me after the meeting. Basically, the budget review has been completed, with maybe a few polishing details left.

A: What kind of action is required?

B: If everyone could take a look at the final review handout, if there are any objections or corrections, let me know. Next week I cast the final approval.

Dialogue 2

A = Chairman   B = Wince   C = Kim

A: Let me take a minute to sum up the main points of this discussion. We can't leave the product on the market; we'll lose more money in the end. We can test special milk powders for each area, but can't leave the powder off the market this week, and work hard on tests for the next month.

B: I don't think we'll be able to turn things around in just one month.

A: You're right. We'll work on just two or three special powders. If they work, we'll start selling again in the right areas. Our advertising will say that we're good people—we'll let profits take a beating before we let anyone get hurt.

C: They should help people to understand that we did our best before—that we never wanted to harm anyone.

A: The plan may not work right away—it may take some time before sales go back up. It's not going to be easy getting the shareholders and management to support us here. I need your full support.

B: Don't worry. You'll have it.

A: Great. If everyone is in agreement, I propose the following: We call a top-level management meeting for tomorrow to push the plan. We'll work on the shareholders after the powder is off the market. It isn't going to be easy.

C: No problem. We are in for the duration.

A: If nobody wants to add anything, we can draw the meeting to a close.

Section 2 Creating your own

Task 1 Role-play a meeting.

Discuss measures to reduce smoking at work.

Task 2 Work in groups. Go through the meeting process, and then make up a dialogue for the given situation.

Tips for meeting process:
- Decide on the objectives and type of meeting (informational/briefing/brainstorming/decision-making);
- Draw up an agenda (also set time limits);
- Decide on roles during the meeting (chairperson, speakers, minute-taker);
- Decide on the style of meeting (formal/informal, structured or not);
- Prepare your contribution to the meeting (content);
- Hold the meeting.

It is a meeting to discuss whether it would be possible to arrange a farewell dinner for the Senior Accountant who has been with the company since its formation 30 years ago and now is due to retire.

Part V Writing

Section 1 The structure for an agenda

(1) The structure of a meeting agenda
- Reference
- Name of the sponsor

- Time of the meeting
- Title of the meeting
- Place of the meeting
- People who will attend the meeting

(2) Events in time sequence
- Event 1
- Event 2
- Event N

Section 2　A sample agenda

A secretary prepares a meeting agenda for the members of the Board of Directors of Myanmar Garment Manufacture Enterprise Ltd. In the meeting, a report, a price list and recent company progress will be discussed.

> Ref: BD/10.26/18
>
> Agenda for the meeting of the Board of Directors to be held in the Boardroom 201 at 2:30 p.m. on Friday, 26th October, 2018. The meeting will consider the following issues:
>
> a. Matters arising from the report
>
> b. The quotation received from Gherzi Machine Tools Ltd. for the supply of equipment
>
> c. To review the progress of the company's recent sales program for its synthetic silk clothes
>
> d. Date and place of the next meeting

Section 3　Writing practice

Write a meeting agenda with the following details given in Chinese.

公司拟定于2018年10月26日星期五上午9点在213会议室召开经理级会议，主要讨论两个内容：一是评估2018年春季销售的进展情况，二是讨论参加应聘高级会计助理岗位的3名申请人的情况。

附申请人情况：

Mr. Tian Grison,31岁,现任贸易促进委员会助理会计;

Mr. Zhou Taylor,27岁,现任N&B有限公司财务经理助理;

Miss Jiang Simpson,26 岁,现任本公司的会计助理。

同时初步确定下次会议的时间和地点。

Part VI Follow-up reading

Passage 1

Read and decide whether the statements following the passage are true (T) or false (F).

How to follow up with a letter after a business meeting

Whether the meeting's been with colleagues or competitors, you're always well-advised to summarize what was discussed and especially what was decided, and to do it in writing as soon as possible afterward. You can combine relevant pieces from a library of business documents, such as the one on "Inc." Magazine's website.

Start with a friendly but clear recap of the date, time and place of the meeting, who attended in what capacities and a brief statement of the meeting's purpose. For example, "Dear Mike, thanks again for spending yesterday morning with me and Steve from our art department, discussing plans for redesign of your packaging."

Review what documents and materials were presented in the meeting and any significant items of discussion about them: "I'm glad you liked Steve's ideas as much as I did. We agreed that the hexagonal carton gives your product a significant change to call attention to the features you're adding next year, but that building it to lie horizontally on the shelf will be more stable and allow us to make both ends just slightly convex, instead of one flat and the other an extended point with no real connection to the product."

Provide reports on all action items agreed in the meeting: "Steve has committed to having the new design specs to our fabrication unit today, and they should be able to give me new cost figures for the horizontal carton by the end of the week. Steve and I will both be disappointed if those figures aren't at least 20 percent below the estimates we had yesterday for the upright, high-pointed carton, since the fabrication will be symmetrical and less complex to fit. We will, however, need a decision from you on whether the belt buckle will be printed or embossed, and whether you want metallic ink on it, before we can firm up the costs."

Set timelines for next steps by all parties: "I made a note that you thought you could get those decisions made today or tomorrow. That would allow us to get back to you by close of business Monday with cost figures firm enough that we can begin to formalize a contract."

Close the letter in as friendly a fashion as is appropriate to the nature of the meeting, and restate plans for any other meetings you've scheduled: "It's always a pleasure meeting with you. I have lunch Tuesday at your office on my calendar, when I'll bring the mockup Steve is working on. Please let me know if Jan will indeed be able to join us."

(From: https://bizfluent.com)

(　　)(1) You are advised to follow up with a letter after a business meeting with just colleagues, but not competitors.

(　　)(2) The tone of the letter should be as serious as possible since it's written in a formal style.

(　　)(3) The documents and materials that were presented in the meeting should be reviewed in the letter.

(　　)(4) Setting timelines for the following steps is quite necessary.

Passage 2

Read the following passage and complete the summary with the words from the passage.

How to chair a meeting

Call the meeting to order. When the meeting reaches its scheduled start time and all of the attendees (or at least all of the important ones) are present, get the attention of everyone in the room. Introduce yourself as the chair and state the purpose of the meeting. Establish the intended time frame for the meeting by informing everyone of the ending time you're shooting for—you may run long or short, but stating your intended time limit ahead of time helps keep the meeting on-track. If some of the attendees aren't familiar with one another, take a moment to conduct a brief roll call and introduce important attendees.

Sum up relevant points from previous meetings. At the start of meetings that are part of a long, ongoing project, you'll want to briefly catch all of the attendees up on the state of the project thus far by quickly summarizing any relevant events or decisions from previous meetings. Not everyone in attendance may be as knowledgeable about the topics of discussion as you are, so quickly bringing everyone up to speed can go a long way towards making your meeting an efficient and effective one.

Allow important attendees to report on the state of affairs. Next, allow people with relevant knowledge to inform the assembly of new or recent developments that have occurred since the last meeting. These can be virtually anything—for instance, new problems facing your business or organization, personnel changes, project developments, and strategy changes can all be addressed here. Meeting attendees will also want to hear about the results of any specific actions that were taken because of decisions made at the last meeting.

Address any unfinished business. If there are any problems that remain unsolved or decisions that haven't been made from the last meeting, make an effort to address these before moving on to new problems. The longer that old problems are put off, the less that any attendee will want to take responsibility for them, so try to pin down and resolve any lingering unfinished business during your meeting. Usually, unfinished business is specifically noted as "undecided" or "tabled for future discussion" in minutes from previous meetings.

Address any new business. Next, bring up new problems, concerns, and issues that need to be discussed. These should be things that naturally stem from the developments that have occurred between any previous meetings and the present. Try to obtain concrete, definite decisions from the attendees—the more items you leave undecided, the more unfinished business you'll have to bring up next meeting.

Summarize the conclusions of the meeting. When you've addressed all past and present business, take a moment to sum up the conclusions of the meeting for everyone in attendance. Break down the results of all the decisions that were made and, if necessary, describe the specific actions that attendees will be expected to take before the next meeting.

End by laying the groundwork for the next meeting. Finally, tell everyone what to expect for the next meeting and if you've already begun to plan it, tell them when and where to expect it to be. This helps give the attendees the sense of continuity from one important project or decision to the next and gives them a time frame for progressing or completing their assigned tasks.

(From: https://smallbusiness.chron.com)

Before the meeting starts, as a chair you are supposed to (1) _____ yourself and the purpose of the meeting to call order. Then at the beginning of the meeting, you need to quickly (2) _____ any relevant events or decisions from previous meetings. Next, you should invite important attendees to (3) _____ the assembly of new or recent developments that have occurred since the last meeting. Later on, if there are unfinished business from the last meeting, make an effort to (4) _____ them before moving on. Next, (5) _____ new problems, concerns, and issues that need to be discussed. When you've addressed all past and present business, take a moment to (6) _____ the conclusions of the meeting. Finally, you are expected to end by laying the groundwork for the next meeting.

Training Assessment

Part I Self-study

Translate the following welcoming speech for new employees into English.

女士们,先生们:

我叫保罗·帕克,是本公司的总经理。首先,请允许我对你们的到来表达真挚的欢迎。正如你们所知,我们公司历史悠久,是轴承业顶尖供应商之一。我想你们一定会为成为这样一个伟大公司的一员而感到骄傲。但是我们不能仅仅沉湎于过去,我们需要吸收新鲜的血液进来,那就是你们。我们需要你们的知识、新想法和新见解。不要浪费这些财富,要及时利用它们。

我当然希望你们努力工作,不仅仅是为公司打工。我希望你们也在为自己、为社会的繁荣而努力工作。要对自己的人生担负起全部责任,从进公司上班那一刻起,要记得那句老话:如果工作需要做,请让我来。

再一次欢迎你们。让我们从今天起共事吧!

Part II BEC exam focus

Listening Test

Questions 1 – 12

- You will hear three telephone conversations or messages.
- Write **one or two words or a number** in the numbered spaces on the notes or forms below.
- You will hear each recording twice.

Conversation 1

(Questions 1 – 4)

- Look at the notes below.
- You will hear a woman giving information about a timetable.

Module 5 Business Meetings

INDUCTION PROGRAMME FOR NEW SALES STAFF	
· Monday	(1) _____
· Tuesday	product development lab
· Wednesday	a. m. (2) _____ department
	p. m. information about (3) _____ in accounts dept.
· Thursday	meet the (4) _____

Conversation 2

(Questions 5 – 8)

- Look at the notes below.
- You will hear a woman leaving a message about some problems with her company's new product.

MESSAGE

To: Jamie
From: Alice
Re:

(5) _____ for Trimco HP4 Problems have been discovered by the (6) _____ staff.

Can't proceed with (7) _____ as planned next month.

Alice travelling to Berlin to join (8) _____ will contact with new information ASAP.

Conversation 3

(Questions 9 – 12)

- Look at the notes below.
- You will hear a manager telling a colleague about what happened in a meeting.

WEBSITE DEVELOPMENT MEETING
Notes

Site most popular with (9) _____

Needs to be more attractive to (10) _____

Changes:
- include the (11) _____
- add link to the (12) _____

Unit 15　Attending a Meeting

Bring your open mind

 Training Objectives

By the end of this unit, you are expected to:
- learn how to communicate properly with others at meetings and conferences;
- learn about the basic vocabulary related to business meetings;
- learn how to take minutes.

 Training Portfolio

Part I　Starting up

Section 1　To discuss

Discuss the following questions with your partner.
(1) How useful is it for people in business to attend conferences? And why?
(2) What is important when attending a business meeting?
(3) What is important when you decide whether to attend a conference or not?

Section 2 To read

Read the following passage and then report the idea that you remember to your classmates and tell what impresses you most.

How to create an effective presentation for a product

Product presentations are a great way to introduce and inform people about your product, by showing them what it is and letting them know why it is unique. However, creating an effective presentation for a product can be tricky, as you will need it to be able to grab and hold the attention of your audience.

If you want to start to create more effective product presentations, there are a few ways that you can go about it:

Define the goal of the presentation. Product presentations can be used for a wide range of reasons. In some cases you may use them to sell the product itself, or in others you may want to educate or train salespeople about it.

By defining the goal of your product presentation, you can tailor it to that objective. That will help you to create a presentation that is more relevant to your audience, and will be more likely to engage them.

Keep your slides simple and focused. The days when presentations were essentially slides with a title and numerous bullet points are long gone—and it has been found that simple and focused slides are far more effective. That is something that you should take to heart in your product presentations, and may even want to limit each slide to a single point.

By keeping the slide simple and focused on a single point, you'll be able to draw attention to it more effectively and drive it home. More importantly the audience will be able to absorb information better when presented in this fashion. Use leverage visuals. Part of the advantage of product presentations is the fact that they will allow you to present information visually—so be sure to take advantage of that fact. In every slide you should think about the best way that you can "show" the message that you're trying to convey using images or other visuals.

Make no mistake. There are lots of ways to visualize data as well, and it is important that you choose the right method.

Use a style that is simple and consistent. While you don't want to use the default styles for presentations, the style that you do use should be simple and consistent. In fact it would help to make decisions about the colors, font, alignment and other elements prior to getting started. At the end of the day the goal should be to come up with a style that is aesthetically pleasing but does not distract the audience from the content of your presentation.

As you do start to create your product presentation, you should make it a point to follow the tips listed above. Not only will they help make it easier for you to structure the presentation, but you will also find that your product presentation is more likely to be able to grab and hold the attention of the audience.

(From: http://passivefamilyincome.com)

Part II Listening in

■ **Task 1 Listen to the following passage and fill in the blanks.**

You should know what (1)_____ you want to achieve in a meeting before it starts and prepare for it by reading any papers (2)_____ beforehand, and carefully thinking about what you want to say. This may sound rather (3)_____, but solid preparation is the key to successful meetings. A great deal of time and energy can be wasted through simple (4)_____ of planning.

During the meeting it is essential to stick to the (5)_____ so as to avoid the common problem of repetition. At the same time you ought to be (6)_____ to other people's ideas and feelings, and never lose your (7)_____. Be prepared to accept and implement a suggestion that is (8)_____ to your own ideas if it is an improvement on them; such honesty and (9)_____ are signs of good leadership and earn respect.

Finally, remember that when a decision is made it is important to act on it and to honor all the (10)_____ you have made in the meeting.

■ **Task 2 Listen to the conversation and decide whether the following statements are true (T) or false (F) according to what you hear.**

(   ) (1) The manager should take at least a sales report of the regional market he is in charge of.

(   ) (2) The data of market trend analysis and countermeasures are of no use.

(   ) (3) Such a conference can help people realize the market situation in other regions.

(   ) (4) Establishing contacts with sales managers from other regions matters much.

(   ) (5) The manager only needs to take an active part in entertainments to do networking at conference.

Part III Language focus

■ **Starting the meeting**

1. Shall we get started/get down to business?
2. Now that everyone is here, I'd like to call the meeting to order.
3. This morning we're going to discuss three problems.

■ **Proceeding to the next item**

1. Shall we move on to the next item on the agenda?
2. Let's turn to the second problem.
3. How about proceeding to the next question?

■ **Guiding people in the discussion**

1. First, I'd like Mr. Hunter to briefly introduce the situation.
2. Could you elaborate on that?
3. Miss Brown, can we have your report now?
4. Would you take the minutes of the meeting, Miss Jones?
5. Would you wind up your statement? We're running out of time.
6. Whose turn is it to take the floor?

■ **Coming to the main point**

1. I think we are getting side-tracked.
2. Shall we get back to the main point?
3. I'm afraid we're getting a bit off the point.
4. Please don't digress from the subject.
5. I'm afraid you're straying from the main point.
6. I see your point, but can we please stick to the main subject here?

■ **Interrupting**

1. I'm sorry to interrupt you, but I'd just like to say that ...
2. If I could make a point here ...
3. Excuse me. I would like to break in here.
4. May I cut in here?
5. I'm sorry to cut you off.
6. Sally, you'll have a chance to give us your point of view in a second. Let John finish first.

■ **Checking understanding**

1. Am I making sense here?

2. Are you with me on this?

3. Do you see what I mean?

4. Are there any questions so far?

■ **Asking for clarification**

1. I'm sorry I didn't quite understand you about …

2. What do you mean by …?

3. I'm not quite with you.

4. I'm sorry. Could you please say that again?

5. I didn't quite follow/catch what you said …

■ **Checking agreement**

1. Are we all agreed (on this)?

2. A: Does everyone support me on this?

   B: You have my full backing on this./I'm fully behind you on this.

3. Are we all for this plan?

   Are we all in favor of this decision?

4. Has anyone got any objection to this proposal?

5. Are you for or against this motion?

6. Those in favor, raise your hands.

7. Those against, put up your hands.

8. Are you abstaining, Mr. Jones?

■ **Declaring results or decisions**

1. I declare the meeting adjourned.

2. I declare the motion carried by a slender majority of eight to six.

3. I declare the motion lost.

4. Let's put it to a vote. Let me take a minute to sum up the main points of this discussion.

5. If nobody wants to add anything, we can draw the meeting to a close.

■ **Giving opinions**

1. I (really) feel that …

2. In my opinion …

3. The way I see things …

■ **Asking for opinions**

1. Do you (really) think that …?

2. (name of participant) Can we get your input?

3. How do you feel about …?

■ **Commenting on opinions**

1. I've never thought about it that way before.

2. Good point!

3. I get your point.

4. I see what you mean.

■ **Agreeing with other opinions**

1. Exactly!

2. That's (exactly) the way I feel.

3. I have to agree with (name of participant).

■ **Disagreeing with other opinions**

1. Up to a point I agree with you, but …

2. (I'm afraid) I can't agree.

■ **Advising and suggesting**

1. We should …

2. Why don't you …?

3. How/What about …?

4. I suggest/recommend that …

■ **Asking for repetition**

1. I didn't catch that. Could you repeat that, please?

2. I missed that. Could you say it again, please?

3. Could you run that by me one more time?

■ **Asking for an opinion**

1. What do you think of this?

2. How do you feel about/like/find this?

3. What's your opinion about this?

4. Is there any other view on this?

5. What does everyone think about this?

6. Could you elaborate on this?

7. Could we have your comments, Mr. Black?

8. Have you got anything to say about this?

9. Whose turn is it to take the floor?

■ **Keeping the meeting on time**

1. Please be brief.

2. I'm afraid that's outside the scope of this meeting.

3. Let's get back on track, why don't we?

4. Why don't we return to the main focus of today's meeting?
5. Keep to the point, please.

Part IV Speaking out

Section 1 Sample dialogues

■ **Dialogue 1**

A and B are talking about how to make a good presentation.

A: I've got a speech to give to our clients Friday morning. Could you give me some advice on how to win them?

B: Sure. First of all, the key to a successful presentation is to keep things simple. People are listening and they usually don't have a long attention span, stick to about three or four points, give them overview of your points and present them one by one, and then summarize at the end. Be straightforward and organized, and you'll be sure to be remembered.

A: What kind of visual should I use to support the presentation? Do you think I should use PowerPoint?

B: You should consider the size and interests of your audiences. In other words, who is listening and what they want, you can put together a PPT with some graphics and animations that will catch people's attention, but be careful not to go overboard.

A: No problem. And you know, when it comes to Friday, I can't help feeling nervous. How can I get over my fear of speaking in public?

B: Well, stage fright is very normal. Most people get nervous before they have to speak in front of large groups. Just prepare well, rehearse beforehand and trust that you will be great!

M: I'll try my best. Thank you so much.

■ **Dialogue 2**

Office head Robert is having a meeting with his two colleagues Joy and Roy discussing about printing the new brochure.

    A = Robert   B = Joy   C = Roy

A: OK, evening everyone. Joy, what have you got for us on the new brochure?

B: A lot of progress since the last meeting. We've had quotes from three design agencies to do the job.

A: And were they within our budget?

B: Yes, well within. And these are some ideas they've put together for us. If we don't like any of these, they'll come up with some more.

A: These are great.

B: Yeah, this is the design I really like. Here Roy, have a look.

C: Mm. Excellent. I agree that this is the best design. If we've got some money left in the budget, why don't we go for better quality?

B: I was wondering about it. What do you think, Robert?

A: How much extra would there be?

B: It might be an extra $1,000. It depends on whether you think it's worth it.

A: Mm. I think it's probably a good idea. When can they print? It's now the last week of October. We must pay by the end of the week.

B: Right, they understand the situation, and they've said if we confirm the order tomorrow, they can get the invoice to us by the end of the week. And the brochures will be ready within two weeks.

A: Excellent.

Section 2 Creating your own

Task 1 Role-play a meeting according to the situation below.

The manager is having a meeting on corporation development with his three group members—Michelle, Wilson and Nelson.

Task 2 Make a presentation for 2 minutes in front of the class based on the given topic.

What is important when ...
(1) attending a meeting
(2) giving a presentation

Part V Writing

Section 1 Tips for writing minutes

- **Identify what the meeting is about.**

Review the agenda including the names of attending participants in order to become familiar with the context of the meeting. The more you know about the upcoming discussions and participants, the more effective your notes will be.

- **Use the agenda to format the minutes.**

Before the meeting begins, prepare a template with the agenda and leave plenty of space for notes. Remember to include all pertinent information, the date and time, agenda, participants, time adjourned, next meeting date, etc. Prepare an attendance checklist especially if you are not familiar with the group or committee.

- **Where possible, the note-taker should not be a participant.**

Be impartial and objective. It is very difficult to take minutes of a meeting that you are expected to participate in. As note-taker you are not in charge of the meeting, the chairperson is. Your focus must be on capturing the discussion of the meeting, not on leading the discussion.

- **Writing minutes is not the same as transcribing.**

Keep your minutes brief and to the point. The minutes of a meeting should be a snapshot of discussions and decisions. Effective minute-taking does not mean you are recording every word that was said, this could lead to missing important points.

- **Attach any documentation given out at the meeting.**

If any materials or brochures were distributed at the meeting, include copies with the meeting notes.

- **Type up minutes as soon as possible.**

It is good practice to put together a draft of the minutes as soon as possible, while it is still fresh in your mind. The longer you put this first draft off, the greater the probability of forgetting something crucial.

- **Proofing**

Be sure to check and double-check your draft before sending to the participants. Keep all rough notes until the minutes have been approved.

- **Record meetings if possible.**

If possible, use a tape recorder to record the meeting and then prepare your notes from the recording.

Section 2 Writing exercises

Fill in the blanks of the following minute with the words given. Change the form where necessary.

| release | enclose | request | adjournment | approve |

Minutes of News Product Designing Committee

Date: May 5, 2015

Chairperson: Jack Stevenson, President

Present: Lucy Anderson, Mary Jane, Peter Black, Alice Brown

Apologies: Teresa Wang

Old business

None

New business

Chief designer Lucy Anderson (1) _____ her new designing Model XP504-GP506, (pictures (2) _____). She explained the new functions of the new model.

The team offered their opinions on these models. All agreed that model XP504 is more acceptable to customers and (3) _____ its trial production.

President (4) _____ that all designers study on the similar product line from other companies and release their new design quickly.

Date of Next Meeting

June 5th 2015

(5) _____

Section 3 Your turn to practice

Write a minute for the recent meeting you attended. Be sure to give a complete record of the meeting, including time, date and place of the meeting. State who attended the meeting and summarize what was discussed or decided at the meeting.

Part VI Follow-up reading

Passage 1

Read and decide whether the statements following the passage are true (T) or false (F).

10 rules for proper business meeting etiquette

- **Arrive early**

Arrive to the location of the business meeting at least 15 minutes early. This allows you to find a seat and get situated before the meeting starts.

- **Follow the agenda**

The chairperson of the meeting should circulate a meeting agenda to each participant at least one week in advance. Participants should call the chairperson to express any concerns about the agenda at least 48 hours prior to the meeting. The chairperson and concerned participant will then have time to determine if changes need to be made. The agenda should also mention the meeting's start and ending times as well.

- **Be prepared**

Each participant should come to the meeting with all of the materials and data he/she will need and an understanding of the meeting topic.

- **Take breaks**

Meetings should have a break every two hours. Breaks should be 20 minutes long, and meal breaks should be 30 minutes long.

- **Follow the dress code**

The chairperson should indicate what kind of attire is required for the meeting, either business casual or business formal, and participants should follow that rule. A representative listing of the attire would be helpful as participants may have differing views on what business casual and business formal is. For example, when listing the meeting as business formal, you can indicate that a button-down shirt and khaki pants are sufficient.

- **Speak in turn**

Keep the meeting organized by only speaking when you have the floor. Ask questions during the designated question period, and raise your hand to be recognized by the chairperson as having the floor. Do not interrupt someone while they are speaking or asking a question.

- **Listen**

You may find that many of the questions you have about a topic are answered by the content of the meeting. Listen attentively to the meeting and take notes.

- **Keep calm**

Avoid nervous habits such as tapping a pen on the table, making audible noises with your mouth, rustling papers or tapping your feet on the floor.

- **Be polite with your phone**

Turn off your cell phone prior to the start of the meeting. If you are expecting an urgent call, then set your phone to vibrate and excuse yourself from the meeting if the call comes in. Unless laptop computers have been approved for the meeting, turn yours off and lower the screen so that you do not obstruct anyone's view.

- **Don't bring guests**

Do not bring unannounced guests to a meeting. If you have someone you would like to bring to a meeting, then contact the chairperson for permission to bring your guest. If permission is not granted, then do not bring him/her.

(From: https://smallbusiness.chron.com)

( ) (1) If a participant has any concerns about the agenda, he or she should call the chairperson at least one day before the meeting.

( ) (2) Each participant should come to the meeting with all of the materials and data he/she needs.

( ) (3) Meetings should have a break every hour and breaks should be a quarter long.

( ) (4) The participant can wear what's comfortable for him/her to the meeting, either business casual or business formal.

( ) (5) If permission is not granted, do not bring unannounced guests to a meeting.

Passage 2

Read and decide whether the statements following the passage are true (T) or false (F).

Business meetings

Many organizations are developing ways of minimizing the time workers spend sitting in meetings in order to give them more hours working at their desks. They realize that reducing the number of meetings is problematic, but some are using a device called a Meeting Meter to determine how much money is wasted through the widespread practice of over-populated and time-inefficient meetings. A general meeting in a big company can cost 9,000 pounds an hour. Even staff in UK government departments have been told to make less elaborate presentations and to get through more quickly.

A solution has often been to take things at breakneck speed or abolish meetings altogether. Olivia Dacourt, CEO of a retail chain, makes a point of not letting anyone sit down in her meetings. "We cover more material in a 15-minute meeting than you'd see in a two-hour sit-down meeting," she says. She drills her employees to shout "pass" if they have no comment to make, thereby saving a hastily mumbled agreement with the previous speaker. In this way, her last staff meeting clocked in at six minutes.

Website designer Barry Hare has gone so far as to charge his clients a meeting tax. If they ask for a meeting, he doubles his design fee of 85 pounds an hour. "Everyone I talk to hates meetings, but they don't know what to do about them," he says, "Well, I've actually done something." Similarly, at JP Products, managers have instigated a No Meetings Day every Friday. The scheme was devised by in-house industrial psychologist Ada Pearson after hearing employees joke about the need for a "meeting-free day".

But abolishing meetings is not as simple as clearing them from your diary. At JP Products some workers have felt the need to get round the No Meetings Day directive by holding spontaneous "huddles" and "nice to knows" to update each other on progress. After her success in reducing the meetings quota, Pearson is under pressure from meeting-weary managers to implement days that are free of mails and telephone calls. But unfortunately she has other priorities—thanks to a lengthy meeting with the chief executive.

(From: https://www.thebalancecareers.com)

(   )(1) Attending meetings has become a common situation in the UK.
(   )(2) Olivia, the CEO of a retail chain encourages the echo of ideas.
(   )(3) Staff attitudes towards meetings have resulted in action to increase their frequency.
(   )(4) The meeting-wearing managers also request limitations on other forms of communication.

Training Assessment

Part I Self-study

Provide a word to fill in the gaps to complete these common phrases used when participating in meetings.

1. May I have a _____? In my opinion, I think we should spend some more time on this point.

2. If I _____, I think we should focus on sales rather than research.

3. Excuse me for _____. Don't you think we should discuss the Smith account?
4. Sorry, that's not quite _____. The shipment isn't due until next week.
5. Well, it's been a good meeting. Has anyone else got anything to _____?
6. I didn't _____ that. Could you repeat your last statement, please?
7. Good _____! I agree that we should focus on locally grown products.
8. That's interesting. I've never thought about it that _____ before.
9. I'm afraid I don't see what you _____. Could you give us some more details?
10. I'm afraid you don't understand my _____. That's not what I meant.
11. Let's get back on _____, why don't we? We need to decide on our strategy.
12. I _____ we put this point off until our next meeting.
13. I'm sorry, Tom, but that's outside the _____ of this meeting. Let's get back on track.
14. I'm afraid I didn't understand your point. Could you _____ that by me one more time?
15. I have to _____ with Alison. That's exactly what I think.

Part II BEC exam focus

Speaking Test

In this part of the test, you are given a discussion topic. You have 30 seconds to look at the task prompt, an example of which is below, and then about three minutes to discuss the topic with your partner. After that, the examiner will ask you more questions related to the topic for two candidates.

Video conferencing

The company you work for is concerned about the amount of time staff spend travelling to meetings in other branches of the company, and is looking at alternatives.

You have been asked to make recommendations about introducing video conferencing.

Discuss the situation together and decide:

(1) what the company needs to know about the meetings that take place at present;
(2) what the advantages and disadvantages of video conferencing might be;
(3) what kinds of practical preparations would be needed before introducing the system.

Follow-on questions
- Would you prefer to have meetings face-to-face or through video conferencing? (Why?)
- In other ways do you think a company could reduce the need for travelling to meetings? (Why?)
- What do you think are the benefits to the staff of business travel? (Why?)
- Do you think modern technology has affected the amount of business travel in recent years? (Why?/Why not?)
- Do you think video conferencing will become more important for meetings in the future? (Why?/Why not?)

Glossary

A

absenteeism　*n.*　（经常性）旷工,旷职
access　*n.*　接近(或进入)的机会,使用,享用权
　　　v.　获得使用计算机数据库的权利
accessible　*a.*　容易取得的,容易接近的,可联系的
accessory　*n.*　配件,附件
accommodate　*v.*　给……提供方便,调节
accommodation　*n.*　设施,住宿
account　*n.*　账,账目,账户
accountability　*n.*　责任心,可说明性
accountancy　*n.*　会计工作,会计职务
accountant　*n.*　会计师
account executive　*n.*　（广告公司）客户经理
accreditation　*n.*　水准鉴定,鉴定认可
acknowledge　*v.*　承认,告知已收到（某物）,承认某人
acquisition　*n.*　收购,被收购的公司或股份
acting　*a.*　代理的
activity　*n.*　业务类型
adapt　*v.*　修改,适应
adjust　*v.*　整理,使适应
adjourn　*v.*　休会
administration　*n.*　实施,经营,行政
administer　*v.*　管理,实施
admission ticket　入场券
adopt　*v.*　采纳,批准,挑选某人作候选人
advertise　*v.*　公布,做广告
advertisement　*n.*　出公告,做广告
advertising agency　广告公司
advertising revenue　广告收入
after-sales service　售后服务
agenda　*n.*　议事日程
agent　*n.*　代理人,经纪人
airfare　*n.*　飞机票价
airline cobranded cards　航空公司联名卡
align　*v.*　结盟
align with　与……结合,联合
all walks of life　各行各业
allocate　*v.*　分配,配给
alternative　*a.*　替代的；备选的；其他的
　　　　　n.　可供选择的事物
amalgamation　*n.*　合并,重组
amortize　*v.*　摊还
ambient light　背景光照明,环境光照明
amenities　*n.*　便利,乐趣,福利设施
analyze　*v.*　分析,研究
analysis　*n.*　分析,分析结果的报告
analyst　*n.*　分析家,化验员
animations　*n.*　动画式广告
annual　*a.*　每年的,按年度计算的
annual leave　年假
annual turnover　年收入
annual general meeting(AGM)　股东年会
anticipate　*v.*　期望
aperitif　*n.*　开胃酒
apparel　*n.*　衣服,服饰
apply　*v.*　申请,请求；应用,运用
applicant　*n.*　申请人
application　*n.*　申请,施用,实施
appointee　*n.*　被任命人
appraisal　*n.*　估量,估价

appreciate　v.　赏识,体谅,增值
appropriate　a.　适当的；合适的；恰当的
　　　　　　　v.　盗用；侵吞；拨(专款等)
approve　v.　赞成,同意,批准
aptitude　n.　天资,才能
arbitrage　n.　仲裁；套汇,套利
arbitration　n.　仲裁
artifact　n.　人造物品
assemble　v.　收集,集合
arts and crafts　工艺品
assembly line　装配线,流水作业线
assess　v.　评定,估价
asset　n.　资产
associate　n.　生意伙伴
assorted　a.　各种各样的
assortment　n.　种类,分类
at regular intervals　定期
attendee　n.　出席者
assist　v.　援助,协助,出席
authentication　n.　认证
authorization　n.　授权
authorized dealership　特许经销商
audience-driven　a.　以受众为导向的
audit　n.　查账,审计
automate　v.　使某事物自动操作
availability　n.　可利用的人或物

B

backing　n.　财务支持,赞助
backhander　n.　贿赂；反手一击
backlog　n.　积压未办之事；没交付的订货
bad debt　死账(无法收回的欠款)
baggage claim area　行李提取处
balance　n.　收支差额,余额
balance of payments　n.　贸易支付差额
balance sheet　n.　资产负债表
bankrupt　a.　破产的
bankruptcy　n.　破产

bank statement　银行结算清单(给帐户的),银行对账单
bar chart　条形图,柱状图
bargain　v.　谈判,讲价
base　n.　基地,根据地
batch　n.　一批,一组,一群
batch production　批量生产
bear market　熊市
bellboy　n.　(酒店里)男侍者
below-the-line advertising　线下广告,尚未被付款的广告
benchmark　n.　基准,参照；标准检查程序
benefit　n.　利益,补助金,保险金得益
bid　n.　出价,投标
bird's view　俯瞰,鸟瞰
billboard　n.　(路边)广告牌,招贴板
black　a.　违法的
black Monday　黑色星期一(1987年10月国际股票市场崩溃的日子)
blue chips　蓝筹股,绩优股
blue-collar　a.　蓝领(工人)的
Board of Directors　董事会
bond　n.　债券
bonus　n.　津贴,红利
books　n.　公司账目
book value　n.　账面价值,(公司或股票)净值
bookkeeper　n.　簿记员,记账人
boom　n.　繁荣,暴涨
boost　v.　提高,增加,宣扬
bottleneck　n.　瓶颈,窄路,阻碍
bounce　v.　拒付,退票
boutique　n.　精品店
brainstorm　n./v.　点子会议,献计策,头脑风暴
branch　n.　分支,分部
brand　n.　商标,品牌
brand leader　占市场最大份额的品牌,名牌
brand loyalty　(消费者)对品牌的忠实

break even 收支相抵,不亏不盈
break even point 收支相抵点,盈亏平衡点
breakthrough *n.* 突破
brief *n.* 简短声明;(争议一方的情况或论点)要点摘录
brochure *n.* 小册子
broker *n.* 经纪人,代理人
bull market 牛市
budget *n.* 预算
bulk *n.* 大量(货物)
　　 a. 大量的
buyout *n.* 买下全部产权

C

camera tripod 相机三脚架
candidate *n.* 求职者,候选人
canteen *n.* 食堂
canvass *v.* 征求意见,劝说
capacity *n.* 生产额,(最大)产量
caption *n.* 照片或图片下的简短说明
capital *n.* 资本,资金
capture *v.* 赢得
cardholder *n.* 持卡人
carry-on item 随身(可登机)行李
cash *n.* 现金,现付款
　　 v. 兑现
cash flow 现金流量
case study 案例分析
catalogue *n.* 目录,产品目录
CEO = Chief Executive Officer (美)总经理
chain *n.* 连锁店
channel *n.* (商品流通的)渠道
charge *v.* 使承担,要(价),记在账上
chart *n.* 图表
checkout *n.* 付款台
chief *a.* 主要的,首席的,总的
C.I.F. 到岸价格;成本、保险费加运费
circular *n.* 传阅的小册子(传单等)

circulate *v.* 传阅
claim *n./v.* 要求,索赔
client *n.* 委托人,顾客
cold *a.* 没人找上门来的,生意清淡的
commercialize *v.* 使商品化
commission *n.* 佣金
commitment *n.* 承诺
commodity *n.* 商品,货物
compensate *v.* 补偿,酬报
compensation *n.* 补偿,酬金
component *n.* 机器元件、组件、部件、部分
concentrated marketing 集中营销策略
configuration *n.* 设备的结构、组合
confirmation number 确认(订单)号码
conflict *n.* 冲突,争论
conglomerate *n.* 综合商社,多元化集团公司
consolidate *v.* 账目合并
consortium *n.* 财团
constant *a.* 恒定的,不断的,经常的
consultant *n.* 咨询人员,顾问,会诊医生
consumable *n.* 消耗品
consumer durables 耐用消费品
consumer goods 消费品,生活资料
contingency *n.* 意外事件
continental breakfast buffet 欧式自助早餐
continuum *n.* 连续时间
contract *n.* 合同,契约
contractor *n.* 承办商,承建人
conversion *n.* 改装,改造
conveyor *n.* (机场)行李输送带,传递,转让
Copenhagen *n.* 哥本哈根(丹麦王国首都)
countermeasure *n.* 对策
core time (弹性工作制)基本上班时间
cost *n.* 成本
cost-effective *a.* 合算的,有效益的
costing *n.* 成本计算,成本会计
credit *n.* 赊购,赊购制度

credit control 赊销管理(检查顾客及时付款的体系)

credit limit 赊销限额

credit rating 信贷的信用等级,信誉评价

creditor n. 债权人,贷方

creditworthiness n. 信贷价值,信贷信用

currency n. 货币,流通

current account 往来账户,活期(存款)户

current assets 流动资产

current liabilities 流动负债

customs formalities 海关手续

customize v. 按顾客的具体要求制造(或改造等);顾客化

cut-throat a. 残酷的,激烈的

cut-price a. 削价(出售)的

CV = curriculum vitae n. 简历,履历

cycle time 循环时间

D

deadline n. 最后期限

deal n. 营业协议,数量
     v. 交易

dealer n. 商人

debit n. 借方,欠的钱
       v. 记入账户的借方

debut n. 首秀,处女秀

debtor n. 债务人

declare v. 申报,声明

decline n./v. 衰退,缓慢,下降

decrease v. 减少

deduct v. 扣除,减去

default n. 违约,未履行

defect n. 缺陷

defective a. 有缺点的

defer v. 推迟

deferred payments 延期支付

deficit n. 赤字

delivery n. 演讲,投递

delivery cycle 交货周期

demand management 需求规划

deposit n. 保证金,押金,存款

depot n. 仓库

depreciate v. 贬值,(对资产)折旧

deputy n. 代理人,副职,代理

devalue v. 货币贬值(相对于其他货币)

differentiation n. 区分,鉴别

dignitary n. 显要人物

dimension n. 尺寸,面积,规模

diplomacy n. 技巧,手段

director n. 经理,主管

direct cost 直接成本

direct mail (商店为招揽生意而向人们投寄的)直接邮件

direct selling 直销,直接销售

directory n. 指南,号码簿

discount n. 折扣,贴现

dismiss v. 让……离开,打发走

dismissal n. 打发走

dispatch n./v. 调遣

display n./v. 展出,显示

dispose v. 安排,处理(事务)

dispose of 去掉,清除

disseminate v. 传播,散布

distribution n. 分配,分发

diversify v. 从事多种经营;多样化

dividend n. 股息,红利,年息

division n. 部门

dog n. 蹩脚货;滞销品

down-market a. 低档商品的

down-time/downtime n. 设备闲置期

D/P = Documents against Payment 付款交单

dramatic a. 戏剧性的

drive n. 积极性,能动

drag v. 拖拉

due a. 到期的;应付的;应得的

    n. 应付款;应得之物
dynamic *a.* 有活力的

E

earnings *n.* 工资,收入
efficiency *n.* 效率
embroider *v.* 刺绣
endorse *v.* 背书,接受
engage *v.* 雇用
engaged *a.* 忙碌的
enticing *a.* 诱人的
entitle *v.* 授权
entitlement *n.* 应得的权利
equity *n.* 股东权益
equity capital 股本
equities *n.* 普通股,股
estimate *v.* 估计(价值)
estimated demand 估计需求
evaluate *v.* 估价,评价
eventual *a.* 最终的
everlasting *a.* 永恒的;永久的
exaggerate *v.* 夸张
exceed *v.* 超过
exclusive *a.* 高档的;豪华的
expenditure *n.* 花费,支出额
expense account 费用账户
expense *n.* 费用,业务津贴
expertise *n.* 专长,专门知识和技能
exposure *n.* 公众对某一产品或公司的知悉
extension *n.* 电话分机

F

facility *n.* 用于生产的设备、器材
facilities layout 设备的布局规划、计划
facilities location 设备安置
fail-safe system 失效保护系统,安全系统
feasibility study 可行性研究
fee *n.* 费用
feedback *n.* 反馈,反馈的信息

field *n.* (作某种用途的)场地
file *n.* 文件集,卷宗,档案,文件
   v. 归档
fill *v.* 充任
finance *n.* 资金,财政
   v. 提供资金
financial *a.* 财政的
financing *n.* 提供资金,筹借资金
finished goods 制成品
firm *n.* 公司
fire *v.* 解雇
fix up 解决,商妥
fiscal *a.* 国库的,财政的
flexible *a.* 有弹性的,灵活的
flextime *n.* 弹性工作时间制
flier(= flyer) *n.* 促销传单
float *v.* 发行股票
flop *n.* 失败
fluctuate *v.* 波动,涨落,起伏
FOB *n.* 离岸价
follow-up *n.* 后续工作
   a. 后续的,增补的
forecast *v.* 预测
framework *n.* 框架,结构
franchise *n.* 特许经销权
   v. 特许经销
franchisee *n.* 特许经营人
franchiser *n.* 授予特许经营权者
fraud *n.* 欺骗
freebie *n.* (非正式的)赠品,免费促销的商品
freelance *n.* 自由作家;自由记者
   a. 自由职业的;特约的
funds *n.* 资金,基金

G

gap *n.* 缺口,空隙
gauge box 标准箱
garment *n.* 服装

gimmick   *n.*   好主意,好点子
go public   首次公开发行股票
grapple with   与……搏斗,尽力解决
grievance   *n.*   申诉,抱怨
gross   *a.*   总的,毛的
        n.   总额,总收入
gross margin   毛利率
gross profit   毛利
gross yield   毛收益
group   *n.*   (由若干公司联合而成的)集团
guarantee   *n.*   保证,保单
            v.   保证
guidelines   *n.*   指导方针,准则

H

handle   *v.*   经营
hand in one's notice   递交辞呈
hands on   直接经验的
hard sell   强行推销
hazard   *n.*   危险,危害行为
head   *n.*   主管,负责
hedge   *n.*   套期保值
hierarchy   *n.*   等级制度,统治集团,领导层
hinder   *v.*   阻碍
hire purchase   分期付款购物法
holder   *n.*   持有者
holding company   控股公司
hostile   *a.*   不友好的,恶意的
HRD   *n.*   人力资源发展部
human resources   人力资源
hype   *n.*   天花乱坠的(夸张)广告宣传

I

identification   *n.*   身份证明(的文件)
impact   *n.*   冲击,强烈影响
impartially   *ad.*   公平地
implement   *v.*   实施,执行
implication   *n.*   隐含意义
incentive   *n.*   刺激;鼓励

income   *n.*   工资或薪金收入,经营或投资的收入
increment   *v.*   定期增加
incur   *v.*   招致,承担
indecisive   *a.*   犹豫不决的
indemnity   *n.*   补偿,赔偿;保障;赔偿物
index   *n.*   指数,索引
retail price index   零售价格指数
indirect cost   间接成本
induction   *n.*   就职
industrial action   (罢工、怠工等)劳工行动
industrial relations   劳资关系
inefficiency   *n.*   低效率,不称职
inflate   *v.*   抬高(物价),使通货膨胀
inflation   *n.*   通货膨胀
infringe   *v.*   违反,违章
initial   *a.*   初步的
innovate   *v.*   革新
input   *n.*   投入
insolvent   *a.*   无力偿清的
installment   *n.*   部分,分期付款
instruction   *n.*   指令
insure   *v.*   给……保险,投保
insurance   *n.*   保险
interest   *n.*   利息,兴趣
interest rate   利率
interim   *n.*   中期,过渡期间
intermittent production   阶段性生产
intertwined   *a.*   缠绕在一起的
interview   *n./v.*   面试
interviewee   *n.*   被面试的人
interviewer   *n.*   主持面试的人,招聘者
intimidated   *a.*   害怕受到威胁的
inventory   *n.*   库存
invest   *v.*   投资
investment   *n.*   投资
investor   *n.*   投资者

invoice n. 发票
         v. 给(某人)开发票
irrevocable a. 不可撤销的,不能改变的
issue n. 发行股票
IT = Information Technology 信息技术
item n. 货物,条目,条款
itinerary n. 行程安排

J

jet lag 时差反应
job lot 库存品
job-lot control 分批节制
job-lot system 工作批量法
job mobility 工作流动
job rotation 工作轮换
joint a. 联合的
joint bank account (几人的)联合银行存款账户
jurisdiction n. 管辖(权)
junk bonds 低档(风险)债券,垃圾债券
junk mail (未经收信人要求的)直接邮寄的广告宣传
just-in-time n. 无库存制度

K

knockdown n. 价格的压低,船的破损
know-how n. 专门技术

L

labor market 劳动力市场
labor relations 劳资关系
labor shortage 劳动力短缺
latest catalogue 最新产品目录
launch v. 推出一种新产品
       n. 新产品的推出
lay-off/layoff n./v. 临时解雇
layout n. 工厂的布局
lead time 完成某项活动所需的时间
leaflet n. 广告印刷传单
lease n. 租借,租赁物
legal a. 合法的

lessee n. 承租人
lesser n. 出租人
ledger n. 分类账
leverage n. 杠杆比率
liability n. 负债
liabilities n. 债务
license n. 许可证
line process 流水线(组装)
link n. 关系,联系,环
liquid a. 易转换成现款的
liquidate v. 清算
liquidity n. 拥有变现力
liquidation n. 清理(关闭公司),清算
liquidator n. 清算人,公司资产清理人
listed a. 登记注册的
listing n. 上市公司名录
literature n. (说明书类的)印刷品,宣传品
litigate v. 提出诉讼
lobby n. (酒店)大堂
loan n./v. 贷款,暂借
logo n. 企业的特有标记
lot n. 批,量
lounge n. (机场、火车站)休息室
lucrative a. 合算的
luggage n. (英)行李

M

Madrid n. 马德里(西班牙首都)
mail shot (英)邮购目录
maintain v. 维持,保持
maintenance n. 维持,坚持
majority shareholding 绝对控股
make n. 产品的牌子或型号
make-to-order a. 根据订货而生产的产品
make-to-stock a. 指那些在未收到订货时就已生产了的产品
management n. 管理,管理部门
managerial a. 管理人员的,管理方面的

management accounts　管理账目

matrix management　矩阵管理

management information system（MIS）　管理信息系统

manning　n.　人员配备

manpower　n.　劳动力

manpower resources　劳动力资源

manual　a.　体力的,人工的,蓝领的

manufacture　v.　（用机器）制造

manufacturer　n.　制造者(厂、商、公司)

manufacturing　a.　制造的

manufacturing industry　制造业

margin　n.　利润

mark-up　v.　标高售价,加价

market　n.　市场;产品可能的销量

marketing mix　综合营销策略,定价、促销、产品等策略的组合

market leader　市场上的主导公司

market niche　小摊位,专业市场的一个小部分

market penetration　市场渗入

market segmentation　市场划分

market share　市场占有率,市场份额

mass-marketing　n.　大众营销术

master production schedule　主要生产计划

material requirements planning（MRP）　计算生产中所需材料的方法

materials handling　材料管理,材料控制

maximize　v.　使增至最大限度、最大化

mass media　大众传媒（如电视、广播、报纸等）

merchandising　n.　（在商店中）通过对商品的摆放与促销进行经营

merge　v.　联合,合并

merger　n.　（公司、企业等的）合并

merit　n.　优点,值得,应受

method study　方法研究

middleman　n.　中间人,经纪人

minimize　v.　使减至最小限度、最小化

minutes　n.　备忘录,会议记录

mission　n.　公司的长期目标和原则

mobility　n.　流动性,可移性

moderately　ad.　中等地,适度地

monopoly　n.　垄断,独占

mortgage　n./v.　抵押

motivate　v.　激励,激发……的积极性

motivated　a.　有积极性的

motivation　n.　提供动机,积极性,动力

motive　n.　动机

N

negotiate　v.　谈判

negotiable　a.　可谈判的,可转让的

net　a.　净的,纯的

network　n.　网络
　　　　v.　建立工作关系

niche　n.　专业市场中的小摊位

notice　n.　通知,辞职申请,离职通知

objective　n.　目标,目的

obsolete　a.　过时的,淘汰的,废弃的

offer　n.　报价,发盘
　　　v.　开价

off-season　a.　淡季的

off-the-shelf　a.　非专门设计的

off-the-peg　a.　标准的,非顾客化的

opening　n.　空位

operating profits　营业利润

operations chart　经营(管理)表

operations scheduling　生产经营进度表

optimize　v.　优化

option　n.　选择权

organogram　n.　组织图

organization chart　公司组织机构图

orient　v.　定向,指引

orientation　n.　倾向,方向;熟悉,介绍情况

outlay　n.　开销,支出,费用

outlet　n.　商店

outgoings n. 开支,开销
outing n. 外出活动
outlined a. 概括的,勾勒的
output n. 产量
outsource v. 外购产品或由外单位制作产品
outstanding a. 未付款的,应收的
over-demand n. 求过于供
overdraft n. 透支
overdraft facility 透支限额
overdraw v. 透支
overheads n. 企业一般管理费用
overhead bin (飞机上)头顶上方的行李架
overhead costs 营业成本
overpay n. 多付(款)
overtime n. 加班
overview n. 概述,概观

P

packaging n. 包装物;包装
parent company 母公司,总公司
participate v. 参加,分享(in)
partnership n. 合伙(关系),合伙企业
patent n. 专利
payoff n. 报酬
payroll n. 雇员名单,工资表
penetrate v. 渗透,打入(市场)
penetration n. 目标市场的占有份额
pension n. 养老金,退休金
perform v. 表现,执行
performance n. 工作情况
performance appraisal 工作情况评估
perk n. 额外待遇(交通、保健、保险等)
personnel n. 员工,人员
petty cash 零用现金
phase out 分阶段停止使用
picking list 用于择取生产或运输订货的表格
pie chart 饼形图
pilot n. 小规模试验

pipeline n. 管道,渠道
plant capacity 生产规模,生产能力
plot v. 标绘,策划
plough back 将获利进行再投资
point of sale(POS) 销售点
policy n. 政策,规定,保险单
porter n. (酒店)行李搬运工
portfolio n. (投资)组合
portfolio management 组合证券管理
potential n. 潜在力,潜势
purchasing power 购买力
PR = Public Relations 公共关系
preference shares 优先股
probation n. 试用期
production cycle 生产周期
production schedule 生产计划
product life cycle 产品生命周期
product mix 产品组合(种类和数量的组合)
productive a. 生产的,多产的,富有成效的
profit and loss account 损益账户
project v. 预测
promote v. 推销
promotion n. 提升,升级
proposal n. 建议,计划
prospect n. 预期,展望
prospectus n. 计划书,说明书
prosperity n. 繁荣,兴隆
protocol n. 礼仪,惯例
prototype n. 原型,样品
publicity n. 引起公众注意
public sector 公有企业
publicity n. 公开场合,名声,宣传
publics n. 公众,(有共同兴趣的)人或社会人士;某一阶层的人们
punctual a. 准时的
punctuality n. 准时
purchase v./n. 购买

245

purchaser   *n.*   买主,采购人

Q

qualify   *v.*   有资格,胜任

qualified   *a.*   有资格的,胜任的,合格的

qualification   *n.*   资格,资格证明

quality   *n.*   质量

quality assurance   质量保证

quality control   质量控制,质量管理

quarterly   *a./ad.*   季度的,按季度

questionnaire   *n.*   调查表,问卷

quote   *n.*   报价,股票牌价

quotation   *n.*   报价,股票牌价

R

Research and Development   研究与开发

radically   *ad.*   根本地,彻底地

raise   *n.*   (美)增薪

　　　v.   增加,提高;提出,引起

range   *n.*   系列产品

rank   *n./v.*   排名

random search   随机检查

rapport   *n.*   密切的关系,轻松愉快的气氛

rate   *n.*   比率,费用

rating   *n.*   评定结果

ratio   *n.*   比率

rationalize   *v.*   使更有效,使更合理

raw   *a.*   原料状态的,未加工的

raw material   原材料

receipt   *n.*   收据

receiver   *n.*   接管人,清算人

accounts receivable   应收账

receivership   *n.*   破产管理;破产清算;破产在管

recession   *n.*   萧条

reckon   *v.*   估算,认为

reconcile   *v.*   使……相吻合,核对,调和

recoup   *v.*   扣除,赔偿,补偿

recover   *v.*   重新获得,恢复

recovery   *n.*   重获,恢复

recreation center   休闲中心

recruit   *v.*   招聘,征募

　　　n.   新招收的人员

recruitment   *n.*   新成员的吸收

in the red   赤字,负债

redundant   *a.*   过多的,被解雇的

redundancy   *n.*   裁员,解雇

reference   *n.*   参考,参考资料

reference number (Ref. No.)   产品的参考号码

refund   *n./v.*   归还,偿还

region   *n.*   地区

reimburse   *v.*   偿还,报销

reliability   *n.*   可靠性

relief   *n.*   减轻,解除,救济

relocate   *v.*   调动,重新安置

remuneration   *n.*   酬报,酬金

redeem   *v.*   兑现

renowned   *a.*   有声望的

rep.   (代表)的缩写

reposition   *v.*   (为商品)重新定位

represent   *v.*   代表,代理

representative   *n.*   代理人,代表

reputation   *n.*   名声,声望

reputable   *a.*   名声/名誉好的

reservation   *n.*   预订,预约

reserve   *n.*   储量金,准备金

resign   *v.*   放弃,辞去

resignation   *n.*   辞职

resistance   *n.*   阻力,抵触情绪

resort   *n.*   度假胜地

respond   *v.*   回答,答复

response   *n.*   回答,答复

restore   *v.*   恢复

retail   *n./v.*   零售

retailer   *n.*   零售商

retained earnings   留存收益

retire   *v.*   退休

retirement *n.* 退休
return *n.* 投资报酬
return on investment（ROI） 投资收入,投资报酬
revenue *n.* 岁入,税收
review *v./n.* 检查
retrieve *v.* 取回,找回
reward *n./v.* 报答,报酬,奖赏
risk capital 风险资本
rival *n.* 竞争者,对手
　　　a. 竞争的
rocket *v.* 急速上升,直线上升,飞升
ROI = Return on Investment 投资回报率
roughly *ad.* 粗略地
round *a.* 整数表示的,大约的
round trip 往返的行程
routine *n.* 惯例,例行公事
royalty *n.* 特许权,专利权税

S

sack *v.* 解雇
sales force 销售人员
sample *n.* 样品
　　　v. 试验;抽样检验
saturation *n.* （市场的）饱和(状态)
saturate *v.* 饱和
savings *n.* 存款
scale *n.* 刻度,层次
scapegoat *n.* 替罪羊
scare *a.* 缺乏的,不足的
scrap *n.* 废料或废品
section *n.* 部门
sector *n.* 部门
securities *n.* 债券及有价证券
segment *n.* 部分
　　　v. 将市场划分成不同的部分
segmentation *n.* 将市场划分成不同的部门
semi-skilled *a.* 半熟练的
session *n.* 开会,会议议程

settlement *n.* 解决,清偿,支付
settle *v.* 安排,支付
share *n.* 股份
shareholder *n.* 股东
shelf-life *n.* 货架期(商品可以陈列在货架上的时间)
shift *n.* 轮班
showroom *n.* 陈列室
simulation *n.* 模拟
shop floor 生产场所
shortlist *n.* 供最后选择的候选人名单
　　　v. 把……列入最后的候选人名单
sign-up bonuses 开卡奖励
skilled employee 熟练工人
skimming *n.* 高额定价,撇奶油式定价
slogan *n.* 销售口号
slump *n.* 暴跌
a slump in sales 销售暴跌
soft-sell *n.* 劝诱销售(术),软销售(手段)
software *n.* 软件
sole *a.* 仅有的,单独的
sole distributor 独家分销商
solvent *a.* 有偿付能力的
sourcing *n.* 得到供货
spare part 零部件
specialize in 主要业务是……
specification *n.* 产品说明
split *v.* 分离
sponsor *n.* 赞助者(为了商品的广告宣传)
spread *n.* （股票买价和卖价的）差额
stable *a.* 稳定的
standard /double room 标准/双人间
staff *n.* 职员
stag *n.* 投机认股者
　　　v. 炒买炒卖
stagnant *a.* 停滞的,萧条的
statute *n.* 成文法

statutory　a.　法定的

steadily　ad.　稳定地,平稳地

stewardess　n.　空中小姐

stock　n.　库存,股票

stock exchange　证券交易所

stockbroker　n.　股票经纪人

stock controller　库房管理者

storage　n.　贮藏,库存量

strategy　n.　战略

strategically　ad.　战略上

streamline　v.　把……做成流线型；使简单化

stretch out　延长

stress　n.　压力,紧迫

strike　n.　罢工

structure　n.　结构,设备

subcontract　v.　分包(工程项目),转包

subordinate　n.　下属,下级
　　　　　　　a.　下级的

subscribe　v.　认购

subsidiary　n.　子公司

subsidize　v.　补贴,资助

subsidy　n.　补助金

substantially　ad.　大量地,大幅度地

summarize　v.　概括,总结

superior　n.　上级,长官

supervisor　n.　监督人,管理人

supervisory　a.　监督的,管理的

supply　n./v.　供给,提供

supplier　n.　供应商

survey　n.　调查

synergy　n.　协作

T

tactic　n.　战术,兵法

tailor　v.　特制产品

tailor-made products　特制产品

take on　雇用

takeover　n.　接管

tariff　n.　关税；价目表

task force　突击队,攻关小队(为完成某项任务而在一起的一组人)

tax allowance　免减税

tax avoidance　避税

taxable　a.　可征税的

taxation　n.　征税

tax-deductible　a.　在计算所得税时予以扣除的

telesales　n.　电话销售,电话售货

temporary　a.　暂时的

temporary post　临时职位

tender　n./v.　投标

territory　n.　(销售)区域

tie　n.　关系,联系

throughput　n.　生产量,生产能力,吞吐量

TQC = Total Quality Control　全面质量管理

track record　追踪记录,业绩

trade　n./v.　商业,生意；交易,经商

balance of trade　贸易平衡

trading profit　贸易利润

insider trading　内部交易

trade mark　商标

trade union　工会

trainee　n.　受培训者

transaction　n.　交易,业务

transfer　n./v.　传输,转让

transformation　n.　加工

transparency　n.　(投影用)透明胶片；透明度

treasurer　n.　司库,掌管财务的人

treasury　n.　国库,财政部

trend　n.　趋势,时尚

trouble-shooting　n.　解决问题

turnover　n.　营业额,员工流动的比率

U

undertake　v.　保证；承担,从事；同意,答应

undifferentiated marketing　无差异性营销策略

uneconomical　a.　不经济的,浪费的

unemployment　*n.*　失业
unemployment benefit　失业津贴
unit　*n.*　单位
unit cost　单位成本
update　*v.*　使现代化
up to date　流行的, 现行的, 时髦的
upgrade　*v.*　升级, 增加
upturn　*n.*　使向上, 使朝上

V

vacancy　*n.*　空缺
vacant　*a.*　空缺的
value　*n./v.*　价值, 估价
valuation　*n.*　价值
value-added　*a.*　有增加值的
variable　*n.*　可变物
variation　*n.*　变化, 变更
VAT = Value Added Tax　增值税
vendor　*n.*　卖主(公司或个人)
venture　*n.*　冒险, 投机
venue　*n.*　地点, 集合地点
viable　*a.*　可行的
viability　*n.*　可行性
vision　*n.*　设想, 公司的长期目标
vocation　*n.*　行业, 职业
vocational　*a.*　行业的, 职业的

W

wage　*n.*　(周)工资
wage freeze　工资冻结
warehouse　*n.*　仓库, 货栈
welfare　*n.*　福利
white-collar　*n.*　白领阶层
wholesale　*n./a./ad.*　批发(的)
wholesaler　*n.*　批发商
withdraw　*v.*　拿走, 收回, 退出
withdrawal　*n.*　拿走, 收回, 退出
work-in-progress　*a.*　在制品(完成部分生产程序)
workload　*n.*　工作量
work order　(原料、半成品、成品的)全部存货总量
work station　工作站
working capital　营运资本, 营运资金
write off　取消
write-off　*n.*　(从账目上)勾销；注销；贬值；报废的东西；

Y

yard goods　按码出售的织物
yen　*n.*　日元(日本货币单位)
yield　*n.*　有效产量

Z

zero defect　合格产品
zero inventory　零存货
zoom　*n.*　变焦；高水平的云视频会议软件

References

(美)艾瑞克,(美)杰西卡,方振宇. 商务英语口语大全[M]. 北京:海豚出版社,2017.

陈小慰. 新编商务英语口试必备手册[M]. 北京:经济科学出版社,2015.

胡英坤,车丽娟. 商务英语写作[M]. 北京:外语教学与研究出版社,2011.

纪淑军. 商务接待英语[M]. 北京:中国人民大学出版社,2010.

金利. 商务英语口语[M]. 北京:化学工业出版社,2016.

孔庆炎等. 文秘英语[M]. 北京:高等教育出版社,2002.

李雪等. 商务英语口语大全[M]. 北京:机械工业出版社,2017.

马龙海,李毅. 商务英语视听说[M]. 北京:外语教学与研究出版社,2015.

冉隆德,刘安洪,罗玲华,陈严春. 商务礼仪接待与外贸基础会话[M]. 广州:暨南大学出版社,2011.

孙宁,于晓言. 商务英语听说[M]. 北京:外语教学与研究出版社,2009.

吴松江,杨帆. 职场英语听说教程(第二册)[M]. 北京:中国人民大学出版社,2014.

姚建华,李政杰. 致用商务英语阅读[M]. 北京:对外经济贸易大学出版社,2014.

张丽丽. 商务英语口语一定要速成[M]. 大连:大连理工大学出版社,2010.

张丽丽. 商务英语口语[M]. 大连:大连理工大学出版社,2011.

庄恩平,Nan M. Sussman. *Intercultural Communication*[M]. 北京:外语教学与研究出版社,2016.

Bennie, Michael. *A Guide to Good Business Communication—How to Write and Speak English Well in Every Business Situation*[M/OL]. Oxford:How To Books Ltd,2009.

Boles, Margaret & Brenda Paik Sunoo. Wanted:Leaders who can lead and write. *Workforce*,December 1997,21.

Cotton, David Falvey & David Simon Kent. 体验商务英语[M]. 北京:高等教育出版社,2005.

Guffey, Ellen Mary. *Essentials of Business Communication*[M]. Mason:South-Western Cengage Learning,2010.

Hughes, John. 新编剑桥商务英语[M]. 北京:经济科学出版社,2008.

Ju, Amanda Crandell. *100 Topics for Business English Situations*[M]. Beijing:Foreign Languages Press,2017.

Kinsman, Michael. Are poor writing skills holding back your career? *California Job Journal*,February 1,2004.

Mackenzie, Ian. *English for Business Studies*[M]. London:Cambridge University Press,2006.

References

Messmer, Max. Skills for a new millennium. *Strategic Finance*, August 1999, 10 – 12.

Moody, Janette, Stewart, Brent & Cynthia Bolt-Lee. Showcasing the skilled business graduate: Expanding the Tool Kit. *Business Communication Quarterly*, March 2002, 23.

Tucker, Mary L. & Anne M. McCarthy. Presentation self-efficacy: Increasing communication skills through service-learning. *Journal of Managerial Issues*, Summer 2001, 227 – 244.

Wood, Lan et al. *PASS Cambridge BEC Vantage* [M]. 北京：经济科学出版社，2002.

https://bizfluent.com.

http://www.hongkongairport.com.

https://www.tripsavvy.com.

http://www.google.com.

https://money.usnews.com.

https://www.wikihow.com.

https://www.thebalancecareers.com.

https://smallbusiness.chron.com.

http://passivefamilyincome.com.

https://careertrend.com.

http://en.wikipedia.org.

http://www.woopidoo.com.

http://www.jobjournal.com.

https://wenku.baidu.com.

https://www.americanexpress.com.

https://www.learnenglishwithwill.com.